BF 683 N4 v.46 1999

Nebraska Symposium on
Motivation.

Nebraska Symposium on
Motivation

Motivation and Child Maltreatment

Volume 46 of
the Nebraska Symposium
on Motivation

University of Nebraska Press
Lincoln and London

Volume 46 of the Nebraska Symposium on Motivation

Motivation and Child Maltreatment

Richard A. Dienstbier
David J. Hansen

Series Editor
Volume Editor

Presenters

Cathy Spatz Widom

Professor of Criminal Justice and Professor of Psychology, University at Albany

Joel S. Milner

Distinguished Research Professor, Professor of Psychology, Director of the Family Violence and Sexual Assault Research Program, and Director of an NIMH funded Family Violence Research Training Program, Northern Illinois University

Dante Cicchetti

Professor of Psychology, Psychiatry, and Pediatrics and Director of the Mount Hope Family Center, University of Rochester

Sheree L. Toth

Associate Director of the Mount Hope Family Center, University of Rochester

Deborah A. Daro

Director of the National Center on Child Abuse Prevention Research of the National Committee to Prevent Child Abuse

John R. Lutzker

The Florence and Louis Ross Professor of Psychology, Chair of the Department of Psychology, and Director of Graduate Training in Psychology, University of Judaism

Ross A. Thompson

Professor of Psychology, University of Nebraska–Lincoln

Motivation and Child Maltreatment is Volume 46 in the series
CURRENT THEORY AND RESEARCH
IN MOTIVATION

Copyright © 2000 by the University of Nebraska Press
All rights reserved
Manufactured in the United States of America
International Standard Book Number
0-8032-2401-X (Clothbound)

∞

"The Library of Congress has cataloged
this serial publication as follows:"
Nebraska Symposium on Motivation.
Nebraska Symposium on Motivation.
[Papers] v. [1]–1953–
Lincoln, University of Nebraska Press.
v. illus., diagrs. 22cm. annual.
Vol. 1 issued by the symposium under
its earlier name: Current Theory and
Research in Motivation.
Symposia sponsored by the Dept. of
Psychology of the University of Nebraska.
1. Motivation (Psychology)
BF683.N4   159.4082   53-11655
Library of Congress

Preface

The volume editor for this 46th edition of the Nebraska Symposium is Professor David J. Hansen. David coordinated the symposium that led to this volume with enthusiasm and dedication. He planned this volume, selected and invited the contributors, and coordinated all aspects of the editing. My thanks to him and to our contributors for their excellent presentations and for the timely production of their chapters.

With this volume we have continued to employ procedures that were designed to facilitate the attending of the symposium by scholars other than our main presenters. Specifically, to allow other scholars the possibility of traveling to the symposium as participants, we invited posters on topics relevant to the main theme of each volume. Since this is a tradition we intend to continue, we urge you, our readers, to consider such poster submissions when you receive future symposium announcements.

This symposium series is supported largely by funds donated in the memory of Professor Harry K. Wolfe to the University of Nebraska Foundation by the late Professor Cora L. Friedline. This symposium volume, like those of the recent past, is dedicated to the memory of Professor Wolfe, who brought psychology to the University of Nebraska. After studying with Professor Wilhelm Wundt, Professor

Wolfe returned to this, his native state, to establish the first undergrad-
uate laboratory of psychology in the nation. As a student at Nebraska,
Professor Friedline studied psychology under Professor Wolfe.

We are grateful to the late Professor Friedline for this bequest
and to the University of Nebraska Foundation for continued financial
support for the series.

Richard A. Dienstbier
Series Editor

Contents

Introduction

David J. Hansen
University of Nebraska–Lincoln

There are at least two great luxuries associated with being coordinator of the Nebraska Symposium on Motivation. One is choosing the topic or major theme of the prestigious and influential conference. The second is selecting the speakers. It is great to sit back and think about all of the leading scholars in the field and decide who you would like to hear speak and have contribute a chapter to the volume. This 46th Annual Nebraska Symposium on Motivation brought together a distinguished panel of scholars who explored issues related to motivation and child maltreatment.

Major societal concern over child abuse and neglect as a significant social problem began as recently as the 1950s and 1960s. The widespread prevalence of child maltreatment, and the numerous problems and consequences associated with it, have been increasingly recognized since then. The increased societal attention to child maltreatment is clearly evident in the research literature, which has grown tremendously since the 1970s. Given all of the recent scholarly attention, we have learned much to guide our understanding of the etiology, treatment, prevention, and consequences of child maltreatment. The Nebraska Symposium's emphasis on the concept of *motivation* provides a valuable perspective for consideration and integration of complex child maltreatment issues. The opportunity provided by the symposium is particularly interesting and unique as "motivation" is not a term or concept that is commonly utilized in the child maltreatment literature.

The eminent panel of symposium scholars provided in their presentations, and the resultant chapters that follow, an informative and stimulating discussion of major perspectives, issues, research, future directions, and challenges in the field today. The speakers addressed a wide range of topics, from etiological perspectives and issues regarding the causes of maltreatment, to potential consequences and mechanisms of impact, to broad-based prevention models and programs, and finally to research strategies and obstacles in intensive intervention efforts with maltreating families.

The chapters appear in the order that the presentations occurred at the symposium. The volume opens with a chapter by Cathy Spatz Widom on perspectives for understanding motivation and possible mechanisms involved in the intergenerational transmission of violence—the phenomenon whereby abused and "victimized" children become perpetrators of violence when they grow up. Widom thoughtfully considers the empirical research on the "cycle of violence" and describes her prospective cohorts' design study with a large sample of abused and neglected children and matched controls who were followed into young adulthood. Theoretical perspectives for explaining motivation and mechanisms are described, and new analyses are presented that serve as an initial attempt to test some of these hypothesized mechanisms using data from the prospective cohorts study. The chapter concludes with a discussion of what has been learned to date and as well as directions for future research.

The examination of the intergenerational transmission of violence is followed by Joel Milner's chapter which examines specific individual (parental) factors that contribute to child abuse. Milner addresses how the abusive parent processes social information, particularly child-related information, and how this may contribute to the etiology of child physical abuse. His social information processing model is used to describe parental cognitive activities believed to mediate verbal and physical aggression against children. Possible relationships between personality factors, external stressors, and the components of information processing are described. Throughout the chapter, the limitations of the model and suggestions for testing and refining the model are presented. In addition, the chapter includes a discussion of the implications of the model for assessment, treatment, and prevention.

From the social-cognitive processes of maltreating parents we proceed to an examination of the self-regulatory processes of maltreated children in the chapter by Dante Cicchetti and Sheree Toth. Issues and parameters for defining maltreatment are discussed. An ecological-transactional model is then presented and used to describe their research on the developmental processes and pathways that result in adaptive or maladaptive outcomes for maltreated children. Investigations of biological, psychological, and social-contextual regulatory processes in children who have experienced maltreatment are discussed to illustrate the mediating and moderating role these influences exert upon developmental outcome. In addition to presenting the extensive research from their laboratory, the authors consider the research of other investigators. Biological, psychological, and sociocultural systems are viewed as the prominent regulators of development. Cicchetti and Toth describe how adaptive or maladaptive development takes place in the dynamic transactions among the evolving capacities of the individual, his or her active self-organizing strivings for adaptation, and the internal and external regulatory context. Resilience is discussed to address the fact that some children exhibit positive adaptation in the face of adversity. The chapter concludes with a discussion of the implications for prevention and intervention as well as future research directions.

The initial chapters have many implications for prevention and intervention in child maltreatment. The next two chapters expand that focus with very specific looks at primary prevention models and programs and at conducting quality applied research on interventions with maltreating families.

In her chapter on child abuse prevention, Deborah Daro discusses the current directions and future challenges we face in our efforts to eliminate maltreatment. Daro describes a conceptual shift in "prevention imagery," away from a horizontal structure and toward a vertical one, with a strong foundation that offers a certain degree of universal screening and assessment. As an alternative to the approach of providing a plethora of separate prevention services, Daro emphasizes rooting all efforts in a common foundation of universal support which may develop and guide the diversified efforts in a more efficient and effective manner. The Healthy Families America program, including its theory of change, goals and objectives, procedures and outcomes, is described to illustrate this perspective and the complex issues involved. Daro also explores how prevention efforts may facilitate change in the health care and child protection systems.

The discussion on intervention shifts from primary prevention toward intervening in families in which abuse has already occurred. John Lutzker's chapter addresses the scarcity of strong applied research data on treatment of child abusive parents, despite the extensive professional attention given to child maltreatment. As Lutzker notes, many treatment programs are available, yet few contribute empirical data to the professional literature in child maltreatment. In fact, treatment and research can have competing agendas (e.g., rapid need for intervention versus a need for thorough baseline data). Lutzker describes the features of good applied research, including specific examples from the literature and his own research on ecobehavioral intervention with maltreating families. He also discusses the obstacles to conducting quality treatment research for abusive families and suggestions for overcoming these challenges while providing and evaluating practical service.

It seemed very fitting, subsequent to the diverse but interrelated presentations, to have a panel discussion that included all of the speakers, to hear them discuss common themes and issues that arose across the presentations, and to provide significant opportunity for audience questions. When I was thinking about how to approach this final part of the symposium, I thought that I wanted someone knowledgeable about the field and insightful about research and conceptual issues who could provide commentary and facilitate a productive discussion among the symposium scholars. Believe it or not, the symposium budget and saving money was not a criterion—I was just fortunate that I found who I was looking for in my own department. Ross Thompson served in the discussant role at the symposium and contributed the final chapter for this volume.

Thompson provides an integrative perspective on the symposium in his discussant's commentary, the final chapter. He organizes his comments around three major themes that arose during the symposium: (a) how maltreatment affects child victims, including the complex and contingent nature of the consequences; (b) how families in which maltreatment has occurred can be healed, including changing representations underlying parental behavior and the relationships that contribute to these representations; and (c) how changes in public policy, including new perspectives on child protection and family preservation, may reduce child maltreatment through prevention efforts and system reform. As Thompson notes, these issues are at the heart of contemporary research on child abuse and neglect.

Overall, the volume clearly communicates that although we have learned much in recent decades about the complexity, etiology, impact, prevention, and treatment of child maltreatment, there is much more to learn. The chapter authors have provided thoughtful commentary on the state of the field and the limits of our understanding and stimulating ideas for where to proceed.

Historical Note

The Nebraska Symposium has a long history focusing on motivation and related topics. Many of the most distinguished scholars in the field have participated over the years. In honor of the completion of the 25th Nebraska Symposium many years ago, Ludy Benjamin and Marshall Jones wrote of the history of the symposium and noted that *even then* the Nebraska Symposium was "the longest lived topical series in American psychology, with a national and international reputation" (Benjamin & Jones, 1979, p. ix).

At the time the Nebraska Symposium planning first began in the early 1950s there were only eight faculty in the Department of Psychology (compared to approximately 24 at present). A major concern for the graduate program was to be able to expose students to a wider variety of information, ideas, and orientations than could be accomplished by the small number of faculty. Thus, the idea of bringing in scholars for lengthy and informative visits developed. The original funding for the Nebraska Symposium for many years came from clinical training grants from the U.S. Public Health Service. These training grants were to provide support for the Clinical Psychology Training Program within the Department of Psychology, which in 1948 was among the first cohort of clinical programs ever to be accredited by the American Psychological Association (APA).

Clinical training grant funding for the Nebraska Symposium on Motivation continued from the early 1950s to the mid-1970s.[1] Thus, it was fitting that in conjunction with the 46th Annual Nebraska Symposium in 1998 we held a "Department of Psychology Celebration" in recognition of the 50th anniversary of APA accreditation of the Clinical Psychology Training Program. The celebration also acknowledged the renovation and reopening of Burnett Hall (the building that houses the Department of Psychology), and included tours, presentations, and workshops by faculty and alumni and the dedication of the Sarata Community Research Room as well as a tree and a bench in memory of Professor Brian Sarata. It culminated with a reception and dinner for many alumni, students, faculty, and friends of the program.

Acknowledgments

There are many people who contributed to this symposium and volume. Of course, the essential players were the invited speakers and authors: Dante Cicchetti, Sheree L. Toth, Debra Daro, John Lutzker, Joel Milner, and Cathy Spatz Widom. It was terrific to hear their presentations, discuss and read their work, and collaborate on this effort. I am also grateful to the discussant, my friend and colleague Ross Thompson, for his ongoing consultation and contributions throughout this experience. Dick Dienstbier, the series editor, was also a valuable resource.

Many current and former graduate students made a variety of contributions to the symposium and volume. Most notably, Deb Hecht and Georganna Sedlar helped from start to finish in *many* ways—from the early days of planning the symposium, to hosting and driving speakers, to help with final proofing of chapters, as well as many other chores throughout the effort. Others who contributed significantly include Mary Fran Flood, Kristine Futa, Becky Colman, and Jen Wyatt.

An enduring influence in making this and many other Nebraska Symposia on Motivation a success has been Claudia Price-Decker, who oversaw most aspects of the scheduling, advertising, and other arrangements. Other staff of the Department of Psychology also contributed significantly, including Becki Barnes, Jamie Longwell, and Norma Jean Green.

Finally, I gratefully acknowledge the help and support of my family. My wife, Mary Kay, and our children, Matt and Marie, contribute in many ways to all of my efforts including this symposium and volume. Thanks.

Note

1. As noted in the preface to this volume, the symposium is currently supported largely by funds donated in the memory of Professor Harry K. Wolfe to the University of Nebraska Foundation by the late Professor Cora L. Friedline.

Reference

Benjamin, L. T., Jr., & Jones, M. R. (1979). From motivational theory to social cognitive development: Twenty five years of the Nebraska Symposium. In R. A. Deinstbier (Ed.), *Human emotion. Nebraska Symposium on Motivation 1978* (pp. ix–xix). Lincoln: University of Nebraska Press.

Motivation and Mechanisms in the "Cycle of Violence"

Cathy Spatz Widom
University at Albany

What an honor to be asked to participate in the Nebraska Symposium on Motivation! As a graduate student in psychology at Brandeis University, I "grew up" on volumes of the Nebraska Symposia. When asked in 1997 to participate, I was touched and enthusiastically agreed.

Since 1986 I have been studying the consequences of early childhood victimization with support from a number of federal agencies (NIJ, NIMH, NIAAA, and NIDA). In this chapter I will focus on only one possible consequence of child abuse and neglect—criminality and primarily on violence.

Numerous theories have been offered to explain the "cycle of violence," or the phenomenon whereby abused and "victimized" chil-

Correspondence should be addressed to: Cathy Spatz Widom, Ph.D., The University at Albany, School of Criminal Justice, 135 Western Avenue, Albany, NY 12222.

This research was supported by grants from the National Institute of Justice (86-IJ-CX-0033, 89-IJ-CX-0007, and 93-IJ-CX-0031), the National Institute of Mental Health (MH49467), the National Institute of Alcohol Abuse and Alcoholism (AA9238, AA11108), and the National Institute of Drug Abuse (DA10060). Points of view are those of the author and do not necessarily represent the position of the United States Department of Justice. The author wishes to thank Jorge Chavez, Jill Harbeck, Jeanne Kaufman, David McDowell, Amie Schuck, and Barbara Luntz Weiler for statistical help and general assistance in the preparation of this manuscript.

dren become the perpetrators of violence when they grow up. People also refer to this phenomenon as the "intergenerational transmission of violence." Very likely there are multiple pathways by which the experiences of early childhood victimization influence later behaviors and particularly whether a person engages in violence. I have divided this chapter into five sections. First, as background, I will briefly discuss the design of my research which utilizes a prospective co-horts design study involving a large sample of abused and neglected children and a matched control group who were followed up into young adulthood. Second, I will summarize the results of recent empirical research on the "cycle of violence," drawing primarily on my findings but also referring to the work of others around the country. Third, I will review a number of theoretical perspectives which have been offered to explain the possible motivations and mechanisms involved in the intergenerational transmission of violence. Fourth, I will present the results of new analyses which have been undertaken as a preliminary test of some of these broad theories. Finally, I will suggest some directions for future research and call attention to some important lessons.

Background to the Study

Over ten years ago, with initial funding from the National Institute of Justice, I began research to address the relationship between early child abuse and neglect and later delinquent and violent criminal behavior using a design that overcame a number of the method-ological limitations of previous research. This study includes 1,575 children from a metropolitan area in the Midwest who have now been followed for a 25-year period after the abuse or neglect incident through official criminal records and a subset of 1,196 who partic-ipated in in-person follow-up interviews. These were documented and substantiated cases of childhood physical and sexual abuse and neglect which occurred early in the lives of these children (ages 11 or under). This prospective design allows us to disentangle the effects of childhood victimization from other potential confounding factors.

This is a prospective cohorts design study (Leventhal, 1982; Schulsinger, Mednick, & Knop, 1981) in which abused and neglected children were matched with nonabused and nonneglected children and followed prospectively into young adulthood. Because of the matching procedure, the subjects are assumed to differ only in the risk factor, that is, having experienced childhood sexual or physical abuse or neglect. Since it is not possible to randomly assign subjects to groups, the assumption of equivalency for the groups is an approximation. The control group may also differ from the abused and neglected individuals on other variables associated with abuse or neglect. (For complete details of the study design and subject selection criteria, see Widom, 1989a).

PHASE I: IDENTIFICATION OF THE SAMPLE AND TRACING OF CRIMINAL HISTORIES (N = 1,575)

The rationale for identifying the abused and neglected group was that their cases were serious enough to come to the attention of the authorities. Only court substantiated cases of child abuse and neglect were included here. Cases were drawn from the records of county juvenile and adult criminal courts in a metropolitan area of the Midwest during the years 1967 through 1971. To avoid potential problems with ambiguity in the direction of causality, and to ensure that the temporal sequence was clear (that is, child abuse or neglect led to subsequent outcomes), abuse and neglect cases were restricted to those in which children were 11 years of age or less at the time of the abuse or neglect incident. Thus, these are cases of early childhood abuse and/or neglect.

Physical abuse cases included injuries such as bruises, welts, burns, abrasions, lacerations, wounds, cuts, bone and skull fractures, and other evidence of physical injury. *Sexual abuse* charges varied from relatively nonspecific charges of "assault and battery with intent to gratify sexual desires" to more specific charges of "fondling or touching in an obscene manner," sodomy, incest, and so forth. *Neglect cases* reflected a judgment that the parents' deficiencies in child care were beyond those found acceptable by community and professional standards at the time. These cases represented extreme failure to provide adequate food, clothing, shelter, and medical attention to children.

A control group was established with children who were matched on the basis of age, sex, race, and approximate family social class during the time period of the study (1967 through 1971). Children who were under school age at the time of the abuse and/or neglect were matched with children of the same sex, race, date of birth (+/- 1 week), and hospital of birth through the use of county birth record information. For children of school age, records of more than 100 elementary schools for the same time period were used to find matches with children of the same sex, race, date of birth (+/- 6 months), class in elementary school during the years 1967 through 1971, and home address, preferably within a five-block radius of the abused or neglected child. Overall, there were matches for 74% of the abused and neglected children.

PHASE II: FOLLOW-UP INTERVIEWS (N = 1,196)

The second phase of the research involved tracing, locating, and interviewing the abused, neglected, or both individuals and controls (approximately 20–25 years later). The follow-up was designed to document long-term consequences of childhood victimization across a number of outcomes (cognitive and intellectual, emotional, psychiatric, social and interpersonal, occupational, and general health). Two-hour follow-up interviews were conducted between 1989 and 1995 and included a series of structured and semi-structured questionnaires and rating scales and a psychiatric assessment using the revised National Institute of Mental Health Diagnostic Interview Schedule (DIS-III-R: Robins, Helzer, Cottler, & Goldring, 1989), permitting assignment of diagnoses according to the *Diagnostic and Statistical Manual of Mental Disorders* (DSM-III-R: American Psychiatric Association, 1987). The DIS-III-R is a fully structured interview schedule designed for use by lay interviewers. Although the DIS-III-R is a structured interview schedule, interviewers received a week of training in the administration of the interview.

The interviewers were not told the purpose of the study or about the inclusion of an abused and/or neglected group or participants' group membership. Similarly, the subjects were not informed about the purpose of the study except in most general terms. Subjects were told that they had been selected to participate as part of a large group of individuals who grew up in that area in the late 1960s and early 1970s. Subjects who participated signed a consent form acknowledging that they were participating voluntarily.

Of the original sample of 1,575 (908 abused and neglected individuals and 667 controls), 1,307 subjects (83%) have been located and 1,196 interviewed (76%). Of the people not interviewed, 43 were deceased (prior to interview), 8 were incapable of being interviewed, 268 were not found, and 60 refused to participate (a refusal rate of 3.8%). Comparison of the current follow-up sample with the original sample indicates no significant differences in terms of percent male, white, abused and/or neglected, poverty in childhood census tract, or mean current age. The interviewed group (follow-up sample) is significantly more likely to have an official criminal arrest record than the original sample of 1,575 (50% of the current sample versus 45% of the original sample). However, this is not surprising since people with a criminal history are generally easier to find, in part because they have more "institutional footprints" to assist in locating them.

Approximately half of the follow-up sample is female (48.7%) and about two-thirds is white (62.9%). The mean age of the sample at the time of the interview was 28.7 (SD=3.84). There were no differences between the abused and neglected group and controls in terms of gender, race/ethnicity, or age. The average highest grade of school completed for the sample was 11.47 (SD = 2.19), although abused and neglected individuals had completed significantly ($p < .001$) less school (M=10.99, SD=1.99) than controls (M=12.09, SD=2.29). At follow-up, two-thirds of the control group had completed high school, whereas less than half (48%) of the abused and neglected children had done so. Occupational status of the sample was coded according to the Hollingshead Occupational Coding Index (Hollingshead, 1975), ranging from 1 (laborer) to 9 (professional). Median occupational level of the sample was semi-skilled workers, and less than 7% of the overall sample was in levels 7–9 (managers through professionals). More of the controls were in higher occupational levels than abused and neglected subjects ($p < .001$).

Characteristics of the design and sample are important for methodological and substantive reasons. However, certain caveats should be kept in mind. Although originally designed to examine the relationship between child abuse, neglect, and later violent behavior and to overcome methodological shortcomings in previous literature, this research has its own limitations. One should be circumspect about these findings and not overgeneralize inappropriately for a number of reasons described below.

Much child abuse and neglect that occurs does not come to the attention of welfare departments, police, or courts. This fact especially applies to official data from the late 1960s and the early 1970s, when it is generally believed that only a fraction of all maltreatment cases were reported. The abuse and neglect cases studied here are those in which agencies have intervened and those processed through the social service systems (Groeneveld & Giovannoni, 1977). These cases were dealt with before most states had adopted mandatory child abuse reporting laws and before the Federal Child Abuse Treatment and Prevention Act was passed.

Furthermore, child abuse researchers have argued that there is bias in the labeling and reporting of child abuse cases and that lower income and minority groups are overrepresented in official reports of child abuse and neglect (Gelles, 1975; Newberger, Reed, Daniel, Hyde, & Kotelchuck, 1977). The design used here does not generally include instances of abuse in higher level socioeconomic families where such abuse may be more likely to be labeled an accident. On the other hand, national surveys of family violence have found that those with the lowest income are more likely to abuse their children (Straus, Gelles, & Steinmetz, 1980). Even though most poor people do not abuse or neglect their children, there is a greater risk of abuse and neglect among the lowest income groups (Gelles & Cornell, 1985). Regardless, one cannot generalize from these findings to unreported cases of abuse and neglect, such as those cases handled unofficially by private medical doctors (Widom, 1988). Similarly, because of the exclusions (Widom, 1989a), these findings are not generalizable to abused and neglected children who were adopted in early childhood.

Empirical Findings Regarding the "Cycle of Violence"

In this chapter, the "cycle of violence" refers to the extent to which abused and neglected children (yesterday's and today's victims) become perpetrators of violence in the future. For the purposes of this chapter and analyses presented here, the findings described here are based only on individuals who participated in the follow-up interviews during the years 1989 through 1995 ($N = 1,196$). Thus, these findings should not be confused with findings in other publications describing the criminal behavior of the entire sample of 1,575 (Maxfield & Widom, 1996; Widom, 1989b).

The results described here focus on delinquent, adult criminal and violent criminal behavior and are based on examinations of official criminal records of arrests during adolescence and young adulthood. These arrest data are from information obtained from complete criminal histories for subjects collected at three levels of law enforcement (local, state, and federal) at two points in time (1986–87 and 1994). Violent crimes include arrests for the following crimes and attempts: assault, battery, robbery, manslaughter, murder, rape, and burglary with injury.

In general, we have found that childhood victimization increases the likelihood of delinquency, adult criminality, and violent criminal behavior (Maxfield & Widom, 1996; Widom, 1989b). I call your attention to five major points.

RISK OF ARREST

Childhood victimization (that is, physical and sexual abuse and neglect) significantly increases a person's risk of arrest as a juvenile, as an adult, and for a violent crime (see Table 1). To place this in perspective, the odds are almost two times higher that an abused and neglected child will be arrested for a crime as a juvenile than a child of the same sex, age, and race who grew up in the same neighborhood or who was born in the same hospital at the same time. In terms of violence, about a fifth of the abused and neglected children have an arrest for violence (significantly higher than the prevalence for the controls, 15.6%).

Our research was conducted in a metropolitan county area in the Midwest, using cases of abuse and neglect that came to the attention of the courts during the years 1967 through 1971. However, others have found similar results. As part of the Rochester Youth Development Study, Thornberry and his colleagues collected information on child abuse and neglect from the Department of Social Services in Rochester, New York for the children who are part of their longitudinal study. Smith and Thornberry (1995), using self-report as well as official arrest information, found that child maltreatment was a significant risk factor for delinquency and self-reported violent behavior, even when gender, race/ethnicity, family structure, and social class were controlled.

Another evaluation of these relationships used maltreated children and two nonmaltreated comparison samples (one from the schools and one from the Department of Health and Social Service

Table 1. *Childhood Victimization and Criminality in Follow-Up Sample* (N = 1,196)

	Abuse/ Neglect (676)	Controls (520)	Odds Ratio
	%	%	
Juvenile Arrest	31.2	19.0	1.9***
Adult Arrest	48.5	36.2	1.6***
Any Arrest	56.5	42.5	1.8***
Violent Arrest	21.0	15.6	1.4*

*p < .05   *** p < .001

records) from another geographic area of the country (Mecklenburg County, North Carolina). In this study, Zingraff and his colleagues (1993) found that maltreated children had higher rates of delinquency and violence complaints than nonmaltreated school and impoverished children.

Thus, in three quite different prospective studies from different parts of the country and using cases from different time periods, childhood abuse and neglect have been found to increase a person's risk of crime and delinquency. This is important because "convergent findings based on such different sampling procedures increase confidence in the generalization of the results" (Cook, 1990).

AGE OF ONSET, FREQUENCY, AND CHRONICITY OF CRIMINAL BEHAVIOR

Abused and neglected children (N = 1,196) are also involved in official criminal behavior more than a year earlier than comparison children (18.1 versus 19.4 years, respectively). Indeed, one of the abused and neglected children was first arrested before age 6. This is important because age of onset is often correlated negatively with the severity of a disorder (the earlier the onset, the more severe the disorder). In the delinquency literature, early onset is associated with increased variety, seriousness, and duration of problems (Loeber & Stouthamer-Loeber, 1987).

We have also learned that abused and neglected children commit more offenses than controls (the average number of arrests was 6.6 versus 4.7, respectively) and are more likely to become recidivists (2–4 arrests; 20.3% versus 13.7%, respectively) and chronic offenders

(5 or more arrests; 22.6% versus 13.7%, respectively) than nonabused and neglected children.

CHILDHOOD VICTIMIZATION, VIOLENCE, AND GENDER

In documenting the relationship between childhood victimization and criminal consequences, it is clear that childhood victimization has pervasive consequences for criminal behavior and violence (see Table 1). We have also found that childhood victimization affects females as well as males, despite the fact that females are traditionally at low risk for being arrested, and particularly being arrested for violent crimes (Maxfield & Widom, 1996).

However, the pattern of increased risk differed for males and females. Compared to controls, abused and neglected females were at increased risk of arrest for a violent crime as a juvenile, as an adult, and during their lifetime, despite the fact that females are generally at lower risk of arrest for violence compared to males. This pattern was not evident for males. Abused and neglected males were *not* at increased risk for violent offending as juveniles or as adults, in comparison to control males, using the dichotomous measure of having an arrest for violence or not.

Since these findings are based on official criminal records, it is possible that these differences represent spurious findings and it is particularly tempting to dismiss these findings about females, because the base rates are so low. However, these findings have also been subjected to more stringent multivariate analyses and the same results were found.

Another possibility is that there may have been increased surveillance of the abused and neglected females in this sample and that this extra attention by the juvenile justice system may have had an unwanted side effect. If the abused and neglected female developed a "chip on her shoulder" (that is, a disposition or inclination to feel resentful or angry), or has become somewhat aggressive in her behavior, then the likelihood that she will be picked up and charged with a "violent crime" may be higher than someone without the chip on her shoulder, and certainly higher than someone without any indications of aggressive behavior. Since few studies have looked at these relationships, it is hard to explain these findings in any conclusive

Table 2. *Childhood Victimization, Gender, and Any Arrest for Violence*

Type of Arrest	Abuse/ Neglect (676)	Controls (520)
	%	%
Juvenile Violent		
Male	9.5	5.4
Female	2.7	0.4*
Adult Violent		
Male	29.9	23.2
Female	8.3	4.1*
Any Violent		
Male	32.2	25.7
Female	9.8	4.1**

$*p < .05$ $**p < .01$

way. Nonetheless, I hope that these speculations will stimulate others to consider these findings and issues when they consider possible mechanisms and to reinforce the need to consider gender differences while examining the cycle of violence (Widom, 2000).

The lack of increased risk for violent offending for abused and neglected males has troubled me for quite some time, given that these findings are so contradictory to expectations. Recently, though, I have been working on a multidimensional modified ecological model to understand the long term consequences of early childhood victimization (Widom, 2000). In this work, I have stressed the importance of contextual factors in understanding outcomes. I began to wonder whether the dependent variable we have typically used in these analyses—any violent arrest—might not be sensitive enough for males. Since very few females are arrested for violence, having an arrest for violence appears to discriminate between abused and neglected and nonabused and neglected females. Perhaps, the reason for the lack of increased risk for violence among males is that having an arrest for violence is not such an unusual occurrence—among a sample such as this—unfortunately. For this reason, perhaps the dichotomous dependent variable (any arrest for violence) is not a good discriminator for males. We reexamined these data using a different dependent variable—the number of arrests for violence (logged). Here we found that abused and neglected males have a significantly larger number of arrests for violence than control males. Thus, there was a gender difference in the effect of childhood victimization on risk for arrest for violence. For females, there is an increased risk for participation (see Table 2). For males, there is an increased risk in the frequency of participation (the number of violent arrests) (see Table 3). Lastly, these findings reinforce for me the critical importance of considering the context surrounding issues under consideration.

CHILDHOOD VICTIMIZATION, VIOLENCE, AND RACE/ETHNICITY

We have also examined the impact of childhood victimization on criminal consequences in African-American and other non-White children compared to White children (see Table 4). We found that abused and neglected African American and other non-White children were at increased risk of arrest for violence. Surprisingly, this increased risk was *not* evident for White abused and neglected children compared to White controls. Indeed, the similarity in the risk of arrest for violence for abused and neglected and control White subjects in this sample was striking (Maxfield & Widom, 1996).

Clearly, the long-term consequences of childhood victimization for violent offending (as measured by official arrest statistics) appear to differ dramatically by race/ethnicity. These differential findings regarding the long-term criminal consequences of abuse and neglect by ethnicity should not be ignored. Wyatt (1990) has written that racial and ethnic minority children can encounter discrimination against their race, color, language, life and family styles, and religious and cultural beliefs. She suggests that these experiences will affect the self-esteem of racial and ethnic minority children and exacerbate the initial and lasting effects of victimization.

In a study of the epidemiology of trauma, Norris (1992) reported complex findings regarding race, which she felt "highlighted the importance of specifying the cultural context in which traumatic events occur." (p. 416) These violence findings suggest the need to examine more fully ethnicity differences in consequences as well as the role of family and community characteristics and responses (see Widom, 2000).

Societal practices can lead to unequal distribution of resources and educational employment opportunities. If there are differences in the community's or system's response to abused and neglected children as a function of differences in ethnic or racial backgrounds,

Table 3. *Mean Number of Violent Arrests Among Abused and Neglected Individuals and Controls in the Follow-up Sample (N = 1,196)*

	Overall		Among Those with at Least One Arrest	
	Abuse/ Neglect	Control	Abuse/ Neglect	Control
Male	0.81	0.46**	2.51	1.77**
Female	0.16	0.05**	1.64	1.20

**p < .01

Table 4. *Childhood Victimization, Ethnicity, and Any Arrest for Violence*

Type of Arrest	Abuse/ Neglect (676)	Controls (520)
	%	%
Juvenile Violent		
White	3.1	2.2
Non-White	10.8	4.5*
Adult Violent		
White	12.3	10.7
Non-White	30.0	19.9*
Any Violent		
White	13.2	11.3
Non-White	33.5	22.4**

Note: Non-White includes Black, Hispanic, American Indian, Asian, and Pacific Islander.
*p < .05   ** p < .01

then, it is important to identify these differences, particularly if they relate to subsequent levels of violence in these children.

Lewis, Shanok, Cohen, Kligfield, & Frisone (1980) compared two samples of adolescents, one sent to a correctional facility and the other admitted to a state psychiatric hospital, in one urban area during a one-year time period. The most powerful distinguishing factor between the two groups was race: 71% of the hospitalized adolescents were white, whereas 67% of the incarcerated adolescents was black. "Our clinical and epidemiological findings indicate clearly that many seriously psychiatrically disturbed, aggressive black adolescents are being channeled to correctional facilities while their equally aggressive white counterparts are directed toward psychiatric treatment facilities" (p. 1216). Not only would this practice reinforce the stereotypes instead of demolishing them, as Comer (1972) suggested, but it would perpetuate the segregation of white and black violently disturbed adolescents.

In another examination of the role of clinical and institutional interventions in children's recovery from sexual abuse, Newberger and Gremy (1995) found that children of color received later and less outpatient therapy than White children, were more likely to be placed outside the home, and to be hospitalized for psychiatric diagnoses. If the abuse or neglect experiences of some children are being identified at a later point in the process, then there is less opportunity to intervene positively in these children's lives and more time for dysfunctional behaviors to become firmly entrenched.

THE CYCLE OF VIOLENCE: DOES VIOLENCE BEGET VIOLENCE?

According to the cycle of violence hypothesis, one would expect that physically abused children (that is, those who experienced violence in childhood) would have the highest rates of arrest for violence when they grow up. To test this hypothesis, arrests for violence were examined as a function of the type of abuse or neglect experienced. It was expected that individuals who experienced physical abuse in childhood would show higher levels of violence than those victimized by sexual abuse or neglect.

Table 5 shows the likelihood that our subjects have an arrest for a violent crime (juvenile or adult) by the type of abuse or neglect (any physical abuse, any neglect, or any sexual abuse) they experienced in childhood. These findings are for the 1,196 individuals in the follow-up interviewed sample (not to be confused with previous findings published for the larger sample of 1,575; see Maxfield & Widom, 1996). Upon inspection of Table 5, it is clear that violence begets violence, but so too does childhood neglect. As expected, victims of childhood physical abuse had a high level of being arrested for violent criminal behavior (26%). However, the risk of arrest for violence for victims of childhood neglect was almost identical (23%). Individuals who had experienced childhood sexual abuse had the lowest rates of arrest for violence, but this might not be surprising since more females are sexually abused and females have lower risk of arrests for violence in general.

In our sample, as well as in national statistics, types of child-

Table 5. *Does Only Violence Beget Violence? Likelihood of Having an Arrest for Violence As a Function of Type of Abuse/Neglect for the Follow-up Sample*

Type of Abuse/Neglect	Any Arrest for Violence (in percent)
Physical Abuse	26.4
Neglect	22.5
Sexual Abuse	12.3
Controls	15.6

Note: Pure cases only (mixed cases omitted). Overall chi square = 11.84, *df* = 3, *p* < .01.

hood experiences of abuse and neglect are not distributed randomly across the population. Here, there were differences in demographic characteristics by type of abuse and neglect: that is, more females were sexually abused, more males were physically abused, and more African Americans were neglected. Since sex, race/ethnicity, and age are themselves related to differences in rates of violent criminal behavior, this makes it necessary to control for the effects of these factors if one wants to carefully "unpack" these relationships. The results of multivariate statistical analyses (which control for sex, race/ethnicity, and age) support the bivariate findings just described. That is, being physically abused *and* being neglected each lead to higher rates of arrest for violent crimes. Being sexually abused as a child was not associated with increased risk of arrest for a violent crime. These multivariate analyses also indicated that demographic characteristics of sex, race, and age were more powerful predictors of arrests for violence than the type of abuse or neglect.

These "cycle of violence" findings illustrate a related and important point—that the cycle of violence is not deterministic or inevitable. On the basis of their literature review, Kaufman and Zigler (1987) reached a similar conclusion several years ago. Other researchers have also called attention to individuals who "break the cycle of violence" (Egeland, Jacobvitz, & Sroufe, 1984; Herrenkohl, Herrenkohl, & Toedter, 1983; Hunter & Kilstrom, 1979). To paraphrase Kaufman and Zigler (1987, p. 190), our findings indicate that childhood physical abuse and neglect put one at increased risk for being arrested for a violent crime, but the path between these two points in time is far from direct or inevitable.

In sum, the "cycle of violence" research indicates that there is a demonstrable increase in risk of arrest for crime and violence associated with childhood abuse and neglect, although the relationship is not at all inevitable or deterministic. However, abused and neglected children are likely to have an earlier age of onset of arrest and a greater likelihood of becoming a chronic offender, compared to nonabused and nonneglected children. These characteristics of their offending have implications for future behavior since they have been found to be important precursors for later development. We have found differences in the patterns of these relationships by gender and race/ethnicity which ultimately will need to be examined further and understood better. Finally, these findings reveal that not only does violence (childhood physical abuse) beget violence, but so too does neglect. These results warrant consideration in a discussion of theories about motivation and mechanisms in the intergenerational transmission of violence.

THE IMPORTANCE OF NEGLECT

The importance of neglect has been recognized for some time, although the systematic study of neglect has not received the attention it deserves. For example, in 1754, Dr. Samuel Johnson wrote in a letter to Lord Chesterfield: "No man is well pleased to have his all neglected, be it ever so little."

Thirty years ago, Maslow (1968) called attention to the importance of satisfying a person's basic needs for food, clothing, shelter, *and* safety. Consider what it means to be growing up without the basic necessities of living—not having enough food, clothing, shelter, or medical attention to provide a secure environment for the developing child. (This is our definition of neglect for these children). Recall Maslow's hierarchy of needs pyramid (see Figure 1):

> Healthy people have sufficiently gratified their basic needs for safety, belongingness, love, respect, and self-esteem so that they are motivated primarily by trends to self-actualization. . . . Assured safety permits higher needs and impulses to emerge and to grow towards mastery. To endanger safety, means regression backward to the more basic foundation. What this means is that in the choice between giving up safety or giving up growth, safety will ordinarily win out. *Safety needs are prepotent over growth needs* (emphasis added). This means an expansion of our

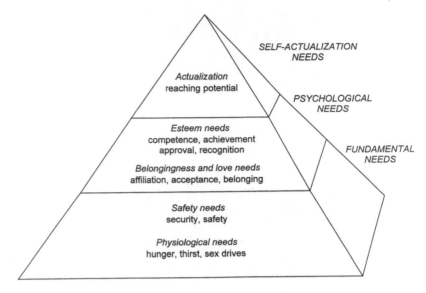

Figure 1. Maslow's hierarchy of needs

basic formula. In general, only a child who feels safe dares to grow forward healthily.

But we know also that curiosity and exploration are "higher" needs than safety, which is to say that the need to feel safe, secure, unanxious, unafraid is prepotent, stronger over curiosity. Both in monkeys and in human children this can be openly observed. The young child in a strange environment will characteristically hang on to its mother and only then, venture out little by little from her lap to probe into things, to explore and to probe. If she disappears and he becomes frightened, the curiosity disappears until safety is restored. He explores only out of a safe harbor. So also for Harlow's baby monkeys. Anything that frightens sends them fleeing back to the mother-surrogate. Clinging there, he can first observe and *then* venture out. If she is not there, he may simply curl up into a ball and whimper. (Maslow, 1968, pp. 49 & 64)

I would suggest that we need to attend as much (or more) to *neglected* children as we do to physically and sexually abused children, especially since we know that neglect is far more common in the United States than physical child abuse. I will not dwell on the need to intervene preventively with neglected and abused children since

Deborah Daro will be discussing this in her chapter and I have made this point elsewhere (Widom, 1998). I will move on to a consideration of some of the potential mechanisms which have been put forth to explain the "cycle of violence" phenomenon.

Motivation and Potential Mechanisms in the "Cycle of Violence"

A variety of theories have been put forth to explain the linkage between childhood victimization and violent behavior. These range from more traditional explanations, such as social learning theory, to more recent models drawing on social information processing models, and extrapolations from the literature on children's or animal's responses to stressful life events.

For the purposes of this chapter, I have selected a number of possible mechanisms which have been proposed to explain the "cycle of violence." Specifically, I will be focusing on five mechanisms which may account for these linkages: (a) social learning; (b) changes in self-concept, attitudes, or attributions; (c) physiological changes and desensitization; (d) attachment; and (e) maladaptive styles of coping. It is also possible that some of these relationships may be spurious.

SOCIAL LEARNING

The fundamental assumption of social learning theory is that behavior is adopted because it is perceived to be functional. From a social learning perspective, it is understandable that successive generations of parents and children can be violent, because we assume that physical aggression in family members provides a likely model for the learning of aggressive behaviors as well as for the appropriateness of such behavior within the family (Bandura, 1973; Feshbach, 1980). All children learn behavior, at least in part, by imitating someone else's behavior.

Thus, the first potential mechanism suggests that children learn to be aggressive through observing aggression in their families and the surrounding society. Observation of behavior is particularly potent when the model observed is of high status (such as a parent) or successful. Given the opportunity to engage in the behavior, it may be practiced and refined. Once learned, behavior can be reinforced or punished (internally or externally) by consequences and this, in turn, can lead to the future enactment or inhibition of the behavior.

According to this view, "each generation learns to be violent by being a participant in a violent family" (Straus, Gelles, & Steinmetz, 1980, p. 121). Aggressive parents tend to produce aggressive children (Bandura & Walters, 1959; Egeland & Sroufe, 1981; Eron, Walder, & Lefkowitz, 1971). More recently, Huesmann and his colleagues (1997) have suggested that children learn "scripts" that guide their actions, perceptions, and interpretations of the world.

From self-report surveys of exposure to violence and adult approval of violence or marital violence (Kalmuss, 1984), studies of children of battered women (Rosenbaum & O'Leary, 1981; Wolfe, Jaffe, Wilson, & Zak, 1985), and studies of television violence and aggressive behavior (Friedrick-Cofer & Huston, 1986), there is some support for the notion that observing violence leads to increased risk of further aggression and violence. However, the mechanism whereby this linkage occurs is not yet fully understood. From our findings presented earlier, not all children who grow up in violent homes become perpetrators of violence when they grow up (at least as defined by official arrest records).

CHANGES IN SELF-CONCEPT, ATTITUDES, OR ATTRIBUTIONAL STYLES

A second possible mechanism is that early childhood victimization may alter the child's self-concept, attitudes, or attributional styles which, in turn, may influence the adolescent's response to later situations. For example, the clinical literature has identified low *self-esteem* as one of the major characteristics of childhood victims (Bagley & Ramsay, 1986; Courtois, 1979; Herman, 1981). Lowered self-esteem may result from childhood victimization directly, by reducing the child's feelings of self-worth, or may be derived from the idea that the child was somehow responsible for the abuse or neglect. However, low self-esteem may also be indirectly related to abuse and neglect as a by-product of lowered cognitive functioning, poor social and interpersonal skills, antisocial and, ultimately, violent behavior.

PHYSIOLOGICAL CHANGES AND DESENSITIZATION

Experiences of early childhood victimization may also lead to bodily changes which, in turn, relate to the development of antisocial and violent behavior. For example, as a result of being beaten continually, or as a result of the severe stress associated with the abuse or neglect, a child might become "desensitized" to future painful or anxiety-provoking experiences. Thus, this desensitization might influence the child's later behavior, making him or her less emotionally and physiologically responsive to the needs of others, callous and *nonempathic*, and without remorse or guilt. This desensitization might then lead to the child's nonresponsiveness to conditioning by punishment (such as found in the psychopath) and ultimately be associated with the person's *need for external stimulation* and inability to tolerate boredom. Under these conditions, successful socialization would be unlikely and, in the right context, violence might be a likely outcome. On the other hand, desensitization might also work to protect the individual from aversive life events in later life; however, whether desensitization occurs and serves a positive or negative function remain empirical questions. We will examine the role of empathy and sensation seeking as possible mediators between childhood victimization and violence.

Another possible mechanism underlying this type of bodily change may be related to stress, which if occurring during critical periods of development, may give rise to abnormal brain chemistry which may lead to aggressive behavior at later points in life (Eichelman, 1990). For example, rats stressed by being immobilized for several hours a day for a period of one month displayed increased aggressive behavior and increased tyrosine hydroxylase in the hypothalamus long after the stress had been discontinued (Lamprecht, Eichelman, Thoa, et al., 1972).

Dorothy Lewis (1992) has suggested an association of childhood victimization with later violent behavior in part through brain neurotransmitters or through an effect on the serotonin system. Based on research findings from studies of nonhuman primates, Higley, Suomi, and their colleagues have suggested that rearing experiences may be associated with changes in central nervous system neurotransmitter activity in both norepinephrine and serotonin monamine systems (1989). Research findings indicate that rearing conditions affect reactivity, and that, in turn, influences levels of both norepinephrine and serotonin (Higley, Melman, & Taub, 1991). Peer-reared monkeys (a laboratory analogue to being neglected or reared without parental figures) showed aggressive behavior and low levels of 5-HIAA (a crude indicator of serotonin turnover) than mother-reared controls (Higley, Hasert, Suomi, & Linnoila, 1991).

While the extent to which one can generalize from this research with nonhuman primates to humans is questionable, the striking similarities between the concepts operationalized in the nonhuman primate literature (stress, anxiety, and rearing conditions of neglect) and in the child development literature (cf. Crittenden & Ainsworth, 1989) invite serious consideration.

ATTACHMENT

Attachment theory has also provided an explanation for the increased risk of aggressive and violent behavior among abused and neglected children. The assumption is that inconsistent, haphazard care or rejection of an infant can make it an insecure-avoidant child, who is likely to interpret neutral or even friendly behavior as *hostile*, and may show inappropriate aggressive behavior. Ainsworth (1989) describes the phenomenon whereby some of these children adopt what she called a "hostile world view."

Along these lines, Dodge, Bates, and Pettit (1990) have suggested that severe physical harm (physical abuse) leads to chronic aggressive behavior by having an impact on the development of social-information-processing patterns, or through the "acquisition of a set of biased and deficient patterns of processing social provocative information" (p. 1679). Dodge et al. found that physically harmed four-year old children showed deviant patterns of processing social information at age five and that these patterns were related to aggressive behavior. The physically harmed children (relative to non-physically harmed children) were significantly less attentive to relevant social cues, more biased toward attributing hostile intent, and less likely to generate competent solutions to personal problems.

Hostility may serve as one of the mechanisms whereby abused and neglected children go on to become violent offenders at a higher rate than nonabused and neglected children. However, abused and neglected children may also develop considerable hostility in a somewhat different context. Abused and neglected children may become angry and hostile in response to increased surveillance by social service and/or juvenile justice agencies. In turn, these angry and hostile feelings may give way to antisocial and violent behavior patterns.

MALADAPTIVE STYLES OF COPING

The final mechanism addressed here involves the hypothesized development of certain styles of coping which may be maladaptive. Characteristics such as lack of realistic long-term goals, being conning or manipulative, pathological lying, or glibness or superficial charm might begin in the child as a means of coping with an abusive home environment. Childhood victimization might lead to the development of early behavior problems, including impulsive behavioral styles which, in turn, translate into inadequate school performance, or less than adequate functioning in occupational spheres. Adaptations or coping styles that may be functional at one point in development (such as running away, avoiding an abusive parent, or desensitizing oneself against feelings) may later compromise the person's ability to draw upon and respond to the environment in an adaptive and flexible way. Evidence for whether abused and neglected children have maladaptive forms of coping is not extensive (see Spaccarelli, 1994 for a review). So far, most of the existing research has examined childhood sexual abuse victims and much of it has focused exclusively on coping through the use of alcohol and/or drugs.

Indeed, substance abuse (alcohol and drug abuse) is assumed to be one of the maladaptive coping strategies adopted by abused and neglected children to help them deal with their childhood traumas and to distance them from the painful realities they experienced. A growing number of studies have reported relationships between childhood victimization and drug abuse (see Miller, 1993; Widom, Weiler, & Cottler, 1999) and have speculated on a number of ways that substance use may serve useful functions for these children.

Substance abuse researchers have also noted the extensive co-occurrence of substance abuse with criminal behavior and violence (Chaiken & Chaiken, 1990; White, 1997). However, it is difficult to study the co-occurrence of these problem behaviors because alcohol and drug abuse diagnoses are often complicated by the presence of antisocial personality disorder, which in turn, includes components of criminal behavior. Hence, problems of definition and diagnosis make it difficult to distinguish among these various problems. Further, engaging in any of these behaviors might increase the likelihood of involvement in another. For example, use of illicit drugs is illegal and, thus, users are at risk for arrest. Drug users have been found to commit other crime to obtain money to buy drugs and may be forced to participate in the illegal drug market, where they may be exposed to potentially violent situations (Goldstein, 1985; White, 1997). Conversely, people who engage in criminal behavior may be exposed to heavy drug using subcultures because of their deviant status (White, 1990). Thus, each behavior may reciprocally influence the other.

In sum, five potential mechanisms involved in the intergenerational transmission of violence have been summarized briefly. The next section of this chapter presents a preliminary attempt to test some of these hypothesized linkages using data from the prospective cohorts design study described earlier (Widom, 1989b). The focus here is on the contributions of family risk factors (social learning theory) and a set of personality characteristics (self-esteem, empathy, sensation-seeking, and hostility) which have been implicated in these theoretical perspectives. However, it should be kept in mind that these are initial examinations, are quite limited, and do not adequately represent the range of possibilities which would be required to thoroughly examine these theories of the intergenerational transmission of violence.

Preliminary Empirical Findings Regarding Mechanisms in the "Cycle of Violence"

The findings described below are presented separately for males and females. This decision was made partly on the basis of the gender differences in findings (see Table 2). However, this decision was also made on the basis of an important theoretical and empirical literature on gender differences in the manifestation of distress (see Dohrenwend & Dohrenwend, 1976; Downey, Feldman, Khuri, & Friedman, 1994; Horwitz & White, 1987; Horwitz, White, & Howell-White, 1996; Widom, 1984) and in coping responses (Pearlin & Schooler, 1978). Typically, females have been reported to respond to stress through depression, anxiety, and psychophysiological symptoms, whereas males respond in externalizing patterns of behavior (for reviews, see Cleary, 1987; Dohrenwend et al., 1980; Hankin, 1990).

SOCIAL LEARNING?

The first set of analyses involved a series of simple tests of the social learning explanation for the "cycle of violence." To do this, the extent to which the cycle of violence relationships might be explained by growing up in a criminal or alcohol and drug abusing household was examined. The assumption was made that growing up in such an environment provides an opportunity to learn antisocial and aggressive behavior, as well as the lack of opportunity to develop prosocial skills and to imitate positive role models.

First, we tested the influence of a series of family risk factors including whether parents were ever arrested, whether siblings were arrested, or whether parents had an alcohol or drug problem. *Parent arrest* was based on the respondent's answer to a question about whether "your parent was ever arrested?" (abuse/neglect = 54.2%, controls = 32.8%). *Sibling arrest* was assessed through the respondent's answer to a question about whether any of their brothers or sisters had ever been arrested (abuse/neglect = 69.5%; controls = 57.5%). *Parental alcohol/drug problems* were assessed by the respondent's answer to the following question in the interview: "Did your (mother/father) ever have a drug or alcohol problem?" The question asked about lifetime parental problems with drugs or alcohol, and was not restricted to the childhood of the respondent (abuse/neglect = 57.7%, controls = 37.8%). *Welfare as a child*, a control variable, was included as a rough indicator of family social class at the time and as an index of childhood poverty. This variable was assessed by the person's response to an interview question which asked: "At any time during your childhood, did either of your parents ever receive welfare payments or food stamps?" (abuse/neglect = 58.8%, controls = 35.3%).

Table 6 reveals that male and female abused and neglected children were more likely than controls to report having grown up in "criminogenic" households, where their parents or siblings were arrested or had problems with alcohol or drugs.

The second step in testing the social learning explanation assessed whether these family risk factors predicted arrests for violence (i.e., number of arrests logged). That is, social learning theory would predict that childhood victimization is associated with increased violence through the indirect mediating effect of what we have called "family risk" factors. Table 7 reveals that family risk factors do *not* predict the number of arrests for violence. It should be pointed out that these equations control for a number of important characteristics—age, race/ethnicity, IQ, and welfare as a child, since the goal of these analyses is to determine whether it is the family risk factors which

Table 6. *Are Family Risk Factors Associated with Childhood Victimization? (Odds Ratios from Logistic Regressions)*

Family Risk Factors	Males (546)	Females (528)
Parent(s) Arrested	2.20***	1.79**
Sibling(s) Arrested	1.85**	ns
Parent(s) Drug/Alcohol Problem	2.38***	1.56*

Note: Regressions control for race/ethnicity, age, IQ, and welfare as a child. Numbers may vary due to missing data. ns = not significant.
*$p < .05$ **$p < .01$ ***$p < .001$

are associated with violence, not the other characteristics frequently associated with childhood victimization.

A series of path analyses were also performed to test the social learning model more directly. Although we found that family risk factors predict childhood victimization, these family risk factors do not predict violent arrests. There were no significant paths from these family risk factors to violence for males or females. Thus, it appears as if the simple hypothesis that children model their parents' antisocial and criminal behavior and thus learn violent behavior does not appear to be an adequate explanation of the cycle of violence.

PERSONALITY CHARACTERISTICS AS MEDIATORS?

The next set of analyses was undertaken to determine the extent to which certain characteristics (hostility, self-esteem, empathy, and sensation-seeking) acted as potential mediators between childhood victimization and violent behavior. Thus, the next set of analyses examined the role of four personality characteristics which have been implicated in theories about the mechanisms involved in the intergenerational transmission of violence. These measures, as well as our measure for substance abuse symptoms, are described below:

Hostility. A 6-item scale taken from the SCL-90, a multidimensional self-report symptom inventory developed by Derogatis (1977). This hostility subscale has acceptable internal consistency (Derogatis & Cleary, 1977).
Self-esteem. A 10-item scale (Rosenberg, 1979) with high internal consistency (.80 or better) and demonstrated construct validity.

Table 7. *Do Family Risk Factors Predict the Number of Violent Arrests?*

Family Risk Factors	Number of Violent Arrests (Logged)	
	Males (546)	Females (527)
Parent(s) Arrested	ns	ns
Sibling(s) Arrested	ns	ns
Parent(s) Drug/Alcohol Problem	ns	ns

Note: OLS regressions control for race/ethnicity, age, IQ, and welfare as a child. ns = not significant.

Empathy. This 5-item scale includes: (1) You worry a lot about the people who are close to you; (2) It hurts you a lot when the people you love are unhappy; (3) You feel responsible for taking care of other people; (4) You take care of yourself before you think about other people's needs; and (5) You are a very sympathetic person. Subjects were asked "how often . . . [each item] is true for you." Response categories ranged from "never true" to "always or almost always true."

Sensation-seeking. This 4-item scale (Zuckerman, Kolin, Price, & Zoob, 1964) includes one item from each factor—Disinhibition, Thrill and Adventure Seeking, Boredom Susceptibility, and Experience Seeking.

Substance abuse. The number of lifetime alcohol and/or drug symptoms, taken from the alcohol and drug abuse modules of the NIMH DIS-III-R (Robins et al., 1989).

The first step was to examine whether abused and neglected children manifest different levels of these personality characteristics than controls as young adults. These findings are presented separately for males and females in Table 8, with controls for race/ethnicity, age, IQ, and welfare as a child (as a proxy for family social class in childhood). As can be seen, abused and neglected males did not differ significantly from control males on these personality characteristics. In contrast, abused and neglected females had higher scores on hostility, empathy, and sensation-seeking than control females, despite controls for race/ethnicity, age, IQ, and welfare as a child.

To determine whether these characteristics are important in explaining the increase in risk for violence associated with abused and neglected children, the next step involved an examination of these individual personality characteristics in relation to arrests for violence. Table 9 presents the results of a series of ordinary least squares

Table 8. *Does Childhood Victimization Predict Personality Characteristics? (OLS Standardized Regression Coefficients)*

Personality Characteristic	Males (546)	Females (531)
Hostility	ns	0.10*
Self-Esteem	ns	ns
Empathy	ns	0.10*
Sensation-Seeking	ns	0.14**

Note: OLS regressions control for race/ethnicity, age, IQ, and welfare as a child. ns = not significant.
*$p < .05$ **$p < .01$

regression analyses predicting the number of arrests for violence (logged), with controls for race/ethnicity, age, IQ, and welfare as a child. For males, none of the personality characteristics predicts violence. However, for females, hostility and sensation-seeking are significant predictors.

Thus, these results suggest a number of tentative conclusions. First, the consequences of early childhood victimization for the development of selected personality characteristics appear to differ by gender. Second, predictors of arrests for violence for males and females are also different. In terms of mechanisms in the intergenerational transmission of violence, these findings suggest that those theories which incorporate hostility and sensation-seeking into explanations of why abused and neglected females become violent have some empirical grounding. On the other hand, these analyses have not shed particular light on understanding the "cycle of violence" among males.

SUBSTANCE ABUSE AS MEDIATOR?

The next set of analyses focused on whether substance abuse is a mediator between childhood victimization and subsequent violent behavior and followed the same steps as in earlier analyses. First, ordinary least squares regressions were performed looking at the extent to which childhood victimization predicted the number of substance abuse (alcohol and drugs) symptoms (logged), controlling for race/ethnicity, age, IQ, and welfare as a child. The second step was to determine whether substance abuse symptoms predicted arrests for violence. Table 10 presents these findings for males and females separately.

Table 9. *Do Certain Personality Characteristics Predict Arrests for Violence? (OLS Standardized Regression Coefficients)*

Personality Characteristic	Number of Arrests for Violence (logged)	
	Males (546)	Females (531)
Hostility	ns	0.11*
Self-Esteem	ns	ns
Empathy	ns	ns
Sensation-Seeking	ns	0.09*

Note: OLS regressions control for race/ethnicity, age, IQ, and welfare as a child. ns = not significant.
*p < .05

Table 10. *Does Substance Abuse Act as a Mediator between Childhood Victimization and Arrests for Violence?*

	Males	Females
Does childhood victimization predict the number of alcohol/drug symptoms?	ns	0.10*
Does the number of alcohol/drug symptoms predict arrests for violence?	0.18***	0.16***

Note: OLS regressions control for race/ethnicity, age, IQ, and welfare as a child. ns = not significant.
*p < .05   ***p < .001

Table 10 shows that childhood abuse and neglect is associated with greater problematic use of substances (a higher number of substance abuse symptoms) for females but not for males. Table 10 also reveals that for both males and females, the number of substance abuse symptoms is a significant predictor of arrests for violence.

Because abused and neglected children are more likely to report having parents arrested and parents with drug and alcohol problems, and because children of parents with alcohol problems are themselves at risk for the development of alcohol problems (Midanik, 1983; Pickens et al., 1991; Winokur & Clayton, 1968), a more complete examination of these relationships would take into account characteristics of the parents as well as of the children (our subjects). Thus, the final step in these analyses was to test a series of structural equation models including parent risk factors, child characteristics (including race/ethnicity, age, and IQ), welfare as a child, and the potential mediators (four personality characteristics and number of substance abuse symptoms). In these analyses, the antecedent variables are all correlated.

In these models, for females, there was a direct path from childhood victimization to increased substance abuse symptoms to increased number of arrests for violence. However, the hypothesized paths through the other potential mediators were not significant. Similarly, for males, there was a direct path from substance abuse symptoms to number of arrests for violence. However, none of the hypothesized personality characteristics or family risk factors was associated with violence. Furthermore, there was no direct path from childhood victimization to violence nor was there an indirect path from childhood victimization to violence through alcohol/drug symptoms for these males.

COPING STRATEGIES AS MEDIATOR?

The final set of analyses examined the role of coping strategies as possible mediators between child abuse and neglect and subsequent violence. Jorge Chavez and I have been examining the role of coping as a potential mediator between child abuse and neglect and adult negative consequences. We initially assumed that abused and neglected children would develop maladaptive coping styles in response to their abusive childhood experiences. However, early in our analyses we found that this was not the case. There were no differences in coping styles between abused and neglected children and matched controls in our sample, with one exception—the use of alcohol and drugs to cope (Chavez & Widom, 1998). Childhood victims of abuse and neglect reported greater use of this particular coping strategy than controls. However, in general, we did *not* find differences in coping strategies between childhood victims and controls. Thus, these findings do not provide support for the general hypothesis that abused and neglected children adopt maladaptive coping strategies which, in turn, lead to increased risk for violence. The one coping strategy used more often by abused and neglected individuals than controls (the use of alcohol and drugs to cope) reinforces the important role of substance use for victims of childhood abuse and neglect.

Conclusions

These findings provide convincing evidence for the cycle of violence. In the most direct and stringent test, being physically abused as a child does increase a person's likelihood of being arrested for criminal violence when they grow up. But, being neglected also increases the likelihood of a person's subsequent violent behavior. The fact that neglected children as well as physically abused children are at increased risk for violence, illustrates and reinforces the importance of examining separately the effects of different types of childhood victimization. In the past, most of the published research has focused on childhood physical and sexual abuse, with relatively little attention paid to neglect. These findings suggest that neglect by itself (life threatening omission of food, clothing, shelter, and medical attention) has serious long-term negative consequences. Here, the large group of neglected children had high rates of arrest for violence and the highest rates of arrests for violence as juveniles.

One possibility is that neglect, almost by definition, means that someone is not taking proper care of the child and that the child lacks supervision. Being out on the streets at inappropriate times gives a child opportunities for getting into trouble. Being out on the streets also places the child in situations where he or she may be picked up by the police and charged with various forms of misbehavior.

Another possibility is that the accumulation of stressful experiences associated with neglect, presumably occurring over a long period of time, leads to these negative consequences, similar to those produced through direct victimization of children by physical abuse. Given that the number of cases of child neglect far outweigh those for physical abuse in national statistics (by a factor of 2:1) (Sedlak, 1990), these findings have implications for the forecasting of future violent behavior.

In terms of potential mechanisms underlying the cycle of violence, these preliminary findings do not provide support for a simple social learning explanation. While these abused and neglected children are more likely to come from what might be considered "criminogenic" families, these family risk factors do not appear to explain the increased risk for arrests for violence.

For females, there appears to be a clear pathway from childhood victimization to violence through increased substance abuse symptoms. On the other hand, for males, none of the direct paths from childhood victimization to violence nor the indirect paths examined here were significant. These surprising findings warrant some comment. First, it is possible that this is simply the wrong model. Prior to the 1970s, the majority of theoretical models were linear or main effects models. I have suggested elsewhere that we need to begin to conceptualize the consequences of childhood victimization in nonlinear ways (Widom, 2000) and to test nonlinear models which may offer further understanding of the intergenerational transmission of violence.

For males, another possibility to be considered is that there may be something about this sample which has influenced these findings. In general, these males are at high risk for a number of problem behaviors (see Luntz & Widom, 1994; Maxfield & Widom, 1996; Widom, Weiler, & Cottler, 1999; Widom, Ireland, & Glynn, 1995). Childhood abuse and neglect may not represent an independent contributor to the risk behavior of males similar to those we have in this sample. We may need to think about thresholds for risk and about saturation models (Widom et al., 1995). We may find that, for some children, childhood victimization experiences represent only one risk factor among a constellation of risk factors characterizing these children. This may be particularly true for children whose cases have come to the attention of the courts for child abuse and neglect. However, this characterization may not be true for middle and upper class children whose cases may not come to the attention of public officials.

Other potential pathways from child abuse and neglect to violence and other coping mechanisms also need to be considered. For example, we are examining the role of running away as a potential mediator between early child abuse and neglect and subsequent delinquent and violent criminal behavior (Kaufman & Widom, 1999). Similarly, we have begun to recognize the potential importance of stressful life events and will be examining the role of these events in the lives of abused and neglected children and subsequent outcomes.

Another possibility not examined here is that childhood victimization may lead to immediate sequelae which then have an irremediable effect on the subsequent development of the child. A child does not need to be struck on the head to sustain brain injuries. Dykes (1986) has described infants who were shaken so vigorously that they sustain intracranial and intraocular bleeding with no signs of external

trauma. Being abused or neglected as a child may result in brain dysfunction as a result of direct brain injury or as a result of malnutrition.
These forms of physical abuse (e.g., battering) or severe neglect (e.g.,
dehydration, diarrhea, and failure to thrive) may lead to developmental retardation which, in turn, may affect school performance
and behavior (e.g., truancy). Some empirical support is provided by
a study of Barbadian children by Galler, Ramsey, Solimano, & Lowell
(1983) who found that malnourished children ages 5 to 11 years old
had significantly lower IQ scores than a matched control group. The
malnourished children also exhibited more attention deficits, poorer
social skills, and less emotional stability in comparison to the controls.
The processes linking childhood victimization with later negative
consequences may have an immediate impact or a delayed outcome,
manifest only some time later.

Some of the consequences associated with childhood victimization may result from the chain of events occurring subsequent
to the victimization rather than from the victimization experience
itself. For example, child abuse and/or neglect may lead to changed
environments or family conditions which, in turn, may increase risk
for delinquency or violence. Being taken away from one's biological
parents, subsequent to the abuse and neglect incident(s), and placed
in foster care may be associated with deleterious effects.

One might also take the position that the relationship between
child abuse, neglect, and violent behavior is spurious, masking a
rather different etiology. For example, Quay (1977) has argued that
certain children may be born with certain biological predispositions
which lead them to seek external stimulation. Theoretically, parents
may react negatively to such a predisposition in their child, with
excessively harsh or inconsistent discipline, rejection, or retreat. In
turn, the child may react by developing antisocial and violent behavior. Patterson and his colleagues (Patterson, 1997; Patterson, De-
Baryshe, & Ramsey, 1989) have described a model which begins with
a troublesome child and/or parents who lack firmness and skills in
discipline, and this leads to coercive cycles of interaction during early
childhood.

While some evidence exists that infants and young children with
different temperaments may elicit different parental behaviors (Bates,
1989) and that children with different temperaments may be singled
out for abuse (e.g. Friedrich & Boriskin, 1976; Herrenkohl & Her-

renkohl, 1981), other researchers have not in general found this to be the case (e.g., Dodge et al., 1990; Silver, Dublin, & Lourie, 1969).

It is also possible that there are certain genetic predispositions to aggressive behavior which are passed on from generation to generation (DiLalla & Gottesman, 1991). However, we do not have data available to test such an hypothesis.

As seen from these preliminary analyses of possible motivations and mechanisms in the cycle of violence, "reality," or some semblance of it, may not be as simple as expected or as hoped. As H. L. Mencken once said: "For every problem, there is one solution that is simple, neat, and wrong." Perhaps the simple notion of a "cycle of violence" needs reconsideration. We may need to move away from "main effects" models where we think about consequences as a direct result of some specific pathogenic experience (e.g. childhood victimization) or process or some inherent biological predisposition or dysfunction. In the future, we need to design studies and utilize analytic techniques which will permit examination of dynamic relationships in more complex ways.

References

Ainsworth, M. S. (1989). Attachments beyond infancy. *American Psychologist,* 44, 709–716.

American Psychiatric Association (1987). *Diagnostic and statistical manual of mental disorders (DSM-III-R).* Washington DC

Bagley, C., & Ramsay, R. (1986). Sexual abuse in childhood: Psychosocial outcomes and implications for social work practice. *Journal of Social Work and Human Sexuality,* 4(1–2), 33–47.

Bandura, A. (1973). *Aggression: A social learning analysis.* Englewood Cliffs NJ: Prentice-Hall.

Bandura, A., & Walters, R. H. (1959). *Adolescent aggression.* New York: Ronald.

Bates, J. E. (1989). Applications of temperament concepts. In G. A. Kohnstamm, J. E. Bates, & M. K. Rothbart (Eds.), *Temperament in childhood* (pp. 321–355). Chichester, England: Wiley.

Chaiken, J. M., & Chaiken, M. R. (1990). Drugs and predatory crime. In M. Tonry & J. Q. Wilson (Eds.), *Crime and justice* (Drugs and crime ed., Vol. 13). Chicago: University of Chicago Press.

Chavez, J. M., & Widom, C. S. (1998). *Childhood victimization, stressful life events, and coping strategies as predictors of substance abuse and violence.* Manuscript in preparation.

Cleary, P. D. (1987). Gender differences in stress-related disorders. In R. C.

Barnett, L. Biener, & G. K. Baruch (Eds.), *Gender and stress* (pp. 144–156). New York: Free Press.

Comer, J. (1972). *Beyond black and white.* New York: Quadrangle.

Cook, T. D. (1990). The generalization of causal connections: Multiple theories in search of clear practice. In L. Sechrest, E. Perrin, & J. Bunker (Eds.), *Research methodology: Strengthening causal interpretations of nonexperimental data (DHHS Publication No. 90–3454,* pp. 9–31). Washington DC: U.S. Department of Health and Human Services, Agency for Health Care Policy and Research.

Courtois, C. A. (1979). The incest experience and its aftermath. *Victimology, 4,* 337–347.

Crittenden, P. M., & Ainsworth, M. S. (1989). Child maltreatment and attachment theory. In D. Cicchetti & V. Carlson (Eds.), *Child maltreatment* (pp. 432–463). New York: Cambridge University Press.

Derogatis, L. R. (1977). *The SCL-90 Manual I: Scoring, administration and procedures for the SCL-90.* Baltimore: Johns Hopkins University of Medicine, Clinical Psychometrics Unit.

Derogatis, L. R., & Cleary, P. A. (1977). Confirmation of the dimensional structure of the SCL-90: A study in construct validation. *Journal of Clinical Psychiatry, 33,* 981–989.

DiLalla, L. F., & Gottesman, I. I. (1991). Biological and genetic contributors to violence—Widom's untold tale. *Psychological Bulletin, 109,* 125–129.

Dishion, T. J., & Patterson, G. R. (1997). The timing and severity of antisocial behavior: Three hypotheses within an ecological framework. In D. M. Stoff, J. Breiling, & J. D. Maser (Eds.), *Handbook of antisocial behavior* (pp. 205–217). New York: Wiley.

Dodge, K. A., Bates, J. E., & Pettit, G. S. (1990). Mechanisms in the cycle of violence. *Science, 250,* 1678–1683.

Dohrenwend, B. P., & Dohrenwend, B. S. (1976). Sex differences in psychiatric disorders. *American Journal of Sociology, 81,* 1447–1459.

Dohrenwend, B. P., Dohrenwend, B. S., Gould, M. S., Link, B., Neugebauer, R., & Wunsch-Hitzig, R. (1980). *Mental illness in the United States: Epidemiological estimates.* New York: Praeger.

Downey, G., Feldman, S., Khuri, J., & Friedman, S. (1994). Maltreatment and childhood depression. In W. M. Reynolds & H. F. Johnson (Eds.), *Handbook of depression in children and adolescents* (pp. 481–508). New York: Plenum Press.

Dykes, L. (1986). The whiplash shaken infant syndrome: What has been learned? *Child Abuse and Neglect, 10,* 211–221.

Egeland, B., Jacobvitz, D., & Sroufe, L. A. (1984). Breaking the cycle of abuse. *Child Development, 59,* 1080–1088.

Egeland, B. E., & Sroufe, L. A. (1981). Developmental sequelae of maltreatment in infancy. In R. Rizley & D. Cicchetti (Eds.), *Developmental perspectives in child maltreatment* (pp. 77–92). San Francisco: Jossey-Bass.

Eichelman, B. (1990). Neurochemical and psychopharmacologic aspects of aggressive behavior. *Annual Review of Medicine, 41,* 149–158.

Eron, L., Walder, L. O., & Lefkowitz, M. M. (1971). *Learning aggression in children.* Boston: Little Brown.

Feshbach, S. (1980). Child abuse and the dynamics of human aggression and violence. In J. Gerbner, C. J. Ross, & E. Zigler (Eds.), *Child abuse: An agenda for action.* New York: Oxford University Press.

Friedrich, W., & Boriskin, J. A. (1976). The role of the child in abuse: A review of the literature. *American Journal of Orthopsychiatry, 46,* 580–590.

Friedrich-Cofer, L., & Huston, A. C. (1986). Television violence and aggression: The debate continues. *Psychological Bulletin, 100,* 364–371.

Galler, J. R., Ramsey, F., Solimano, G., & Lowell, W. E. (1983). The influence of malnutrition on subsequent behavioral development. II. Classroom behavior. *Journal of the American Academy of Child Psychiatry, 24,* 16–22.

Gelles, R. J., (1975). The social construction of child abuse. *American Journal of Orthopsychiatry, 43,* 363–371.

Gelles, R. J., & Cornell, C. P. (1985). *Intimate violence in families.* Beverly Hills CA: Sage.

Goldstein, P. J. (1985). The drugs/violence nexus: A tripartite conceptual framework. *Journal of Drug Issues, 15,* 493–506.

Goldstein, P. J. (1991). Frequency of cocaine use and violence: A comparison between men and women. In C. Schade & S. Schober (Eds.), *Epidemiology of Cocaine Use and Abuse. National Institute on Drug Abuse Research Monograph.* Rockville MD: NIDA.

Groeneveld, L. P., & Giovannoni, J. M. (1977). Disposition of child abuse and neglect cases. *Social Work Research and Abstracts, 13,* 24–30.

Hankin, J. R. (1990). Gender and mental illness. *Research in Community and Mental Health, 6,* 183–201.

Herman, J. (1981). *Father-daughter incest.* Cambridge MA: Harvard University Press.

Herrenkohl, E. C., Herrenkohl, R. C., & Toedter, L. J. (1983). Perspectives on the intergenerational transmission of abuse. In R. J. Finkelhor, R. J. Gelles, G. T. Hotaling, & M. A. Straus (Eds.), *The dark side of families* (pp. 305–316). Beverly Hills CA: Sage.

Herrenkohl, R. C., & Herrenkohl, E. C. (1981). Some antecedents and developmental consequences of child maltreatment. In R. Rizley & D. Cicchetti (Eds.), *New directions for child development: Developmental perspectives on child maltreatment* (Vol. 11, pp. 57–76). San Francisco: Jossey-Bass.

Higley, J. D., Hasert, M. F., Suomi, S. J., & Linnoila, M. (1991). A nonhuman primate model of alcohol abuse: Effects of early experience, personality and stress on alcohol consumption. *Proceedings of the National Academy of Sciences USA, 88,* 7261–7265.

Higley, J. D., Melman, P., & Taub, D. (1991). CSF monoamine and adrenal correlates of aggression in feral living rhesus monkeys. *Biological Psychiatry, 29*(50A), 16.

Higley, J. D., & Suomi, S. J. (1989). Temperamental reactivity in nonhuman primates. In G. A. Kohnstamm, J. E. Bates, & M. K. Rothbart (Eds.), *Temperament in childhood* (pp. 153–167). New York: John Wiley.

Hollingshead, A. B. (1975). *Four factor index of social status.* New Haven CT: Yale University. Working Paper.

Horwitz, A. V., & White, H. R. (1987). Gender role orientations and styles of pathology among adolescents. *Journal of Health and Social Behavior, 28,* 158–170.

Horwitz, A. V., White, H. R., & Howell-White, S. (1996). The use of multiple outcomes in stress research: A case study of gender differences in responses to marital dissolution. *Journal of Health and Social Behavior, 37,* 278–291.

Huesmann, L. R., Moise, J. R., & Podolski, C. L. (1997). The effects of media violence on the development of antisocial behavior. In D. M. Stoff, J. Breiling, & J. D. Maser (Eds.), *Handbook of Antisocial Behavior* (pp. 181–193). New York: Wiley.

Hunter, R. S., & Kilstrom, N. (1979). Breaking the cycle in abusive families. *American Journal of Psychiatry, 136,* 1320–1322.

Kalmuss, D. (1984). The intergenerational transmission of marital aggression. *Journal of Marriage and the Family, 46,* 11–19.

Kaufman, J. G., & Widom, C. S. (1999). Childhood victimization, running away, and delinquency. *Journal of Research in Crime and Delinquency, 36,* 347–370.

Kaufman, J., & Zigler, E. (1987). Do abused children become abusive parents? *American Journal of Orthopsychiatry, 57,* 186–192.

Lamprecht, F., Eichelman, B., Thoa, N., et al. (1972). Rat fighting behavior: Serum dopamine-beta hydroxylase and hypothalamic tyrosine hydroxylase. *Science, 177,* 1214–1215.

Leventhal, J. M. (1982). Research strategies and methodologic standards in studies of risk factors for child abuse. *Child Abuse and Neglect, 6,* 113–123.

Lewis, D. O. (1992). From abuse to violence: Psychophysiological consequences of maltreatment. *Journal of the American Academy of Child and Adolescent Psychiatry, 31,* 383–391.

Lewis, D. O., Shanok, S. S., Cohen, R. J., Kligfield, M., & Frisone, G. (1980). Race bias in the diagnosis and disposition of violent adolescents. *American Journal of Psychiatry, 137,* 1211–1216.

Loeber, R., & Stouthamer-Loeber, M. (1987). Family factors as correlates and predictors of juvenile conduct problems and delinquency. In M. Tonry & N. Morris (Eds.), *Crime and justice: An annual review of research* (pp. 29–149). Chicago: University of Chicago Press.

Luntz, B. K., & Widom, C. S. (1994). Antisocial personality disorder in abused and neglected children grown up. *American Journal of Psychiatry, 151,* 670–674.

Maslow, A. H. (1968). *Toward a psychology of being.* New York: Van Nostrand.

Maxfield, M. G., & Widom, C. S. (1996). The cycle of violence: Revisited six years later. *Archives of Pediatrics and Adolescent Medicine, 150,* 390–395.

Midanik, L. (1983). Familial alcoholism and problem drinking in a national drinking survey. *Addictive Behaviors, 8,* 133–141.

Miller, B. (1993). Investigating links between childhood victimization and alcohol problems. In S. E. Martin (Ed.), *Alcohol and interpersonal violence: Fostering multidisciplinary perspectives* (NIH Publication No. 93–3496). Rockville MD: U.S. Government Printing Office. (NIAAA Research Monograph No. 24)

Newberger, C. M., & Gremy, I. M. (1995, July). *The role of clinical and institutional interventions in children's recovery from sexual abuse.* Paper presented at the Fourth International Family Violence Research Conference, Durham NH.

Newberger, E. H., Reed, R. B., Daniel, J. H., Hyde, J. N., & Kotelchuck, M. (1977). Pediatric social illness: Toward an etiological classification. *Pediatrics, 50,* 178–185.

Norris, F. H. (1992). Epidemiology of trauma: Frequency and impact of different potentially traumatic events on different demographic groups. *Journal of Consulting and Clinical Psychology, 60,* 409–418.

Patterson, G. R., & Yoerger, K. (1993). Development models for delinquent behavior. In S. Hodgins (Ed.), Mental Disorders and Crime (pp. 140–172). Newbury Park CA: Sage.

Patterson, G. R., DeBaryshe, B. D., & Ramsey, E. (1989). A developmental perspective on antisocial behavior. *American Psychologist, 44,* 329–335.

Pearlin, L. I., & Schooler, C. (1978). The structure of coping. *Journal of Health and Social Behavior, 19,* 2–21.

Pickens, R. W., Svikis, D. S., McGue, M., Lykken, D. T., Heston, L. L., & Clayton, P. J. (1991). Heterogeneity in the inheritance of alcoholism. *Archives of General Psychiatry, 48,* 19–28.

Quay, H. C. (1977). Psychopathic behavior: Reflections on its nature, origins, and treatment. In I. Uzgiris & F. Weizmann (Eds.), *The structuring of experience* (pp. 371–383). New York: Plenum Press.

Robins, L. N., Helzer, J. E., Cottler, L., & Goldring, E. (1989). *National Institute of Mental Health Diagnostic Interview Schedule, Version III Revised (DIS-III-R).* St. Louis MO: Washington University.

Rosenbaum, A., & O'Leary, K. D. (1981). Marital violence: Characteristics of abusive couples. *Journal of Consulting and Clinical Psychology, 49,* 63–71.

Rosenberg, M. (1979). *Conceiving the self.* New York: Basic Books.

Schulsinger, F., Mednick, S. A., & Knop, J. (Eds.). (1981). *Longitudinal research: Methods and uses in behavioral sciences.* Boston: Martinus Nijhoff.

Sedlak, A.J. (1990) *Technical amendments to the study findings—National Incidence and Prevalence of Child Abuse and Neglect (NIS-2) 1988.* Washington DC: U.S. Department of Health and Human Services.

Silver, L. R., Dublin, C. C., & Lourie, R. S. (1969). Does violence breed violence? Contributions from a study of the child abuse syndrome. *American Journal of Psychiatry, 126,* 152–155.

Smith, C., & Thornberry, T. P. (1995). The relationship between childhood maltreatment and adolescent involvement in delinquency. *Criminology, 33*, 451–481.

Spaccarelli, S. (1994). Stress, appraisal, and coping in child sexual abuse: A theoretical and empirical review. *Psychological Bulletin, 116*(2), 340–362.

Straus, M. A., Gelles, R. J., & Steinmetz, S. K. (1980). *Behind closed doors: Violence in the American family*. Garden City NY: Anchor Press.

White, H. R. (1990). The drug use delinquency connection in adolescence. In R. Weisheit (Ed.), *Drugs, crime and the criminal justice system* (pp. 215–256). Cincinnati OH: Anderson , Criminal Justice Division.

White, H. R. (1997). Alcohol, illicit drugs, and violence. In D. Stoff, J. Brieling, & J. D. Maser (Eds.), *Handbook of antisocial behavior* (pp. 511–523). New York: John Wiley & Sons.

Widom, C. S. (Ed.). (1984). *Sex roles and psychopathology*. New York: Plenum Press.

Widom, C. S. (1988). Sampling biases and implications for child abuse research. *American Journal of Orthopsychiatry, 58*, 260–270.

Widom, C. S. (1989a). Child abuse, neglect and adult behavior: Research design and findings on criminality, violence, and child abuse. *American Journal of Orthopsychiatry, 59*, 355–367.

Widom, C. S. (1989b). The cycle of violence. *Science, 244*, 160–166.

Widom, C. S. (1998). Child victims: Searching for opportunities to break the cycle of violence. *Applied and Preventive Psychology, 7*, 225–234.

Widom, C. S. (2000). Understanding the consequences of childhood victimization. In R. M. Reece (Ed.), *The Treatment of Child Abuse* (pp. 339–361). Baltimore MD: Johns Hopkins University Press.

Widom, C. S., Weiler, B. L., & Cottler, L. B. (1999). *Childhood victimization and drug abuse: A comparison of prospective and retrospective findings. Journal of Cousulting and Clinical Psychology, 67*, 867–880.

Widom, C. S., Ireland, T., & Glynn, P. J. (1995). Alcohol abuse in abused and neglected children followed-up: Are they at increased risk? *Journal of Studies on Alcohol, 56*, 207–217.

Winokur, G., & Clayton, P. J. (1968). Family history studies. IV: Comparison of male and female alcoholics. *Quarterly Journal of Studies on Alcohol, 29*, 885–891.

Wolfe, D. A., Jaffe, P., Wilson, S. K., & Zak, L. (1985). Children of battered women: The relation of child behavior to family violence and maternal stress. *Journal of Consulting and Clinical Psychology, 53*, 657–665.

Wyatt, G. E. (1990). Sexual abuse of ethnic minority children: Identifying dimensions of victimization. *Professional Psychology: Research and Practice, 21*, 338–343.

Zingraff, M. T., Leiter, J., Myers, K. A., & Johnsen, M. C. (1993). Child maltreatment and youthful problem behavior. *Criminology, 31*, 173–202.

Zuckerman, M., Kolin, E. A., Price, L., & Zoob, I. (1964). Development of a Sensation Seeking Scale. *Journal of Consulting Psychology, 28*, 477–482.

Social Information Processing and Child Physical Abuse: Theory and Research

Joel S. Milner
Department of Psychology
Northern Illinois University

Explanatory models of child physical abuse have included constructs from a variety of domains, ranging from individual and family characteristics to community and cultural factors (Milner & Crouch, 1999; Tzeng, Jackson, & Karlson, 1991). Organizational models of child abuse have described these domains as representing different ecological levels of influence (Belsky, 1980, 1993). Factors at each ecological level are believed to have either potentiating or compensatory influences that may be transient or enduring in their effects on the risk for child abuse (Cicchetti & Rizley, 1981). Reviews are available that provide descriptions of contributing and compensating factors at the individual (e.g., Milner, 1998; Milner & Crouch, 1999; Milner & Dopke, 1997), family (e.g., Milner, 1998), community (e.g., Limber & Nation, 1998), and societal (e.g., Tolan & Guerra, 1998) levels.

Although factors at each ecological level are believed to contribute to the etiology of child physical abuse, this chapter examines

Material presented in this chapter represents a description and extension of a previously proposed social information processing model of child physical abuse (Milner, 1993, 1995).

Correspondence concerning this chapter should be addressed to Joel S. Milner, Center for the Study of Family Violence and Sexual Assault, Department of Psychology, Northern Illinois University, DeKalb IL 60115.

contributing factors at the individual level, with a detailed examination of how abusive and at-risk parents may process child-related information. More specifically, a social information processing model is used to describe parental cognitive activities believed to mediate verbal and physical aggression directed at children. Putative relationships between the information processing model components, stress, and personality factors are discussed.

Brief Historical Overview

The current use of social information processing models to describe cognitive mediators of behavior has its roots in social cognitive learning theories (e.g., Bandura, 1986; Markus & Zajonc, 1985; Mischel, 1973) and related social skills models (e.g., Lang, 1977; McFall, 1982; Patterson, 1971). These approaches typically include the view that, based on experiences, individuals develop cognitive schemata that moderate their future responses to environmental events.

Cognitive behavioral and social learning models have been used to explain aggression in a variety of groups, such as aggressive children (e.g., Akhtar & Bradley, 1991; Crick & Dodge, 1994, 1996), adult rapists (e.g., Laws & Marshall, 1990; Lipton, McDonel, & McFall, 1987; McFall, 1990), and male spouse abusers (e.g., Holtzworth-Munroe, 1991; Mihalic & Elliott, 1997). Similarly, in the child maltreatment field, cognitive behavioral approaches have been used to explain child neglect (e.g., Crittenden, 1993), child sexual abuse (e.g., Howells, 1981), and child physical abuse (e.g., Azar, 1986, 1989, 1997; Newberger & Cook, 1983; Parke & Collmer, 1975; Rosenberg & Reppucci, 1983; Twentyman, Rohrbeck, & Amish, 1984; Wolfe, 1987).

Although the authors who first used cognitive behavioral models to explain child physical abuse proposed a mediating role for cognitive factors, their focus tended to be on a small number of cognitions, such as parental awareness of child-related events (Newberger & Cook, 1983) or parental expectations and attributions about child-related behaviors (Azar, 1986, 1989; Larrance & Twentyman, 1983; Twentyman et al., 1984, Wolfe, 1987). Since a large number of abuse-related cognitive factors had been described in the family violence literature (e.g., Milner & Chilamkurti, 1991; Milner & Crouch, 1999), a comprehensive social information processing model was needed to organize and describe the cognitions thought to mediate physically abusive behaviors. In addition, a model was needed that described how cognitions may be related to each other and how cognitive activities may be impacted by events from other ecological levels (e.g., child-related stress) and personality factors (e.g., depression).

Social Information Processing Model

In an attempt to meet the need for a comprehensive cognitive behavioral model of child physical abuse, a social information processing model was proposed that provided an overview of the domains of parental cognitive activities thought to be associated with child physical abuse (Milner, 1993, 1995). In addition, the model provided descriptions of child-related cognitive distortions, biases, and errors in each domain (cognitive stage of information processing) that may cause caretakers to verbally and physically assault their children. The purpose of this chapter is to describe and expand upon earlier presentations of the social information processing model of child physical abuse. Following the description of the model, a detailed discussion of the empirical support for the various components of the model will be provided.

As indicated in Table 1, the components of the model consist of preexisting schemata, three cognitive processing stages, and a fourth cognitive/behavioral stage of response execution. The three cognitive stages include *perceptions* of social behavior; *interpretations* and *evaluations* that give meaning to social behavior; and *information integration* and *response selection* activities. The fourth stage involves *response implementation* and *monitoring* processes. Preexisting schemata and cognitive activities at one or more of the first three cognitive processing stages are thought to impact events at the response implementation and monitoring stage.

PREEXISTING SCHEMATA

The social information processing model assumes that abuse-related preexisting cognitive schemata (information structures that exist prior to the processing of new information) influence parental perceptions and child-related cognitions at other processing stages. This assumption is based on the view that all parents develop and maintain global (related to all children) and specific (related to their own children) child-related beliefs and values that guide their parenting

Table 1. *Components of a Social Information Processing Model of Child Physical Abuse*

Preexisting schemata
Stage 1: Perceptions
Stage 2: Interpretations and evaluations
Stage 3: Information integration and response selection
Stage 4: Response implementation and monitoring

behavior. Thus, parenting behavior is thought to be theory driven (e.g., based on preexisting beliefs about parenting behavior and about children) as well as context driven (impacted by situational factors, such as type of child behavior observed and level of environmental stress). The assumption that preexisting schemata provide a basis for theory-driven parenting behavior is similar to views that parents have internal working models or models of relating that guide their parenting behavior (Bowlby, 1982; Zeanah & Anders, 1987).

The social information processing model proposes that abusive, compared to nonabusive, parents hold more inaccurate and biased preexisting cognitive schemata involving beliefs and values that impact the way they perceive, evaluate, integrate, and respond to information related to children. Abuse-related beliefs and values about child rearing are thought to be acquired most often in the family of origin (e.g., value of physical punishment in child rearing) and from cultural norms (e.g., legitimacy of using force in relationships). However, general abuse-related schemata are also believed to develop as a consequence of negative interactions with children. This latter possibility allows for instances where situational stimuli can acquire idiosyncratic meanings that are incorporated into cognitive frameworks that impact a parent's responses to future situations.

In addition to maintaining different general beliefs about child-rearing practices, abusers are thought to maintain different types of person-specific schemata, which involve beliefs about others and oneself (Fiske & Taylor, 1991). For example, abusive, compared to nonabusive, parents may have different dispositional beliefs about their children's abilities and motivations (e.g., child-related expectations and attributions) and about their own parenting skills (e.g., self-efficacy and control expectancies) that impact how they view and treat their children.

With respect to other-person schemata, abusive, compared to nonabusive, parents are thought to have more erroneous preexisting beliefs (higher or lower expectations) about when the physical maturation and cognitive development of their child should occur (e.g., developmental milestones). Similarly, physically abusive, relative to nonabusive, parents may exhibit more errors in their beliefs about the age at which their child should be able to successfully carry out complex sequences of behaviors. The assumption is that the abusive parent will be more likely to expect that their child can perform sequences of behaviors that are not developmentally appropriate for the child.

Abuse-related schemata about the self are thought to involve the abusive parents' low self-esteem and lack of confidence in their parenting ability. In addition, self-efficacy is thought to be related to the types of causal attributions made (Bandura, 1986). Thus, parents with high levels of perceived self-efficacy may attribute parenting failures to a lack of effort, whereas parents with low levels of perceived self-efficacy may attribute parenting failures to low ability, which may lead to more expectations of failure in future parenting activities.

Abusive, compared to nonabusive, parents may enter the parenting role with other specific attributional beliefs (e.g., attributions of hostile intent and external control orientations). In a discussion of parents' attributional beliefs, Bugental (1993) suggested that some individuals (including physically abusive parents) have threat-oriented schema that structure how they perceive and react to caregiving situations. Parents with threat-oriented schema are believed to assess children's behavior for evidence of threat more frequently. Bugental asserts that parents who maintain threat-oriented schema may make more external attributions about the control of events and may enter parent-child interactions believing that the child has more control over outcomes than the parent.

In addition to ideational components, Turk and Speers (1983) suggested that preexisting cognitive schemata include affective components. Bucci (1997) described these emotions as image-action schemata that operate in or outside of awareness and differ from ideational schemata in their strong association with motoric and visceral systems. As discussed here, affective schemata are thought to consist of emotions that were experienced during previous events and are associated with specific beliefs about prior events. Thus, in addition to the beliefs held by an individual, associated moods are thought to influence how information is perceived, interpreted, organized in memory, and accessed (Arsenio & Ford 1985; Turk & Speers, 1983). In the case of physically abusive parents, it is proposed that preexisting schemata, such as the expectation of child noncompliance following discipline, often have associated negative affect (e.g., anger, hostility, anxiety, and depression in the parent) that influences how information is retrieved and how new information is perceived, processed, and acted upon.

Although the examples of schemata reviewed in this section are not assumed to be exhaustive, they are thought to be representative of abuse-related preexisting schemata that may help explain why abusive, relative to nonabusive, parents process and respond to child-related behavior in more negative ways. Further, abusive parents may be more likely to use their preexisting schemata, compared to situational cues, when they are interpreting and evaluating situations that involve ambiguous child behaviors, problematic but developmentally appropriate child behaviors, and minor child transgressions. Abusive parents are also thought to be more likely to use preexisting schemata if they are experiencing high levels of distress (especially if there is a combination of general parental stress and specific child-related stress) and/or if they are experiencing negative affect (either general affect or affect associated with preexisting cognitions).

STAGE 1: PERCEPTIONS

The first stage, the input stage, of the model suggests that abusive, relative to nonabusive, parents have deficits, distortions, biases, and errors in their perceptions of their children's behavior. First, it is proposed that physically abusive, compared to nonabusive, parents are less attentive to and are less aware of their children's behavior. More specifically, it is suggested that abusive parents often fail to encode information related to their children's behaviors. For example, abusive parents may fail to notice minor changes (e.g., improvements) in behavior when their child attempts to comply with the parent's request for a desired behavior. Second, it is suggested that abusive parents engage in selective attention; attention that is congruent with their preexisting schemata (beliefs and moods). Abusive, compared to nonabusive, parents may be more likely to observe noncompliant child behaviors because they expect noncompliant behaviors from their children. Next, it is hypothesized that abusive parents are different in their cue detection accuracy. In this case, the problem is not that abusive, relative to nonabusive, parents are inattentive to environmental information, rather the problem is that information is encoded inaccurately. For example, abusive, compared to nonabusive, parents may make more errors in their recognition of children's emotional expressions, especially if the emotions are expressed at a low intensity. Further, in cases where they correctly recognize children's emotional expressions they may more often incorrectly evaluate the intensity of the emotion.

A limitation of the present discussion is that few hypotheses have been made with respect to the reasons for encoding failures. That is, if an abusive parent fails to encode child-related information, is this failure due to dispositional differences (such as a general limitation in attentional capacity) or to attentional differences that exist only under certain conditions (such as when the parent is experiencing stress)? A general assumption is that when physically abusive parents are stressed they are more inattentive than nonabusers. However, the exact role of stress on encoding is not known. In contrast to the view that stress disrupts encoding, it may be that under stress physically abusive parents become hypervigilant and are more accurate encoders when viewing children and/or related stimuli because such stimuli are aversive and threatening to them.

Finally, although it is expected that parental perceptions of children's behavior are impacted by negative affective states (e.g., anxiety, depression), the nature and extent of these relationships in abusive parents are not known. Nevertheless, Gil (1970) and Lahey, Conger, Atkeson, and Treiber (1984) concluded that when mothers are depressed (a characteristic of many physically abusive mothers, Milner, 1998), they have a lower threshold for perceived child misbehavior, suggesting that preexisting affective states may moderate child-related perceptions. Alternatively, what researchers have reported as a lower threshold for perceived misbehavior in abusive parents may be due to different evaluations of children's behavior (Stage 2) and not to actual differences in the information perceived.

STAGE 2: INTERPRETATIONS AND EVALUATIONS

The second stage of the model proposes that physically abusive, relative to nonabusive, parents will display differences in their interpretations and evaluations of their children's behavior. Abusive parents are believed to make quantitatively and, sometimes, qualitatively different judgements on various dimensions of their children's behavior. It is expected that abusive parents will interpret noncompliant child behavior as being more serious, wrong, and blameworthy. Likewise, it is expected that abusive, compared to nonabusive, parents will be more likely to view negative behaviors as due to internal, stable, and global child factors, and will be more likely to view the behavior as being motivated by hostile intent.

Although attributional differences are expected when negative child behaviors are being evaluated, attributional differences between abusers and nonabusers are predicted to be greatest in parent-child interactions that represent ambiguous child behaviors, problematic but developmentally appropriate child behaviors, and minor child transgressions. Further, in each of these situations, it is thought that interpretations and evaluations are more likely to be influenced by the parents' preexisting schemata, which in the case of abusive parents are more likely to involve inaccurate and biased schemata.

In the proposed model, differences in the evaluation of the wrongness of children's behavior are believed to be critical mediators of abusive behavior. If a parent observes negative child behavior and attributes responsibility and negative intent to the child, it may be that the child's behavior must also be evaluated as wrong for negative consequences to follow. That is, the parent may observe negative behavior, attribute responsibility to the child, and attribute negative intent to the child, but because the parent does not evaluate the behavior as very wrong, there is little or no resulting disciplinary action. For example, a father may acknowledge that his male child is inappropriately aggressive (engaging in fighting in the classroom), attribute responsibility to his child, and perceive negative intent; but because of preexisting beliefs that young boys should "stand-up and fight for themselves," the father may not evaluate the behavior as wrong. On the other hand, if a minor transgression (failing to clear the dinner table) is viewed as wrong or very wrong, then the parental disciplinary response may be relatively severe. Thus, parental evaluations of wrongness may be a critical mediator of parental disciplinary actions.

Abusers, compared to nonabusers, are also assumed to make different predictions of child compliance following selected child transgressions and parental discipline techniques. These situation-specific expectation differences are believed to exist separate from more global, preexisting child-related expectation differences (e.g., expectations related to a child's general abilities). As predicted for perceptions at Stage 1, abusive, relative to nonabusive, parents' interpretations and expectations are thought to become more distorted and biased as their distress levels increase and when they experience negative affect.

STAGE 3: INFORMATION INTEGRATION AND RESPONSE SELECTION

The third stage of the model suggests that abusive, compared to nonabusive, parents fail to adequately integrate child-related information. It is proposed that abusers use different information-weighting and integration rules. This processing difference is viewed as a mediating factor in the response selection decision, separate from the contributions of preexisting schema and inaccurate and biased cognitions. Specifically, physically abusive parents are thought to be less likely to use situational information in their evaluation of their child's behavior. Thus, even if social information is perceived and interpreted correctly, abusive parents may ignore important information. For example, abusive parents may be aware of mitigating events (information that lessens the child's responsibility) related to a child's transgression, but because they fail to adequately integrate this information (e.g., big brother bumped little Johnny causing Johnny to spill the milk), the mitigating information has little or no impact on their disciplinary decision.

The lack of information integration may allow the abusive parent to maintain explanations of their child's behavior that are consistent with their own dispositional beliefs (e.g., belief that they have a problem child), which are associated with the use of power-assertive behaviors (verbal and physical assault). Further, increased levels of parental distress and negative affective states are believed to decrease the likelihood that the abusive parent will use mitigating information.

Finally, the response selection process will be limited to the response choices (parenting skills) that are available to a parent, which will be determined by their degree of knowledge of various parenting techniques and their ability to generate appropriate child management strategies. It is assumed that abusive, compared to nonabusive, parents have more skill deficits and less ability to creatively generate appropriate child management techniques. Relationships are also expected between the response selection process, stress, and negative affect. That is, stress and negative affect are thought to interfere with the response selection process in both abusive and nonabusive parents, but they are believed to have a relatively greater impact on abusive parents.

STAGE 4: RESPONSE IMPLEMENTATION AND MONITORING

The fourth stage of the model involves the parent's ability to implement a parenting skill, including the ability to monitor and modify their parenting behavior as needed. More specifically, physically abusive, compared to nonabusive, parents are thought to lack well-developed skills and/or abilities to adequately implement child-directed responses, which may include less ability to monitor and to modify their responses.

In addition, many factors are believed to impact the parent's implementation and monitoring abilities. For example, cognitive factors, such as expectations of child noncompliance (Stage 2), may reduce the likelihood that a discipline technique will be carefully implemented or monitored by the parent. Likewise, parental distress and negative affect may decrease the parent's ability to adequately implement or maintain some types of disciplinary strategies (such as approaches that include explaining rules to a child). Failure to achieve child compliance when the abusive parent uses techniques other than power assertion may serve to confirm the parent's child-related biases, increasing the likelihood that power assertive techniques will be used in the future.

AUTOMATIC AND CONTROLLED PROCESSING

In the social information processing model of child physical abuse (Milner, 1993), conceptualizations of automatic and controlled processing developed by Shiffrin and Schneider (1977, 1984; Schneider & Shiffrin, 1977) are used to explain possible relationships between the stages of the model. Although all parents are believed to use automatic and controlled processing, differences in abusive parents' preexisting schemata and perceptions of their children, which have been previously discussed, are believed to produce different outcomes when automatic and controlled processing are used.

Automatic processing is viewed as a cognitive process that occurs outside of awareness (Schneider & Shiffrin, 1977; Shiffrin & Schneider, 1977, 1984). It places few demands on attention and is difficult to modify or suppress. Automatic processing acts in parallel to other processes; and, once initiated, the processing generally continues to completion. With repeated use, automatic processing may result in shorter response latencies, which may explain, in part, the immediate and explosive reactions sometimes observed in physically abusive parents. In addition, abusers, compared to nonabusers, are thought to engage in more automatic processing of child-related data in ambiguous, everyday living, and/or stressful situations.

Automatic processing can be divided into two types: actional and informational. Actional automatic processing describes cognitive processes that direct internal activities (e.g., leads the parent to a conclusion regarding the child) or that lead directly to response selection and implementation (e.g., the child's crying leads immediately to parental physical discipline). Informational automatic processing does not lead directly to a response, but is viewed as providing an internal linkage between specific cognitions (e.g., a parental attribution of hostile child intent following a child's negative behavior may automatically trigger an expectation of child noncompliance following discipline for the transgression).

In contrast, controlled processing takes place in awareness, requires substantial attention, and is easily modified (Schneider & Shiffrin, 1977; Shiffrin & Schneider, 1977, 1984). Controlled processing may be especially useful in ambiguous and novel situations that require moment-to-moment decisions. If controlled processing (as opposed to automatic processing) is used in ambiguous and novel child-related situations, it is assumed that the parent will be more likely to reduce the influence of preexisting schema, to use mitigating information, and to respond in an appropriate fashion.

As indicated earlier, actional automatic processing may occur at

Stage 1 (perception of child) and lead directly to Stage 4 (parental response). That is, child behavior viewed as undesirable by a parent may initiate an automatic processing sequence that leads directly to a specific response selection. Although in some situations such efficiency may be adaptive and result in appropriate response choices, in other situations the rapid response may produce inappropriate outcomes if important information is overlooked. For example, the use of actional automatic processing by physically abusive parents may explain how mitigating information related to the child's behavior can be overlooked. In such a case, perceived child misbehavior leads directly to a parental response, skipping the information integration stage (Stage 3) where mitigating information about the seriousness, wrongness, and blameworthiness of the behavior may be considered.

The use of automatic processing is thought to be influenced by the individual's responses (physiological arousal) to stress. The greater physiological reactivity to stressful stimuli believed to be experienced by abusive, relative to nonabusive, parents (Milner & Crouch, 1999; Milner & Dopke, 1997) is thought to increase the abusers' use of automatic processing, which increases the likelihood of power assertive responses based on inaccurate and biased preexisting schemata. Further, when child-related stimuli are associated with parental emotions (e.g., anger or hostility), it is assumed that emotion triggered automatic processing can activate other cognitions and affect related to the child, which for abusive parents are more likely to be negative cognitions and emotions. This view is analogous to propositions made in general models of aggression. For example, in a cognitive-neoassociationistic model of aggression, Berkowitz (1990) postulated that the physiological arousal and negative affect experienced upon exposure to aversive stimuli can automatically activate associated cognitions and behavioral responses.

However, if controlled processing is used, controlled processing may attenuate or block the cognitive and behavioral responses associated with stress and negative affect (Clark & Isen, 1982). Therefore, with respect to parenting behavior, controlled processing is thought to enhance the likelihood of an appropriate behavioral response, resulting from such activities as increased efforts at integrating information and/or implementing and monitoring a response.

Although relatively simple examples of parental processing activities can be generated using descriptions of automatic and controlled processing, it should not be concluded that most processing relationships are simple and straightforward. During information processing, there may be a large number of automatic and controlled processing events occurring within and between the stages in the model. Automatic and controlled processing events are also assumed to be both nomothetic and idiographic in nature, making a complete exposition of abuse-related information processing events very difficult.

Research Related to the Social Information Processing Model Components

The research literature provides varying degrees of support for the contention that physically abusive, relative to nonabusive, parents are different in their preexisting schemata and cognitions at the different stages of the proposed social information processing model of child physical abuse. Following a discussion of methodological issues common to the child abuse studies, a discussion of the research describing preexisting schemata believed to be common to physically abusive parents will be presented. These discussions will be followed by a review of research data on abusive parents' cognitions at each stage of the model.

METHODOLOGICAL ISSUES

As the research literature is summarized, specific research concerns will be described. There are, however, several general problems that should be mentioned prior to beginning the literature review. These problems involve theoretical, definitional, sampling, and design issues. First, it should be noted that most of the studies reviewed here were not conducted to directly test the social information processing model, and in some instances the research does not appear to be linked to any specific cognitive model. Thus, some of the studies only marginally inform the model. Another limitation is that terms are not always defined in a consistent manner across studies nor in the same manner as in the social information processing model. For example, in some studies parental perceptions of child behavior refer to parental evaluations of child behavior (e.g., Mash, Johnston, & Kovitz, 1983; Reid, Kavanagh, & Baldwin, 1987), whereas, in other studies (Camras et al., 1988; During & McMahon, 1991; Kropp & Haynes, 1987) and in the present social information processing model, parental perceptions refer to the parents' attention to and accurate identification of social stimuli.

Another problem with the cited studies is that different criteria are used to define the child abuse study groups. Results are based on at-risk parents (e.g., Azar, 1997, Chilamkurti & Milner, 1993), physically abusive parents (e.g., Larrance & Twentyman, 1983), and mixed groups of physically abusive and neglectful parents (e.g., Newberger & Cook, 1983). Even when studies use the same category of parents (e.g., physically abusive parents), definitions often vary. For example, some physically abusive parents are self-identified abusive parents from Parents Anonymous programs (e.g., Frodi & Lamb, 1980), whereas other abusive parents are confirmed physically abusive parents from social services agencies (e.g., Trickett & Kuczynski, 1986). Studies also show a gender bias because in almost all studies only abusive mothers are studied, and, in many cases generalizability is limited by the use of small samples of abusive mothers (e.g., $n = 5$, Wood-Shuman & Cone, 1986).

Further, when parents reported for child physical abuse are studied, there are potential confounding effects of the abuse report, the investigation, the confirmation (which may include court action), and the intervention on their cognitions. In addition, when identified physically abusive parents are studied, it is not known if observed cognitive differences preceded the abusive behavior or were a consequence of the abuse. Only a modest number of studies have used at-risk parents (e.g., Chilamkurti & Milner, 1993; Dolz, Cerezo, & Milner, 1997; Dopke & Milner, in press; Milner & Foody, 1994; Milner, Halsey, & Fultz, 1995), a population which requires study to demonstrate that cognitive and behavioral factors precede abusive behavior. However, when at-risk parents are studied, there are problems with attenuation in whatever criteria are used to define the parents as at-risk as well as the possibility that some of the at-risk parents may have been abusive. Finally, even though there is an increasing awareness that demographic variables need to be controlled, many authors fail to use adequately matched abusive and comparison groups, resulting in confounded designs. That is, when demographic differences exist between the study groups, it is not known if observed differences in the dependent variables under investigation are due to abuse/nonabuse group differences and or to demographic (e.g., education) group differences.

EVIDENCE FOR PREEXISTING COGNITIVE SCHEMATA

Investigators have studied several beliefs and values associated with child discipline that are thought to represent abusive parents' preexisting schemata. For example, since abusive parents are reported to use more severe discipline (see literature reviews in sections on Stages 3 and 4), it has been assumed that abusive, relative to nonabusive, parents place a higher value on the more severe forms of discipline (e.g., physical discipline). Most study findings, however, have not supported this hypothesis. For example, although Trickett and Susman (1988) found that abusive, relative to comparison, parents rated material punishment (e.g., removal of privileges) as more effective and reasoning as less effective as disciplinary techniques, no overall difference in the value of spanking was observed. Likewise, Kelley, Grace, and Elliott (1990) reported no differences between abusive (court-referred) and nonabusive parents in the level of acceptability of spanking or timeout with spanking, even though differences were found between at-risk (self-referred) and nonabusive parents. Evans (1980) and Starr, Jr. (1982) also failed to find differences between abusive and nonabusive parents' attitudes toward punishment.

Despite these negative findings, additional research is needed because uncontrolled factors may have impacted the results of studies that have attempted to examine abusive parents' beliefs in the value of harsh disciplinary strategies. For example, identified physically abusive parents may give more socially acceptable responses when asked to indicate their beliefs in the value of power assertive (verbal and physical assault) disciplinary techniques because of concerns about the lack of confidentiality and about continuing to be identified and labeled as abusive (Kelley et al., 1990). Beliefs in the value of power assertive disciplinary strategies also warrant further study because beliefs in the "goodness" of corporal punishment have been associated with the use of violent discipline in general population mothers (Lenton, 1990).

Separate from general beliefs about the value of different disciplinary techniques, abusive parents are thought to have a number of negative beliefs related to the characteristics of their children (other-person schemata), and studies generally support this view. Abusive, relative to nonabusive, mothers report that their children have less intellectual ability (Reid et al., 1987), are more problematic (Mash et al., 1983), and are more hyperactive, aggressive, and conduct-disordered (Reid et al.). In each of these studies, the abusive parents' beliefs were not confirmed by independent raters, suggesting a cognitive bias on the part of the abusive parent. Congruent with these findings, Oates, Forrest, and Peacock (1985) found that abusive parents, relative to teachers, more frequently reported their children as having an abnormal level of behavior problems, and Stringer and LaGreca (1985) reported a significant correlation between abuse potential and reported behavior problems in sons, albeit not daughters. Thus, abusive and high-risk parents appear to have inaccurate and biased beliefs about their children's abilities and behaviors that represent preexisting biased schemata. These inaccurate and biased beliefs are thought to be separate from the well-documented findings that following maltreatment abused, compared to nonabused, children display higher rates of affective and behavioral problems (e.g., Malinosky-Rummell & Hansen, 1993).

Physically abusive, compared to nonabusive, parents are thought to have different preexisting expectations regarding child behaviors. Early in the development of child abuse theory, Gil (1970) suggested that physically abusive parents have more exacting standards for children's behaviors than nonabusive parents. Twentyman's cognitive behavioral model (Twentyman et al., 1984) is based on the specific notion that abusive parents enter parent-child interactions with unrealistically high expectations. Unfortunately, studies of abusive parents' child-related expectations (which are reviewed later when studies on Stage 2 of the model are discussed) are inconsistent in their findings with respect to whether or not abusive and high-risk, relative to comparison, parents have different preexisting child-related expectations (e.g., Azar, Robinson, Hekimian, & Twentyman, 1984; Caselles & Milner, 2000; Chilamkurti & Milner, 1993; Gaines, Sandgrund, Green, & Power, 1978; Kravitz & Driscoll, 1983; Larrance & Twentyman, 1983; Oates et al., 1985; Perry, Wells, & Doran, 1983; Spinetta, 1978; Starr, Jr., 1982; Twentyman & Plotkin, 1982). However, as the literature review will indicate, there may be specific expectation differences that are higher or lower based on the nature and context of the situation. For example, high-risk, compared to low-risk, mothers have been reported to expect less child compliance following discipline for major transgressions and more compliance following discipline for minor transgressions (e.g., Chilamkurti & Milner, 1993).

Few studies are available that directly assess abusive parents' preexisting beliefs about their parenting abilities and related control expectancies (self schemata). Abusive, compared to nonabusive, parents have been found to have less confidence in their parenting ability, as indicated by their predictions of the likelihood of achieving child compliance following discipline. What is unclear is the degree to which the abusive parents' lack of confidence in achieving compliance is due to their preexisting beliefs about parenting skills (self-efficacy) and/or to the abusers' negative views of their children.

Indirect evidence that abusive parents may have different schema regarding their parenting self-efficacy is available from studies of constructs thought to be associated with parenting self-efficacy. For example, abusive and high-risk, relative to nonabusive, mothers have lower self-esteem and ego-strength on general measures (e.g., Evans, 1980; Fulton, Murphy, & Anderson, 1991; Melnick & Hurley, 1969; Oates & Forrest, 1985; Perry et al., 1983; Shorkey & Armendariz, 1985) and on a measure that focused on emotional stability in relationships (Milner, 1988).

With respect to control orientations, Wiehe (1986) found that abusive, compared to nonabusive, mothers report a more external locus of control. This finding has been replicated with high- and low-risk mothers (Ellis & Milner, 1981; Stringer & LaGreca, 1985) and high- and low-risk male and female nonparents (Conyngham, 1998), suggesting that the external control orientation is a dispositional belief that predates abuse. Somewhat surprising was a related finding that high-risk, compared to low-risk, individuals had a lower desire for control (Conyngham). Although this finding needs replication, it was speculated that high-risk and abusive individuals may have a lower desire for control because they have a dispositional belief that life events are not under their control.

With respect to other attributional differences regarding control and intent, the literature (which is reviewed later when studies on Stage 2 of the model are discussed) provides a mixed picture with regard to whether abusive and high-risk, relative to comparison, parents make different attributions regarding their children's positive and negative behaviors (Bauer & Twentyman, 1985; Bradley & Peters,

56

1991; Diaz, Neal, & Vachio, 1991; Dopke & Milner, 2000; Foody, 1993; Larrance & Twentyman, 1983; Miller & Azar, 1996; Milner & Foody, 1994; Rosenberg & Reppucci, 1983; Schellenbach, Monroe, & Merluzzi, 1991; Valle, 1998). Nevertheless, since the general parenting literature indicates that attributions of intent and beliefs regarding children's blameworthiness can impact the parents' choice of disciplinary response (e.g., Bacon & Ashmore, 1986; Dix & Grusec, 1985; Dix & Lochman, 1990), additional studies should be conducted to determine the attributional patterns of abusive and at-risk parents.

The model suggests that preexisting beliefs often have associated negative affective states (image-action schemata) that can influence information processing. There is a paucity of data on the possibility that associations between specific beliefs and emotions exist in abusive and high-risk parents, albeit data can be found that indirectly support this possibility. For example, the impact of preexisting affective states on parental cognitions has been studied in nonabusive parents (e.g., Dix, Reinhold, & Zambarano, 1990). Mothers in an angry condition, compared to an emotionally-neutral condition, expected more negative child behaviors and believed that obtaining child compliance would be more difficult. Interestingly, abusive and at-risk, relative to comparison, parents are reported to experience more anger and arousal when they observe children's misbehavior (e.g., Schellenbach et al., 1991; Trickett & Kuczynski, 1986) and when they observe a crying child (e.g., Frodi & Lamb, 1980; Pruitt & Erickson, 1985).

Preexisting positive affective states may also be relevant to understanding child physical abuse. For example, effective parenting is thought to be warm and empathic (Dix, 1991). Empathy has been defined as the ability to identify another's thoughts and feelings, to take the other's perspective, and to demonstrate emotional responsiveness (Feshbach, 1989; Letourneau, 1981). Empathy is believed to facilitate behavior (e.g., helping behavior) that is incompatible with aggression (e.g., Feshbach; Feshbach & Feshbach, 1982). Letourneau reported that dispositional empathy correlated positively with giving help or comfort to a child and negatively with parental aggression. In addition, the perspective-taking component of empathy may reduce the misinterpretations of others' behavior (e.g., as intentional and malicious; Feshbach & Feshbach; Miller & Eisenberg, 1988), decreasing the likelihood that anger will be experienced. Conversely, preexisting negative schemata (e.g., negative beliefs about children) as well as misperceptions of others' behavior (e.g., attributions of hostile intent) may inhibit empathic responding (Miller & Eisenberg) and increase the likelihood that anger will be experienced.

Although mixed results were reported in one study (Rosenstein, 1995), numerous studies using demographically matched groups have reported dispositional empathy differences between abusive and nonabusive mothers (e.g., Frodi & Lamb, 1980; Letourneau, 1981; Melnick & Hurley, 1969; Wiehe, 1986). In a study of high- and low-risk mothers that attempted to document preexisting dispositional empathy differences, Milner et al. (1995) failed to find the expected differences. However, within the high- and low-risk groups, there were differences in the mothers' emotional reactions to child stimuli. High-risk mothers did not show a significant change in empathy from baseline when they observed a crying infant, whereas the low-risk mothers displayed a significant increase in empathy. In contrast, the high-risk mothers reported significant increases from baseline in sadness, distress, and hostility when they observed the crying infant; the low-risk mothers reported no changes on these dependent variables. Although it is not known if the high-risk mothers reported more negative affect because of preexisting beliefs about the meaning of the crying infant stimulus (they were not asked), the findings are congruent with such a possibility and this relationship should be investigated.

A major problem with using the parental evaluation, attribution, and expectation research as an indication of the existence of preexisting schemata is that reported differences in these cognitions may be due to factors other than biased preexisting schemata. Reported evaluation, attribution, and expectation differences between abusive and comparison parents may be due to factors such as selective perceptions of child behaviors at Stage 1 or biased evaluations and expectations at Stage 2. Distinctions are also complicated by the possibility that abusive parents' perceptions and evaluations of their children may have developed during previous information processing sequences that involved the child and became preexisting schemata for subsequent information processing activities. To the extent that schemata were developed as a result of abusive encounters, the schemata would not predate abusive behavior and, therefore, would not be useful risk markers to identify high-risk, but not yet abusive, individuals.

58

MOTIVATION AND CHILD MALTREATMENT

In summary, descriptive data provide some support for the proposition that physically abusive, relative to nonabusive, parents have different preexisting beliefs and values (e.g., biased beliefs about their children's characteristics and beliefs about external locus of control) that guide their child-rearing behavior. A limitation of the studies is that the data are based primarily on the assessment of parents following the abuse of their child. Data demonstrating that certain parenting beliefs and values precede the occurrence of abuse are generally lacking. In addition, the mere finding of an association between preexisting schemata and child abuse is not sufficient to demonstrate that preexisting beliefs mediate physically abusive behaviors. Despite this problem, it should be noted that outside of the family violence field, research supports the view that preexisting schemata determine the kind of information that receives attention and the manner in which information is encoded (Markus & Zajonc, 1985). Thus, the search for abuse-related preexisting schemata and the documentation of their relationship to other cognitive processing activities and child-directed behaviors should continue.

EVIDENCE FOR STAGE 1: PERCEPTIONS

With respect to parental perceptions, the social information processing model proposes that physically abusive parents are less attentive to and are less aware of their children's behavior, which in some cases is due to encoding problems and in other instances due to errors in cue recognition. A lack of parental awareness is a major feature of Newberger and Cook's (1983) cognitive developmental model of child maltreatment. Although Newberger and Cook used a broader definition of awareness than is used in the present social information processing model, they suggested that maltreating parents have less awareness of and appreciation for the complexity of children's needs, especially when they conflict with parents' needs. In the context of the present social information processing model, parental needs may be viewed as moderating the extent of perceptual errors.

More than three decades ago, Young (1964) concluded that abusive parents' use of punishment appeared to be independent of the child's behavior. In a study of abusive and nonabusive mothers, Frodi and Lamb (1980) found that abusive parents were more physiologically reactive to both a crying and a smiling infant, leading to the conclusion that the abusive parent perceives the child as an aversive stimulus regardless of the child's behavior. Similarly, Wahler and Dumas (1989) stated that abusive mothers have attentional problems: they respond to both positive and negative child behavior as the same stimulus class. Wood-Shuman and Cone (1986) reported differences in abusive, at-risk, and comparison mothers' descriptions of normal behavior and concluded that abusive mothers have "faulty stimulus discrimination" abilities with regard to their evaluations of children's behavior.

Although the above observations are congruent with the view that abusers have faulty stimulus discrimination abilities that are perceptual in nature, the purported perceptual differences may be due to other processing differences. That is, abusive parents may perceive the behavior correctly but may engage in processing activities that discount or ignore certain child behaviors (e.g., prosocial behaviors). More specifically, it is unclear if the data described above represent perceptual deficits (Stage 1); differences in evaluations and interpretations (Stage 2) of correctly perceived behavior; a skipping of the intermediate stages of processing (automatic processing); or difficulties in parental abilities to monitor and modify responses (Stage 4).

Crittenden (1981) reported that abusive parents exhibit behavior patterns in their interactions with their infants which suggest that they do not perceive infant cues. Aragona (1983) reported that abusive parents are less responsive to temporal changes in their child's behavior, which may result from a lack of parental awareness. A limitation is that, since Crittenden and Aragona found only that abusive mothers failed to modify their behavior in response to changes in the child's behavior, it is unclear if the abusive mothers failed to change their behavior because they did not perceive child cues (Stage 1) or if they failed to respond to their child's behavior for some other reason (e.g., the mothers perceived child cues but ignored their meaning, Stage 3).

Several studies have reported on the abusive mother's ability to accurately encode child-related information (cue detection accuracy), or more specifically, to recognize children's affective states. Kropp and Haynes (1987) found that abusive, compared to nonabusive, mothers generally made more errors in infant emotion recognition and were more likely to identify negative infant emotions as positive. In contrast, using a different emotion recognition task, Camras et al. (1988) and During and McMahon (1991) did not find that abusive and nonabusive mothers differed in their abilities to identify children's emotions. During and McMahon also failed to find abusive and nonabusive parent differences in the identification of adults' emotional expressions.

Camras et al. (1988) suggested that the failure to replicate emotion recognition differences in abusive parents may be due to methodological differences between studies. For example, Camras et al. used full-frontal facial expressions, whereas Kropp and Haynes (1987) provided facial expressions at various angles, which may be more difficult to evaluate. Similarly, During and McMahon (1991), who failed to find expected differences, suggested that future studies use procedures that produce less explicit emotional expressions. The assumption is that, as explicitness decreases, abusive parents may have relatively greater difficulty identifying emotions.

Although differences in the emotion recognition abilities of abusive and high-risk, relative to comparison, mothers need further study because of the mixed results reported thus far, the view that abusive and high-risk parents may make more errors in their encoding of emotions remains a viable hypothesis. In addition, the social information processing model suggests that as stress increases, abusive and high-risk parents will show less ability to correctly identify emotional expressions. This possibility has not been investigated.

If abusive and high-risk, relative to comparison, parents are shown to make more errors in emotion recognition, the extent to which an inability to recognize emotional states represents a perceptual problem (Stage 1) or is a limitation in the ability to interpret correctly perceived information (Stage 2) remains unclear. For example, George and Main (1980) speculated that abusive mothers may lack the ability to interpret or, alternately, they may be unwilling to interpret child-related cues.

In contrast to the perspective that abusive and high-risk, relative to comparison, parents have faulty stimulus discrimination abilities that are perceptual in nature, one study reported data suggesting a different conclusion, at least in a specific context. Using a signal detection paradigm, Dopke and Dunsterville (1998) conducted an analogue study that assessed the ability of high- and low-risk college students to identify compliant and noncompliant child behaviors. Although there were no high- and low-risk group differences in the "hit rates" for the identification of compliant behaviors, low-risk participants were more likely to miss noncompliant child behaviors. If replicated, these findings suggest that low-risk, relative to high-risk, individuals may tend to overlook child noncompliant behaviors. What is unclear is whether the failure to observe child noncompliant behavior is a perceptual issue (selective perception of the environment, Stage 1) or if the low-risk individual perceives the information but evaluates it differently (Stage 2).

Although it is not always known which part of the social information processing model the data support, available theory and research are congruent with the notion that abusive parents are less aware of their children's behavior and supports a call for research that can clarify the extent that abuse-related perceptual differences exist separate from other processing differences. The hypothesis that abusive parents' perceptual difficulties are more evident when changes in a child's behavior are subtle has not been adequately studied. Likewise, studies are needed on the possibility that an increase in the level of stress and the existence of negative affect can reduce the abusive parent's ability to correctly perceive child behavior more than in comparison parents.

EVIDENCE FOR STAGE 2: INTERPRETATIONS AND EVALUATIONS

The social information processing model proposes that abusive, compared to nonabusive, parents have more inappropriate and inaccurate child-related expectations. In an early attempt to describe physically abusive parents, Kempe, Silverman, Steele, Droegemueller, and Silver (1962) indicated that abusive parents had unrealistically high expectations of their children. A decade later, Spinetta and Rigler (1972) reviewed the literature and concluded that abusive parents had inappropriate (early) child expectations. As previously mentioned, Twentyman's (Twentyman et al., 1984) cognitive behavioral model of child physical abuse was based on the assumption that abusive parents have unrealistically high expectations of their children, and these high expectations mediate child abuse. Supporting this view, several studies, which used matched comparison groups, have reported that abusive, compared to nonabusive, parents have higher child-related expectations (Larrance & Twentyman, 1983; Oates et al., 1985).

Other researchers, however, have reported different findings.

Kravitz and Driscoll (1983), who generally found that there were no expectation differences, also reported that abusive, compared to nonabusive, parents had a few child-related expectations that were either too high or too low. Spinetta (1978) also reported mixed results. In contrast, Twentyman and Plotkin (1982) and Perry et al. (1983) found that mothers and fathers in abusive families expected slower child development, whereas Starr, Jr. (1982) and Gaines et al. (1978) failed to find differences between abusive and nonabusive parents in their expectations of children's development. Azar et al. (1984) found no differences on a measure of developmental milestones but did report that abusive parents had higher expectations on a measure of complex sequences of child behavior.

Given the diversity of findings, the extent to which abuse-related expectation differences exist with respect to developmental milestones and complex child behaviors remains unclear. Further, the degree to which any observed expectation differences may reflect preexisting schemata, as opposed to beliefs that develop after abuse occurs, is not known. Finally, data on the impact of stress and negative affective states on abusive, at-risk, and comparison parents' expectations of child behavior with respect to developmental milestones and complex sequences of child behaviors are lacking.

Studies examining parental expectations related to child compliance following discipline have found that abusive and high-risk, compared to matched groups of low-risk, mothers had higher or lower expectations of child compliance as a function of the type of transgression (Chilamkurti & Milner, 1993) and as a function of the type of transgression and discipline combination (Caselles & Milner, 2000). For example, high-risk mothers expected less future compliance following discipline for moral transgressions and more future compliance following discipline for personal transgressions. That is, high-risk mothers had lower expectations that their children would cease to engage in more serious behavior (e.g., stealing) and higher expectations that their children would not engage in less serious, more common child behaviors (e.g., writing on the hand with a pen). Low-risk mothers had the opposite expectations (Chilamkurti & Milner).

Higher expectations of child compliance following discipline for minor transgressions may be unrealistic, especially since children of both high- and low-risk mothers indicate that compliance is less likely following discipline for minor transgressions (e.g., Chilamkurti & Milner, 1993). If such expectations are unrealistic, they may result in the high-risk and abusive parent perceiving a discipline failure when the child repeats the minor transgression, resulting in the child being viewed as oppositional and defiant or simply "bad." The parent may subsequently use this view to justify the use of power assertion techniques. Finally, data are needed on the impact of stress on abusive, at-risk, and comparison parents' expectations of child compliance across different types of child transgressions and disciplinary techniques.

Collectively, the data suggest that in some areas abusive parents may have higher and/or lower expectations of their child's behavior, supporting the social information processing model's view that abusive parents have inappropriate expectations of child behavior. It is also apparent that the type of expectation under investigation (developmental milestone, child compliance) and the context in which the expectation occurs (e.g., unstructured situation, following discipline) need additional study to more adequately determine the types and extent of the abusive parent's inappropriate expectations.

As part of parental evaluations, differences in the abusive parent's attributions have been mentioned by many authors (e.g., Feshbach, 1980; Pollock & Steele, 1972; Twentyman et al., 1984) as potential mediators of child abuse. Congruent with this view, Larrance and Twentyman (1983) reported that abusive parents made internal and stable attributions for negative child behavior and external and unstable attributions for positive child behavior. Comparison parents made the opposite attributions for negative and positive child behaviors. In addition, abusive parents were more likely to attribute hostile intent to the child. Supporting this latter finding, Bauer and Twentyman (1985) reported that abusive parents view children's behavior as more intentionally annoying.

Although the research designs and the questions asked were not always the same as in the Larrance and Twentyman (1983) study, other investigators have reported data that provide support for the Larrance and Twentyman findings. For example, Bradley and Peters (1991) reported differences in the attributional styles of abusive mothers. Diaz et al. (1991) and Miller and Azar (1996) reported attributional differences in high-risk, relative to low-risk, mothers. Dopke and Milner (2000) reported that high-risk, relative to low-risk, mothers showed greater attributional changes, especially in their stable, global, and intentional attributions, after repeated child noncompliance following discipline for negative behavior. High-risk mothers also appraised the child noncompliance as more stressful and reported more negative affect. Although Dopke and Milner found co-occurring changes of attributions and negativity, the possible impact of negative affectivity on attributions was not directly studied. However, a study of nonabusive parents revealed that mothers in an angry condition, compared to an emotionally-neutral condition, made more negative attributions for children's noncompliance (Dix et al., 1990).

In contrast to the above reports, several authors failed to find differences between abusive and high-risk, relative to comparison, mothers in their overall attributional styles (e.g., Foody, 1993; Kravitz & Driscoll, 1983; Milner & Foody, 1994; Rosenberg & Reppucci, 1983; Valle, 1998; Webster-Stratton, 1985), though trends were sometimes reported. Although the reasons for the inconsistent findings are unknown, Bradley and Peters (1991), who found differences, speculated that the differences may be due to the "great diversity" of participants used in the study criterion groups. In addition, whether or not abuse-related attribution differences are found may be due, in part, to the context in which attributions are measured. For example, although Milner and Foody (1994) did not find overall attributional differences, they did find differences between high- and low-risk mothers following the introduction of mitigating information for negative child behavior (this research is reviewed in the next section). It is also interesting to note that Schellenbach et al. (1991) reported that maternal differences in the ratings of intentionality of child behavior were evident only when abuse potential interacted with stress, supporting a moderating role for stress.

Abusers, relative to nonabusers, are thought to differ in their evaluations of the seriousness and wrongness of children's behavior. Supporting this view, research has shown that abusive mothers evaluate mildly aversive children's behavior (e.g., begging for candy) and daily living scenes (e.g., playing with a dog) as more negative than at-risk and comparison mothers (Wood-Shuman & Cone, 1986). Chilamkurti and Milner (1993) and Caselles and Milner (2000) found that abusive and high-risk mothers viewed their child's transgressions as more wrong overall. Further, evaluation of wrongness interacted with the type of transgression and risk group, so that minor child transgressions were viewed as more wrong by the abusive and high-risk parents. Likewise, Valle (1998) found that abusive mothers evaluated minor child transgression as more serious and more wrong than did nonabusive mothers.

Caselles and Milner (2000) expected but failed to find a risk group by stress (crying infant) interaction, which meant that a situational stress manipulation did not differentially increase the abusive parents' evaluation of the wrongness of their children's behavior. Although additional data on the relationship between the abusive parents' affective state and their evaluation of the seriousness and wrongness of children's behaviors are needed, nonabusive mothers in an angry condition, compared to nonabusive mothers in an emotionally-neutral condition, have been found to evaluate child behaviors as more serious (Dix et al., 1990), and this difference was more pronounced when the child's behavior was ambiguous than when the behavior was clearly negative.

Although the data indicate that abusive and at-risk parents view child transgressions, especially minor transgressions, as more wrong and more serious, the extent to which the evaluations of wrongness and the seriousness of transgressions are linked to the use of power assertion disciplinary techniques in abusive parents remains to be determined. As with expectations and interpretations, the possible role of chronic and situational stress in moderating parental evaluations and the role of affective factors (e.g., depression and anger) on parental child-related evaluations need additional study.

EVIDENCE FOR STAGE 3: INFORMATION INTEGRATION AND RESPONSE SELECTION

As previously mentioned, more than three decades ago Young (1964) reported that punishment of children in abusive families appeared to be independent of any specific behavior of the child, suggesting that either the abusive parent has problems with encoding child-related information (Stage 1) or is making biased interpretations (State 2) or is failing to integrate information that is perceived (Stage 3). With respect to indiscriminant responding to children, theoretical support for problems at both the interpretation and information integration and response selection stages is provided by Newberger and Cook (1983). These authors view maltreating parents as having less of the cognitive resources needed to facilitate interpretation and resolution of conflicts. Likewise, Hansen, Pallotta, Tishelman, Conaway, and MacMillan (1989) concluded that abusive parents have less ability to generate appropriate child management strategies.

A central hypothesis of Stage 3 of the social information processing model is that, prior to their response selection, abusive parents may not integrate available information, such as mitigating data, even when information is perceived correctly. Foody (1993) investigated the effects of mitigating information on abusive and nonabusive mothers' attributions for children's behaviors. Although many attributional differences were expected, the introduction of mitigating information only produced group differences on the attributions of stability. That is, when mitigating information was present, comparison mothers' attributions became more specific (less global), whereas abusive mothers' attributions did not change.

In a similar study, Milner and Foody (1994) investigated the effects of mitigating information on high- and low-risk participants' attributions of children's behaviors. Although no overall group differences in attributions were found, the interaction between risk group status and receipt of mitigating information was significant for several attributions. As expected, low-risk participants showed a significant change toward unstable and unintentional attributions following the receipt of mitigating information related to the child's behavior, whereas high-risk participants did not change the degree of their stable/unstable or intentional/unintentional attributions following the receipt of mitigating information. Both low- and high-risk participants made more external attributions after receiving the mitigating information (albeit the absolute change was greater for the low-risk mothers). No significant differences were found for specific/global attributions.

Follow-up questioning revealed that the high- and low-risk groups did not differ in their ability to correctly remember the mitigating information during a recall period (albeit a trend was present), indicating that both groups were statistically similar in their perception (Stage 1), storage, and retrieval of the mitigating information (Milner & Foody, 1994). This finding supports the view that the high-risk participants did not integrate mitigating information that they had in their conscious awareness. While not uniform, the data indicate that abusive and high-risk, compared to nonabusive and low-risk, mothers' judgements regarding the child's blameworthiness for their behavior is less likely to be impacted by situational child-related information.

Although the Foody (1993) and Milner and Foody (1994) studies provide some support for differences in abusive, high-risk, and nonabusive parents' use of mitigating data, additional research is needed on abusive parents in a variety of situations where mitigating information may be present. Further, the putative reasons (e.g., lack of integration of information or automatic processing which skips the integration stage) for the differential impact of mitigating information on abusers and nonabusers judgments need to be studied. A design issue also warrants mention. In the Foody (1993) and Milner and Foody (1994) studies, mitigating information was presented in an additional sentence in a brief vignette. It is possible that in situations where the mitigating information is more difficult to observe or obtain (e.g., imbedded in a complex social situation or distal versus proximal to the parent) and/or if stress is present, the abusive, compared to the nonabusive, parent will be even less likely to consider the mitigating information.

Finally, one of the most widely accepted beliefs in the family violence field is that physically abusive parents lack parenting skills (e.g., Kelly, 1983; Walker, Bonner, & Kaufman, 1988; Wolfe, 1987; Wolfe, Kaufman, Aragona, & Sandler, 1981), a view that has been maintained in the proposed social information processing model. For example, Walker et al. stated that child physical abuse frequently results from the parent's inability to "generate suitable management alternatives." Many interventions are based on the view that abusive parents lack parenting skills (Azar, 1997), and case studies have shown that abusive parents benefit from structured training designed to improve parenting skills (e.g., MacMillan, Guevremont, & Hansen, 1988; MacMillan, Olson, & Hansen, 1991; Wolfe et al., 1982).

Group studies have reported skill deficits in maltreating parents. Azar et al. (1984) reported that abusive and neglectful, relative to comparison, mothers demonstrated poorer problem solving skills for child-related problems. Hansen et al. (1989) reported that abusive and neglectful parents, compared to nonmaltreating community and clinic parents, were deficient in problem-solving skills. Abusive parents generated fewer and less adequate solutions in five child and nonchild situations, albeit no differences were found for child care problems. Hansen et al. concluded that maltreating parents may "lack creativity and skill for 'brainstorming' solutions" (p. 365). At present it is unclear to what degree the abusive parent's problem-solving deficits are child-related or are more general in nature, albeit the data on nonchild-related situations described by Hansen et al. suggest that abusive parent problem-solving deficits extend beyond child-related issues.

With respect to the use of discipline techniques, Trickett and Kuczynski (1986) found that abusive parents used punishment as their predominant strategy in response to initial child noncompliance, whereas nonabusers did not show any predominant response to initial child noncompliance. This relatively uniform use of punishment following initial child noncompliance provides support for the view that abusive parents are less likely to show flexibility in their disciplinary response selection and may indicate that they are less responsive to contextual factors. In a study of child noncompliance in high and low-risk mothers, Dopke and Milner (2000) failed to find the expected group differences in disciplinary choices following child noncompliance, though changes in attributions were observed in the high-risk mothers. The mixed findings regarding abusive and high-risk mothers' responses to child noncompliance indicates that additional research is needed to determine the extent of the differences between abusers and high-risk mothers in their response selections and if findings will vary as a function of other factors, such as the nature of the child's transgression.

Parenting skill problems are suggested by research indicating that abusive mothers, compared to nonabusive mothers, initiate fewer interactions with their children (Wasserman, Green, & Allen, 1983) and have lower rates of interaction (e.g., Bousha & Twentyman, 1984; Burgess & Conger, 1978; Dietrich, Starr, & Kaplan, 1980; Schindler & Arkowitz, 1986). Schindler and Arkowitz concluded that most evidence supports the view that the lower rates of parent-child interaction observed in abusive parents represent specific skill deficits abusers have in dealing with their children.

Many studies appear to support the view that physically abusive parents have parenting skill deficits. However, as previously noted, these studies must be viewed as preliminary because many findings are based on both abusive and neglectful parents or on modest sample sizes. Another limitation is that, with only a few exceptions (e.g.,

Trickett & Kuczynski, 1986), researchers assess parenting skills using vignettes, which may or may not be related to actual parenting behavior. It is also not known to what extent parental differences at earlier processing stages contribute to reported skill deficits. That is, reported limitations in response selection may be due to a skill deficit or to cognitions (e.g., expectations of child noncompliance) that may limit parental response selections, resulting in an apparent difference in parenting skills.

Although stress has been shown to impact an individual's coping skills in situations other than parent-child interactions, the extent to which stress impacts a parent's selection of child management alternatives is unclear. One study provides initial support for the role of stress in moderating parenting behavior. Schellenbach et al. (1991) reported that when stress was present parents with high abuse potential were judged to be more controlling, punishing, and rejecting in their parenting behavior than when stress was not present. These data are congruent with the view that stress may impact the response choice of the parent, limiting the choice to more serious disciplinary techniques. If additional research supports this finding, it still must be determined if the response choice is directly impacted by the stress or if the choice of disciplinary techniques is mediated by the effects of stress on other social information processing events.

Although more data are needed, negative affective states appear to be associated with disciplinary choice. For example, based on interview data, Dietrich, Berkowitz, Kadushin, and McGloin (1990) reported that the majority of abusive parents indicated that they felt angry prior to the abusive incident and lost their tempers immediately before the physical abuse occurred. Using nonabusive parents, Dix et al. (1990) reported that when they were in an angry condition, relative to an emotionally-neutral condition, mothers expected that greater sternness would be needed to gain child compliance, and this difference was more pronounced when the child's behavior was ambiguous than when it was clearly negative.

EVIDENCE FOR STAGE 4: RESPONSE IMPLEMENTATION AND MONITORING

Although studies reviewed in the previous section and elsewhere (e.g., Milner, 1998; Milner & Crouch, 1999; Milner & Dopke, 1997) indicate that abusive, compared to nonabusive, parents may have limited parenting skills, few studies have directly investigated the physically abusive parent's ability to effectively implement specific disciplinary techniques. Nevertheless, data are available which are consistent with the view that abusive, compared to nonabusive, parents show less flexibility in their responses to children's behavior. Based upon observations of mother-child interactions, Crittenden (1981) reported that abusive mothers could be distinguished from neglectful, problematic, and adequate mothers on the basis of the rigidity of their response patterns. Similarly, other investigators have reported that abusive, compared to nonabusive, mothers more often fail to modify their behavior in response to changes in their children's behaviors (Aragona, 1983; Crittenden; Letourneau, 1981). Consequently, although more data are needed, authors have concluded that physically abusive parents may not be able to "change their own behavior" when alternative child management techniques are needed to successfully manage their child's behavior (e.g., Walker et al., 1988).

The reports that abusive and high-risk, relative to comparison, mothers engage in more intrusive and interfering parenting behaviors and have higher rates of noncontingent responses to prosocial behaviors (e.g., Cerezo & D'Ocon, 1995; Cerezo, D'Ocon, & Dolz, 1996; Dolz et al., 1997; Lorber, Felton, & Reid, 1984; Lyons-Ruth, Connell, Zoll, & Stahl, 1987; Schmidt & Eldridge, 1986) are perhaps the strongest evidence that abusive and high-risk parents have more problems in effectively implementing and monitoring their responses to their children. Although the available data are relatively uniform in indicating that both abusive and high-risk, relative to comparison, parents have more problems in implementing and monitoring their parenting responses, more research is needed. Specifically, research is needed to determine the extent to which these differences represent specific implementation and monitoring deficits or if they are due to the impact of abuser-related differences in preexisting schema, perceptions, and/or interpretations and evaluations.

The proposed social information processing model also assumes that high levels of parental distress can interfere with the parent's ability to adequately implement and monitor parenting behavior. For example, if attentional resources are limited by stress, then the implementation and monitoring activities may be limited because of encoding problems (Stage 1). Further, stress has been assumed to have effects on both interpretations and evaluations (Stage 2) and integration and response selection activities (Stage 3) that may impact the parenting behavior at Stage 4. However, except for the previously mentioned study by Schellenbach et al. (1991), which found that stress increased the degree of punitive disciplinary responses in mothers with high abuse potential, the effects of stress on the abusive and high-risk parent's implementation and monitoring techniques have not been investigated.

Studies are also lacking on the hypothesized impact of negative affective (e.g., depression and anger) and other personality factors (e.g., self-esteem) on the implementation and monitoring of parenting behaviors in abusive and high-risk parents. Data are available which indicate that, after controlling for intelligence, high-risk, compared to low-risk, mothers show inferior performance on a neuropsychological measure of conceptual ability, cognitive flexibility, and problem solving ability. Most relevant to the present discussion was the finding that these differences were not significant after maternal depression and anxiety were statistically controlled (Nayak & Milner, 1998). Thus, in this study, problems in conceptual ability, cognitive flexibility, and problem solving ability in high-risk mothers may not have represented cognitive limitations but may have been indicative of the higher levels of depression and anxiety that are commonly reported in abusive and high-risk mothers (Milner & Dopke, 1997). The problem with such an interpretation is one of directionality. It is not known whether the negative affect caused the inferior performance or if cognitive limitations resulted in the parents experiencing depression and anxiety. Nevertheless, these data are consistent with the speculation that negative affect may have an impact on cognitive activities related to the implementation and monitoring of parenting behaviors.

Further, it is not known to what extent negative affect and other personality factors may interact with stress to reduce the parents' ability to adequately implement and monitor their child directed responses. In the aforementioned study (Nayak & Milner, 1998), which reported a relationship between cognitive performance and negative affect, stress (a crying child) was a manipulated variable, but no stress interactions were found. In contrast, data from outside of the family violence literature indicate that relationships between cognitive performance, personality variables, and stress exist. For example, there is evidence that low self-esteem is positively correlated with poor problem-solving performance under stressful conditions (Hubbs-Tait & Blodgett, 1989), which suggests the need for additional studies using abusive and high-risk parents. Likewise, data are needed on whether negative affect associated with preexisting schemata may interact with other components of the information processing model to produce a differential impact on abusers' and nonabusers' ability to implement and monitor their parenting behaviors.

Research Needs

In each of the preceding sections, gaps in our knowledge of the cognitive and behavioral factors that are associated with child physical abuse have been discussed. Some of the major research needs, which were previously described, will be summarized in this section. With respect to preexisting schemata, we need to determine which types of cognitive and affective schemata are associated with child physical abuse. At each stage the social information processing model, additional research is needed to determine with more specificity which cognitions are associated with child physical abuse and the relative strengths of these associations. The possible interactive effects of social information processing factors at the different stages of the model should be examined. We also do not know if selected social information processing problems are associated with specific levels of child development.

To the extent that child abuse related preexisting schemata can be demonstrated to exist, the impact of these schemata on cognitive activities at different stages of the social information processing model needs to be studied. The possible role of preexisting schemata in determining the response choice outcome when automatic versus controlled processing occurs in response to stimuli needs to be explored. Further, the relationships between components of the model and contextual factors (e.g., level of stress, level of social support) and personal factors (e.g., depression, self-esteem) needs additional exploration.

In addition to studying child physical abusers, high-risk parents should be studied to determine if cognitive differences observed in abusive parents can be found prior to the abuse event. All research findings need to be replicated using demographically diverse parent groups, including fathers, to demonstrate the degree of generalizability of findings. Perhaps most important is the need for research to demonstrate a relationship between components of the social information processing model and observable parent behaviors in the natural environment.

As social information processing differences between high-risk, abusive and nonabusive parents are established, investigators can use these results to explore the impact of the parents' cognitions on children's thinking. For example, in a study that used high- and low-risk mothers and their children (Chilamkurti & Milner, 1993), many of the cognitive differences (e.g., evaluations of wrongness) observed between the high- and low-risk parents were observed in the children of the high- and low-risk parents. The possibility that the children of high-risk and abusive parents acquire selected beliefs and processing styles from their parents may be one mechanism for the intergenerational transmission of child abuse. If abused children incorporate the cognitive styles of their abusive parent, these cognitions may also contribute to the increased peer aggression reported in physically abused children.

Implications for Intervention

Since the preceding summary indicates many gaps exist in our knowledge of the cognitive and behavioral factors that associated with child physical abuse, any attempt to provide a detailed discussion of treatment (intervention and prevention) implications of the social information processing model would be premature. As has been pointed out by others, for social skills training to be successful, we first must have an adequate description (taxonomy) of the problem situations and related skill deficits that are most characteristic of the target population (Freedman, Rosenthal, Donahoe, Schlundt, & McFall, 1978). At present, this description is incomplete.

In addition to the need for information about the different model components (and their interactions), we need to understand the factors that may limit the effectiveness of cognitive-behavioral interventions. We need to know to what extent controlled processing is a skill that can be taught and how it can be taught. For example, assuming that information is correctly perceived and evaluated, how can parents be taught to consider mitigating information? If controlled processing skills can be taught, what are the constraints (cognitive, affective, environmental) on the use of controlled processing? That is, to what extent are factors such as low self-esteem, low self-efficacy, external locus of control, negative affect, stress, and lack of social support constraints that reduce the likelihood of controlled processing? To what extent is it necessary to treat factors that constrain controlled processing before other interventions are attempted?

Some suggestions as to what the answers might be to these questions can be found outside of the family violence literature. For example, interventions have been designed to prevent selective attention and cognition distortions that are due to preexisting schemata. An intervention that challenges such negative biases while introducing controlled processing of positive interpersonal material is called "synthesis teaching," a method developed for use with depressed, socially isolated mothers whose children have behavior problems (Wahler & Dumas, 1989). More generally, in the field of social psychology, many authors have discussed how an individual's motivation, cognitive capacity, and situational factors impact an individual's controlled processing and make suggestions about how these factors may be modified (e.g., Higgins & Kruglanski, 1996).

Assuming that the major components of the social information processing model can be supported and that appropriate focused interventions are available, changes might be needed in some of the current approaches to intervention. The use of highly focused parent-education programs or specific skill building programs may be ineffective if problems existing at other stages of the social information processing model are not also addressed. For example, behavioral training alone may not result in significant behavior change if preexisting beliefs, perceptions (Stage 1), interpretations, evaluations, and expectations (Stage 2) lead automatically to the use of disciplinary techniques involving verbal or physical assault. In this case the newly acquired behavior (e.g., new disciplinary technique) would not be selected. Likewise, teaching a parent to recognize that mitigating information (Stage 3) is present may not be adequate if automatic processing or the lack of ability to integrate information results in mitigating data being ignored.

The interactive nature of parental personality factors, including parental distress, with information processing and related parenting behavior may also need to be considered. For example, if parental distress constrains controlled processing, then interventions such as stress management may need to be implemented before the parent can benefit from cognitive-behavioral interventions. Indeed, to the extent that different components of the model are supported, the assessment of physically abusive parents will need to include an evaluation of cognitive, affective, and environmental factors and their interactions for each parent. These idiographic assessments could then be used to guide the selection of specific treatment techniques and to plan an optimal order for interventions. This approach is in contrast to a "one size fits all" approach to treatment and prevention and is congruent with recent suggestions that interventions use a consultation approach (Wekerle & Wolfe, 1998), which actively involves the parent and fosters the identification of key problems with respect to factors such as a parental beliefs, expectations, arousal, and skill deficits.

References

Akhtar, N., & Bradley, E. J. (1991). Social information processing deficits of aggressive children: Present findings and implications for social skills training. *Clinical Psychology Review, 11*, 621–644.

Aragona, J. A. (1983). Physical child abuse. An interactional analysis (Doctoral dissertation, University of South Florida, 1983). *Dissertation Abstracts International, 44*, 1125B.

Arsenio, W. F., & Ford, M. E. (1985). The role of affective information in social-cognitive development: Children's differentiation of moral and conventional events. *Merrill-Palmer Quarterly, 31*, 1–17.

Azar, S. T. (1986). A framework for understanding child maltreatment: An integration of cognitive behavioural and developmental perspectives. *Canadian Journal of Behavioural Science, 18*, 340–355.

Azar, S. T. (1989). Training parents of abused children. In C. E. Schaefer & J. M. Briesmeister (Eds.), *Handbook of parent training: Parents as co- therapists for children's behavior problems* (pp. 414–441). New York: John Wiley & Sons.

Azar, S. T. (1997). A cognitive behavioral approach to understanding and treating parents who physically abuse their children. In D. A. Wolfe, R. J. McMahon, & R. DeV. Peters (Eds.), *Child abuse: New directions in prevention and treatment across the lifespan* (pp. 79–102). Thousand Oaks CA: Sage.

Azar, S. T., Robinson, D. R., Hekimian, E., & Twentyman, C. T. (1984). Unrealistic expectations and problem-solving ability in maltreating and comparison mothers. *Journal of Consulting and Clinical Psychology, 52*, 687–691.

Bacon, M. K., & Ashmore, R. D. (1986). A consideration of the cognitive activities of parents and their role in the socialization process. In R. D.

Ashmore & D. M. Brodzinsky (Eds.), *Thinking about the family: Views of parents and children* (pp. 3–33). Hillsdale NJ: Lawrence Erlbaum.

Bandura, A. (1986). *Social foundations of thought and action: A social cognitive theory.* Englewood Cliffs NJ: Prentice-Hall.

Bauer, W. D., & Twentyman, C. T. (1985). Abusing, neglectful, and comparison mothers' responses to child-related and non-child-related stressors. *Journal of Consulting and Clinical Psychology, 53,* 335–343.

Belsky, J. (1980). Child maltreatment: An ecological integration. *American Psychologist, 35,* 320–335.

Belsky, J. (1993). Etiology of child maltreatment: A developmental-ecological analysis. *Psychological Bulletin, 114,* 413–434.

Berkowitz, L. (1990). On the formation and regulation of anger and aggression: A cognitive-neoassociationistic analysis. *American Psychologist, 45,* 494–503.

Bousha, D. M., & Twentyman, C. T. (1984). Mother-child interactional style in abuse, neglect, and control groups: Naturalistic observations in the home. *Journal of Abnormal Psychology, 93,* 106–114.

Bowlby, J. (1982). *Attachment and loss: Vol. 1. Attachment* (2nd ed.). New York: Basic Books.

Bradley, E. J., & Peters, R. D. (1991). Physically abusive and nonabusive mothers' perceptions of parenting and child behavior. *American Journal of Orthopsychiatry, 61,* 455–460.

Bucci, W. (1997). Symptoms and symbols: A multiple code theory of somatization. *Psychological Inquiry, 17,* 152–172.

Bugental, D. B. (1993). Communication in abusive relationships. *American Behavioral Scientist, 36,* 288–308.

Burgess, R. L., & Conger, R. D. (1978). Family interaction in abusive, neglectful, and normal families. *Child Development, 49,* 1163–1173.

Camras, L. A., Ribordy, S., Hill, J., Martino, S., Spaccarelli, S., & Stefani, R. (1988). Recognition and posing of emotional expressions by abused children and their mothers. *Developmental Psychology, 24,* 776–781.

Caselles, C., & Milner, J. S. (2000). Evaluations of child transgressions, disciplinary choices, and expected child compliance in a no-cry and a crying-infant condition in physically abusive and comparison mothers. *Child Abuse & Neglect, 24,* 477–491.

Cerezo, M. A., & D'Ocon, A. (1995). Maternal inconsistent socialization: An interactional pattern in maltreated children. *Child Abuse Review, 4,* 14–35.

Cerezo, M. A., D'Ocon, A., & Dolz, L. (1996). Mother-child interactive patterns in abusive families: An observational study. *Child Abuse & Neglect, 20,* 573–587.

Chilamkurti, C., & Milner, J. S. (1993). Perceptions and evaluations of child transgressions and disciplinary techniques in high- and low-risk mothers and their children. *Child Development, 64,* 1801–1814.

Cicchetti, D., & Rizley, R. (1981). Developmental perspectives on the etiology, intergenerational transmission, and sequelae of child maltreatment. In

R. Rizley & D. Cicchetti (Eds.), *Developmental perspectives on child maltreat-ment* (pp. 31–55). San Francisco: Josey-Bass.

Clark, M. S., & Isen, A. M. (1982). Toward understanding the relationship between feeling states and social behavior. In A. H. Hastorf & A. M. Isen (Eds.), *Cognitive social psychology* (pp. 73–108). New York: Elsevier North Holland.

Conyngham, H. (1998). *Control expectancies in high- and low-risk individuals.* Unpublished manuscript, Northern Illinois University, DeKalb.

Crick, N. R., & Dodge, K. A. (1994). A review and reformulation of social information-processing mechanisms in children's social adjustment. *Psychological Bulletin, 115,* 74–101.

Crick, N. R., & Dodge, K. A. (1996). Social information-processing mechanisms on reactive and proactive aggression. *Child Development, 67,* 993–1002.

Crittenden, P. M. (1981). Abusing, neglecting, problematic, and adequate dyads: Differentiating by patterns of interaction. *Merrill-Palmer Quarterly, 27,* 201–218.

Crittenden, P. M. (1993). An information-processing perspective on the behavior of neglectful parents. *Criminal Justice and Behavior, 20,* 27–48.

Diaz, R. M., Neal, C. J., & Vachio, A. (1991). Maternal teaching in the zone of proximal development: A comparison of low- and high-risk dyads. *Merrill-Palmer Quarterly, 37,* 83–107.

Dietrich, D., Berkowitz, L., Kadushin, A., & McGloin, J. (1990). Some factors influencing abusers' justification of their child abuse. *Child Abuse & Neglect, 14,* 337–345.

Dietrich, K. N., Starr, R. H., & Kaplan, M. G. (1980). Maternal stimulation and care of abused infants. In T. M. Field, S. Goldberg, D. Stern, & A. M. Sostek (Eds.), *High-risk infants and children* (pp. 25–41). New York: Academic Press.

Dix, T. (1991). The affective organization of parenting: Adaptive and maladaptive processes. *Psychological Bulletin, 110,* 3–25.

Dix, T., & Grusec, J. E. (1985). Parent attribution processes in the socialization of children. In I. E. Sigal (Ed.), *Parental belief systems: The psychological consequences for children* (pp. 201–233). Hillsdale NJ: Lawrence Erlbaum.

Dix, T., & Lochman, J. E. (1990). Social cognition and negative reactions to children: A comparison of mothers of aggressive and nonaggressive boys. *Journal of Social and Clinical Psychology, 9,* 418–438.

Dix, T., Reinhold, D. P., & Zambarano, R. J. (1990). Mothers' judgements in moments of anger. *Merrill-Palmer Quarterly, 36,* 465–486.

Dolz, L., Cerezo, M. A., & Milner, J. S. (1997). Mother-child interactional patterns in high- and low-risk mothers. *Child Abuse & Neglect, 12,* 1149–1158.

Dopke, C. A., & Milner, J. S. (2000). Impact of child noncompliance on stress appraisals, attributions, and disciplinary choices in mothers at high- and low-risk for child physical abuse. *Child Abuse & Neglect, 24,* 493–504.

78

MOTIVATION AND CHILD MALTREATMENT

Dopke, C. A., & Dunsterville, E. (1998). *Information processing of child compliance and noncompliance in individuals at high- and low-risk for child physical abuse.* Unpublished manuscript, Northern Illinois University, DeKalb.

During, S. M., & McMahon, R. J. (1991). Recognition of emotional facial expressions by abusive mothers and their children. *Journal of Clinical Child Psychology, 20,* 132–139.

Ellis, R. H., & Milner, J. S. (1981). Child abuse and locus of control. *Psychological Reports, 48,* 507–510.

Evans, A. L. (1980). Personality characteristics and disciplinary attitudes of child-abusing mothers. *Child Abuse & Neglect, 4,* 179–187.

Feshbach, N. (1989). The construct of empathy and the phenomenon of physical maltreatment of children. In D. Cicchetti & V. Carlson (Eds.), *Child maltreatment: Theory and research on the causes and consequences of child abuse and neglect* (pp. 349–373). New York: Cambridge University Press.

Feshbach, N., & Feshbach, S. (1982). Empathy training and the regulation of aggression: Potentialities and limitations. *Academic Psychology Bulletin, 4,* 399–413.

Feshbach, S. (1980). Child abuse and the dynamics of human aggression and violence. In G. Gerbner, C. Ross, & E. Zigler (Eds.), *Child abuse: An agenda for action* (pp. 48–60). New York: Oxford University Press.

Fiske, S. T., & Taylor, S. E. (1991). *Social cognition* (2nd ed.). New York: McGraw-Hill.

Foody, R. (1993). Attributions, mitigating information, and physical child abuse (Doctoral dissertation, Northern Illinois University, 1993). *Dissertation Abstracts International, 50–08B,* 4389.

Freedman, B. J., Rosenthal, L., Donahoe, C. P. , Schlundt, D. G., & McFall, R. M. (1978). A social-behavioral analysis of skill deficits in delinquent and nondelinquent adolescent boys. *Journal of Consulting and Clinical Psychology, 50,* 697–705.

Frodi, A. M., & Lamb, M. E. (1980). Child abusers' responses to infant smiles and cries. *Child Development, 51,* 238–241.

Fulton, A. M., Murphy, K. R., & Anderson, S. L. (1991). Increasing adolescent mothers' knowledge of child development: An intervention program. *Adolescence, 26,* 73–81.

Gaines, R., Sandgrund, A., Green, A. H., & Power, E. (1978). Etiological factors in child maltreatment: A multivariate study of abusing, neglecting, and normal mothers. *Journal of Abnormal Psychology, 87,* 531–540.

George, C., & Main, M. (1980). Abused children: Their rejection of peers and caregivers. In T. Field, S. Goldberg, D. Stern, & A. Sostek (Eds.), *High-risk infants and children: Adult and peer interactions* (pp. 293–312). New York: Academic Press.

Gil, D. G. (1970). *Violence against children.* Cambridge MA: Harvard University Press.

Hansen, D. J., Pallotta, G. M., Tishelman, A. C., Conaway, L. P., & MacMillan, V. M. (1989). Parental problem-solving skills and child behavior problems:

A comparison of physically abusive, neglectful, clinic, and community families. *Journal of Family Violence, 4,* 353–368.

Higgins, E. T., & Kruglanski, A. W. (1996). *Social psychology: Handbook of basic principles.* New York: Guilford Press.

Holtzworth-Munroe, A. (1991). Applying the social information processing model to maritally violent men. *The Behavior Therapist, 14,* 128–132.

Howells, K. (1981). Adult sexual interest in children: Considerations relevant to theories of aetiology. In M. Cook & K. Howells (Eds.), *Adult sexual interest in children* (pp. 54–94). New York: Academic Press.

Hubbs-Tait, L., & Blodgett, C. J. (1989). The mediating effects of self-esteem and coronary-prone behavior on problem solving and affect under low and high stress. *Behavioral Medicine, 15,* 101–110.

Kelly, J. A. (1983). *Treating child-abusive families: Intervention based on skills-training principles.* New York: Plenum Press.

Kelley, M. L., Grace, N., & Elliott, S. N. (1990). Acceptability of positive and punitive discipline methods: Comparisons among abusive, potentially abusive, and nonabusive parents. *Child Abuse & Neglect, 14,* 219–226.

Kempe, C. H., Silverman, F. N., Steele, B. F., Droegemueller, W., & Silver, H. K. (1962). The battered child syndrome. *Journal of the American Medical Association, 181,* 105–112.

Kravitz, R. I., & Driscoll, J. M. (1983). Expectations for childhood development among child-abusing and nonabusing parents. *American Journal of Orthopsychiatry, 53,* 336–344.

Kropp, J. P., & Haynes, O. M. (1987). Abusive and nonabusive mothers' ability to identify general and specific emotion signals of infants. *Child Development, 58,* 187–190.

Lahey, B. B., Conger, R. D., Atkeson, B. M., & Treiber, F. A. (1984). Parenting behavior and emotional status of physically abusive mothers. *Journal of Consulting and Clinical Psychology, 52,* 1062–1071.

Lang, P. J. (1977). Psychological assessment of anxiety and fear. In J. D. Cone & R. P. Hawkins (Eds.), *Behavioral assessment: New directions in clinical psychology* (pp. 178–195). New York: Brunner/Mazel.

Larrance, D. T., & Twentyman, C. T. (1983). Maternal attributions and child abuse. *Journal of Abnormal Psychology, 92,* 449–457.

Laws, D. R., & Marshall, W. L. (1990). A conditioning theory of the etiology and maintenance of deviant sexual preference and behavior. In W. L. Marshall, D. R. Laws, & H. E. Barbaree (Eds.), *Handbook of sexual assault: Issues, theories, and treatment of the offender* (pp. 209–229). New York: Plenum Press.

Lenton, R. L. (1990). Techniques of child discipline and abuse by parents. *Canadian Review of Sociology and Anthropology, 27,* 157–185.

Letourneau, C. (1981). Empathy and stress: How they affect parental aggression. *Social Work, 26,* 383–389.

Limber, S. P., & Nation, M. A. (1998). Violence within the neighborhood and community. In P. K. Trickett & C. J. Schellenbach (Eds.), *Violence against children in the family and the community* (pp. 171–193). Washington DC: American Psychological Association.

Lipton, D. N., McDonel, E. C., & McFall, R. M. (1987). Heterosocial perception in rapists. *Journal of Consulting and Clinical Psychology, 55*, 17–21.

Lorber, R., Felton, D. K, Reid, J. B. (1984). A social learning approach to the reduction of coercive processes in child abusive families: A molecular analysis. *Advances in Behavior Research and Therapy, 6*, 29–45.

Lyons-Ruth, K., Connell, D. B., Zoll, D., & Stahl, J. (1987). Infants at social risk: Relations among infant maltreatment, maternal behavior, and infant attachment behavior. *Developmental Psychology, 23*, 223–232.

MacMillan, V. M., Guevremont, D. C., & Hansen, D. J. (1988). Problem-solving training with a multiply distressed abusive and neglectful mother: Effects on social insularity, negative affect, and stress. *Journal of Family Violence, 3*, 313–326.

MacMillan, V. M., Olson, R. L., & Hansen, D. J. (1991). Low and high deviance analogue assessment of parent-training with physically abusive parents. *Journal of Family Violence, 6*, 279–301.

Malinosky-Rummell, R. R., & Hansen, D. J. (1993). Long-term consequences of childhood physical abuse. *Psychological Bulletin, 114*, 68–79.

Markus, H., & Zajonc, R. B. (1985). The cognitive perspective in social psychology. In G. Lindzey & E. Aronson (Eds.), *Handbook of social psychology: Vol. 1. Theory and method* (3rd ed., pp. 137–230). New York: Random.

Mash, E. J., Johnston, C., & Kovitz, K. (1983). A comparison of the mother-child interactions of physically abused and non-abused children during play and task situations. *Journal of Clinical Child Psychology, 12*, 337–346.

McFall, R. M. (1982). A review and reformulation of the concept of social skills. *Behavioral Assessment, 4*, 1–33.

McFall, R. M. (1990). The enhancement of social skills: An information-processing analysis. In W. L. Marshall, D. R. Laws, & H. E. Barbaree (Eds.), *Handbook of sexual assault: Issues, theories, and treatment of the offender* (pp. 311–330). New York: Plenum Press.

Melnick, B., & Hurley, J. R. (1969). Distinctive personality attributes of child-abusing mothers. *Journal of Consulting and Clinical Psychology, 33*, 746–749.

Mihalic, S. W., & Elliott, D. (1997). A social learning theory model of marital violence. *Journal of Family Violence, 12*, 21–47.

Miller, L. P. R., & Azar, S. T. (1996). The pervasiveness of maladaptive attributions in mothers at-risk for child abuse. *Family Violence & Sexual Assault Bulletin, 12*(3–4), 31–37.

Miller, P. A., & Eisenberg, N. (1988). The relation of empathy to aggressive and externalizing/antisocial behavior. *Psychological Bulletin, 103*, 324–344.

Milner, J. S. (1988). An ego-strength scale for the Child Abuse Potential Inventory. *Journal of Family Violence, 3*, 151–162.

Milner, J. S. (1993). Social information processing and physical child abuse. *Clinical Psychology Review, 13*, 275–294.

Milner, J. S. (1995). La aplication de la teoria del procesamiento de informacion social al problema del maltrato fisco a ninos. *Infancia y Aprendizaje, 71,* 125–134.

Milner, J. S. (1998). Individual and family characteristics associated with intrafamilial child physical and sexual abuse. In P. K. Trickett & C. J. Schellenbach (Eds.), *Violence against children in the family and the community* (pp. 141–170). Washington DC: American Psychological Association.

Milner, J. S., & Chilamkurti, C. (1991). Physical child abuse perpetrator characteristics: A review of the literature. *Journal of Interpersonal Violence, 6,* 345–366.

Milner, J. S., & Crouch, J. L. (1999). Child physical abuse: Theory and research. In R. L. Hampton (Ed.), *Family violence: Prevention and treatment* (pp 33–65). Newbury Park CA: Sage.

Milner, J. S., & Dopke, C. A. (1997). Child physical abuse: Review of offender characteristics. In D. A. Wolfe, R. McMahon, & R. Peters (Eds.), *Child abuse: New directions in prevention and treatment across the life-span* (pp. 25–52). Thousand Oaks CA: Sage.

Milner, J. S., & Foody, R. (1994). The impact of mitigating information on attributions for positive and negative child behavior by adults at low- and high-risk for child-abusive behavior. *Journal of Social and Clinical Psychology, 13,* 335–351.

Milner, J. S., Halsey, L. B., & Fultz, J. (1995). Empathic responsiveness and affective reactivity to infant stimuli in high- and low-risk for physical child abuse mothers. *Child Abuse & Neglect, 19,* 767–780.

Mischel, W. (1973). Toward a cognitive social learning reconceptualization of personality. *Psychological Review, 80,* 252–283.

Nayak, M., & Milner, J. S. (1998). Neuropsychological functioning: Comparison of parents at high- and low-risk for child physical abuse. *Child Abuse & Neglect, 22,* 687–703.

Newberger, C. M., & Cook, S. J. (1983). Parental awareness and child abuse and neglect: A cognitive-developmental analysis of urban and rural samples. *American Journal of Orthopsychiatry, 53,* 512–524.

Oates, R. K., & Forrest, D. (1985). Self-esteem and early background of abusive mothers. *Child Abuse & Neglect, 9,* 89–93.

Oates, R. K., Forrest, D., & Peacock, A. (1985). Mothers of abused children: A comparison study. *Clinical Pediatrics, 24,* 9–13.

Parke, R. D., & Collmer, C. W. (1975). Child abuse: An interdisciplinary analysis. In E. M. Hetherington (Ed.), *Review of child development research* (Vol. 5., pp. 509–590). Chicago: University of Chicago Press.

Patterson, G. R. (1971). *Families: Applications of social learning theory to family life.* Champaign IL: Research Press.

Perry, M. A., Wells, E. A., & Doran, L. D. (1983). Parent characteristics in abusing and nonabusing families. *Journal of Clinical Child Psychology, 12,* 329–336.

Pollock, C., & Steele, B. (1972). A therapeutic approach to the parents. In

C. Kempe & R. Helfer (Eds.), *Helping the battered child and his family* (pp. 3–21). Philadelphia: Lippincott.

Pruitt, D. L., & Erickson, M. T. (1985). The Child Abuse Potential Inventory: A study of concurrent validity. *Journal of Clinical Psychology, 41,* 104–111.

Reid, J. B., Kavanagh, K., & Baldwin, D. V. (1987). Abusive parents' perceptions of child problem behaviors: An example of parental bias. *Journal of Abnormal Child Psychology, 15,* 457–466.

Rosenberg, M. S., & Reppucci, N. D. (1983). Abusive mothers: Perceptions of their own and their children's behavior. *Journal of Consulting and Clinical Psychology, 51,* 674–682.

Rosenstein, P. (1995). Parental levels of empathy as related to risk assessment in child protective services. *Child Abuse & Neglect, 19,* 1349–1360.

Schellenbach, C. J., Monroe, L. D., & Merluzzi, T. V. (1991). The impact of stress on cognitive components of child abuse potential. *Journal of Family Violence, 6,* 61–80.

Schindler, F., & Arkowitz, H. (1986). The assessment of mother-child interactions in physically abusive and nonabusive families. *Journal of Family Violence, 1,* 247–257.

Schmidt, E., & Eldridge, A. (1986). The attachment relationship and child maltreatment. *Infant Mental Health Journal, 7,* 264–273.

Schneider, W., & Shiffrin, R. M. (1977). Controlled and automatic human information processing: I. Detection, search, and attention. *Psychological Review, 84,* 1–66.

Shiffrin, R. M., & Schneider, W. (1977). Controlled and automatic human information processing: II. Perceptual learning, automatic attending, and a general theory. *Psychological Review, 84,* 127–190.

Shiffrin, R. M., & Schneider, W. (1984). Automatic and controlled processing revisited. *Psychological Review, 91,* 269–276.

Shorkey, C. T., & Armendariz, J. (1985). Personal worth, self-esteem, anomia, hostility and irrational thinking of abusing mothers: A multivariate approach. *Journal of Clinical Psychology, 41,* 414–421.

Spinetta., J. (1978). Parental personality factors in child abuse. *Journal of Consulting and Clinical Psychology, 46,* 1409–1414.

Spinetta, J., & Rigler, D. (1972). The child-abusing parent: A psychological review. *Psychological Bulletin, 77,* 296–304.

Starr, R. H., Jr. (1982). A research-based approach to the prediction of child abuse. In R. H. Starr, Jr. (Ed.), *Child abuse prediction: Policy implications* (pp. 105–134). Cambridge MA: Ballinger. Stringer, S. A., & LaGreca, A. M. (1985). Child abuse potential. *Journal of Abnormal Child Psychology, 13,* 217–226.

Tolan, P. H., & Guerra, N. (1998). Societal causes of violence against children. In P. K. Trickett & C. J. Schellenbach (Eds.), *Violence against children in the family and the community* (pp. 195–209). Washington DC: American Psychological Association.

Trickett, P. K., & Kuczynski, L. (1986). Children's misbehaviors and parental discipline strategies in abusive and nonabusive families. *Developmental Psychology, 22,* 115–123.

Trickett, P. K., & Susman, E. J. (1988). Parental perceptions of child-rearing practices in physically abusive and nonabusive families. *Developmental Psychology, 24,* 270–276.

Turk, D. C., & Speers, M. A. (1983). Cognitive schemata and cognitive processes in cognitive-behavioral interventions: Going beyond the information given. In P. C. Kendall (Ed.), *Advances in cognitive- behavioral research theory* (Vol. 2., pp. 1–31). New York: Academic Press.

Twentyman, C. T., & Plotkin, R. C. (1982). Unrealistic expectations of parents who maltreat their children: An educational deficit that pertains to child development. *Journal of Clinical Psychology, 38,* 497–503.

Twentyman, C. T., Rohrbeck, C. A., & Amish, P. L. (1984). A cognitive-behavioral model of child abuse. In S. Saunders, A. M. Anderson, C. A. Hart, & G. M. Rubenstein (Eds.), *Violent individuals and families: A handbook for practitioners* (pp. 87–111). Springfield IL: Charles C. Thomas.

Tzeng, O. C. S., Jackson, J. W., & Karlson, H. C. (1991). *Theories of child abuse and neglect: Differential perspectives, summaries, and evaluations.* New York: Praeger.

Valle, L. A. (1998). *Child physical abuse: Cognitive and affective responses to children's transgressions.* Unpublished doctoral dissertation, Northern Illinois University, DeKalb.

Wahler, R. G., & Dumas, J. E. (1989). Attentional problems in dysfunctional mother-child interactions: An interbehavioral model. *Psychological Bulletin, 105,* 116–130.

Walker, C. E., Bonner, B. L., & Kaufman, K. L. (1988). *The physically and sexually abused child: Evaluation and treatment.* Elmsford NY: Pergamon.

Wasserman, G. A., Green, A., & Allen, R. (1983). Going beyond abuse: Maladaptive patterns of interaction in abusing mother-infant pairs. *Journal of American Academy of Child Psychiatry, 22,* 245–252.

Webster-Stratton, C. (1985). Comparison of abusive and nonabusive families with conduct-disordered children. *American Journal of Orthopsychiatry, 55,* 59–69.

Wekerle, C., & Wolfe, D. A. (1998). Windows for preventing child abuse and partner abuse: Early childhood and adolescence. In P. K. Trickett & C. J. Schellenbach (Eds.), *Violence against children in the family and the community* (pp. 339–369). Washington DC: American Psychological Association.

Wiehe, V. R. (1986). Empathy and locus of control in child abusers. *Journal of Social Service Research, 9,* 17–30.

Wolfe, D. A. (1987). *Child abuse: Implications for child development and psychopathology.* Newbury Park CA: Sage.

Wolfe, D. A., Kaufman, K., Aragona, J., & Sandler, J. (1981). *The child management program for abusive parents.* Winter Park FL: Anna.

Wolfe, D. A., St. Lawrence, J., Graves, K., Brehony, K., Bradlyn, D., & Kelly, J. A. (1982). Intensive behavioral parent training for a child abusive mother. *Behavior Therapy, 13,* 438–451.

Wood-Shuman, S., & Cone, J. D. (1986). Differences in abusive, at-risk for abuse, and control mothers' descriptions of normal child behavior. *Child Abuse & Neglect, 10,* 397–405.

Young, L. (1964). *Wednesday's children: A study of child abuse and neglect.* New York: McGraw-Hill.

Zeanah, C. H., & Anders, T. F. (1987). Subjectivity in parent-infant relationships: A discussion of internal working models. *Infant Mental Health Journal, 8,* 237–250.

Developmental Processes in Maltreated Children

Dante Cicchetti and Sheree L. Toth

Mt. Hope Family Center
University of Rochester

Due in large part to the theoretical, empirical, and practical importance of understanding the immediate and long-term consequences
of child abuse and neglect, examinations of the developmental sequelae of child maltreatment have burgeoned in recent decades (see,
e.g., Cicchetti & Carlson, 1989; Cicchetti & Lynch, 1995; Cicchetti &
Toth, 1997; Finkelhor & Kendall-Tackett, 1997; Malinosky-Rummell
& Hansen, 1993; Toth & Cicchetti, 1998; Wolfe & Wekerle, 1997).
Presently there exists complete consensus among theoreticians, researchers, practitioners, and social policy advocates that the experience of child maltreatment, whether through sexual abuse, physical
abuse, emotional abuse, and/or neglect, exerts a deleterious impact
on the biological and psychological development of maltreated children across the life course and represents a gross violation of the rights
of vulnerable children (see, e.g., Cicchetti & Toth, 1993, 1995; Cicchetti
& Tucker, 1994; Dodge, Pettit, & Bates, 1997; Egeland, 1997; Emery

The research reported herein was supported by grants from the William T. Grant
Foundation, the John D. and Catherine T. MacArthur Network on Early Childhood, the
National Center on Child Abuse and Neglect, the National Institute of Mental Health,
and the Spunk Fund, Inc. We thank the many children and families who participated
in these investigations, as well as the colleagues who have collaborated with us on
this work.

& Laumann-Billings, 1998; Kendall-Tackett, Williams, & Finkelhor, 1993; Melton & Flood, 1994; National Research Council, 1993; Perry, Pollard, Blakley, Baker, & Vigilante, 1995; Thompson, 1995; Trickett & McBride-Chang, 1995).

However, much less progress has been achieved in elucidating the processes and mechanisms that contribute to the range of developmental outcomes observed in maltreated children (National Research Council, 1993). Existing research reveals that psychological and biological functioning are not uniformly affected by the experience of child maltreatment. Moreover, several studies have begun to demonstrate that some maltreated children may develop in a resilient fashion, despite the significant adversity they have experienced (Cicchetti, Rogosch, Lynch, & Holt, 1993; Moran & Eckenrode, 1992). Consequently, it is essential that research on the sequelae of maltreatment increasingly strives to explicate the mechanisms that exacerbate the difficulties, or serve to lessen the harmful consequences, typically associated with child maltreatment. Thus, investigations of the processes and pathways contributing to these outcomes are essential in order to provide a more comprehensive portrayal of the impact that maltreatment exerts on developmental processes and to inform interventions for maltreated children.

Similarly, in order to elucidate the developmental processes that are implicated in the consequences of child maltreatment, longitudinal research must be conducted. Although factors such as insufficient funding for maltreatment research (National Research Council, 1993; Thompson & Wilcox, 1995), the mobility of maltreating families, and attrition associated with mandated reporting requirements when families thought to be comparison families are found to be maltreaters (e.g., a child designated initially as a nonmaltreated comparison subject may experience maltreatment over the course of a longitudinal investigation) often conspire against the investigator, longitudinal research must occur if genuine progress is to be achieved regarding an understanding of the developmental course of child maltreatment (Cicchetti & Manly, 1990; National Research Council, 1993). Longitudinal research is further impeded by difficulties related to differentiating the effects of maltreatment from those associated with co-occurring risk factors such as poverty, substance abuse, and domestic violence (Downey & Coyne, 1990; Emery & Laumann-Billings, 1998).

In addition, research on maltreatment to date has emphasized behavioral outcomes. Although the physiological impact of maltreatment has not received much attention, further examination of the neurobiological sequelae of abuse and neglect may enhance our understanding of the mechanisms underlying pathological development in maltreated children (Cicchetti & Tucker, 1994; Perry et al., 1995). Adverse life circumstances, exemplified by abuse and neglect, influence psychological and physiological processes. Rather than adhering to a unidimensional belief in the deterministic role that unfolding biology exerts on behavior, theoreticians and researchers in the fields of developmental neuroscience and developmental psychopathology have begun to assert that brain structure and function and their subsequent influence on behavior possess self-organizing properties that can, in fact, be altered by experiences that occur during sensitive periods of development across the life course (Cicchetti & Tucker, 1994; Eisenberg, 1995; Nelson & Bloom, 1997). Physiological and behavioral responses to maltreatment are expected to be interrelated and to lead children to make choices and respond to experiences in ways that support pathological development (Cicchetti & Tucker, 1994; Pollak, Klorman, & Cicchetti, 1998).

Finally, the heterogeneity in the outcomes of maltreated children suggests that maltreatment does not affect each developmental domain in a similar fashion (e.g., some maltreated children may manifest deficits across all areas of functioning, whereas others may be affected in only a few areas). As noted above, some maltreated children have been shown to evidence adaptive functioning even in the face of the great adversity they have experienced (Cicchetti et al., 1993). The varied outcomes that have been observed among maltreated children despite similar experiences of adversity underscore the importance of conducting research not only on the processes and pathways to maladaptive functioning but also on the predictors of resilience in maltreated children. The incorporation of knowledge derived from investigations of the processes and pathways to developmental outcome in maltreated children, the longitudinal course of maltreatment on development, the effects of maltreatment on the interrelation between biological and psychological processes, and the predictors of competent adaptation in maltreated individuals hold considerable potential for suggesting effective prevention and intervention strategies for maltreated individuals, as well as for those at risk for perpetrating maltreatment (Kitzman et al., 1997, Olds et al., 1997; Post et al., 1998; Toth & Cicchetti, 1993).

Goals of the Chapter

We begin by discussing definitional parameters of child maltreatment and the sample characteristics of children who have participated in studies presented in this chapter. We then describe an ecological-transactional model, which we subsequently use to conceptualize research emanating from our laboratory on the developmental processes that eventuate in adaptive or maladaptive biological and psychological outcomes in children who have been maltreated. Although we focus on research from our laboratory, we refer to the work of other investigators as it relates to the findings that emerge from our investigations. The diversity in outcome manifested by maltreated children is intriguing and requires a comprehensive theory of development, as well as a multifaceted research strategy to fully capture these varied processes. In the penultimate section of the chapter, we discuss research on resilience in maltreated children. We conclude by examining the implications of the work reported herein for prevention and intervention.

Defining Child Maltreatment

Although child maltreatment is a major societal problem that has direct implications for the welfare and normal development of children, there remains a lack of consensus on what constitutes maltreatment and how it should be defined (Aber & Zigler, 1981; Emery & Laumann-Billings, 1998; Juvenile Justice Standards Project, 1977; McGee & Wolfe, 1991). Despite vigorous debate over these issues, little progress has been made in producing clear, reliable, valid, and useful definitions of child abuse and neglect (Cicchetti & Barnett, 1991; Cicchetti & Rizley, 1981; National Research Council, 1993). The problems in constructing effective operational definitions include such factors as lack of social consensus concerning what forms of parenting are unacceptable or dangerous, uncertainty about whether to define maltreatment based on adult behavior, child outcome, or some combination of the two, controversy over whether criteria of harm or endangerment should be included in definitions of maltreatment, and confusion about whether similar definitions should be used for scientific, legal, and clinical purposes (Aber & Zigler, 1981; Cicchetti & Barnett, 1991; Cicchetti & Rizley, 1981).

With respect to a definition with utility for research purposes, several scientists have suggested that an operationalization of maltreatment that focuses on the specific acts that endanger children may be most appropriate (see, e.g., Barnett et al., 1993; Cicchetti & Barnett, 1991; Zuravin, 1991). Such an approach would allow researchers to concentrate on identifiable behaviors that comprise the child's caretaking environment rather than on the uncertain consequences of those parental actions, such as some form of harm that may or may not be demonstrable (Aber & Cicchetti, 1984; Barnett et al.). The challenge for researchers, then, is to develop precise operational definitions that minimize reliance on professional opinion. This lack of consensus about what constitutes maltreatment makes clear communication and collaboration among respective fields problematic and contributes to difficulties in interpreting results of various investigations across laboratories.

In general, four categories of child maltreatment are usually distinguished from each other: (a) *physical abuse*, which involves the infliction of bodily injury on a child by other than accidental means; b) *sexual abuse*, which includes sexual contact or attempted sexual contact between a caregiver or other responsible adult and a child for purposes of the caregiver's sexual gratification or financial benefits; (c) *neglect*, which includes both the failure to provide minimum care and the lack of supervision; and (d) *emotional abuse*, which involves persistent and extreme thwarting of a child's basic emotional needs. McGee and Wolfe (1991) have expanded on the notion of emotional maltreatment to offer an operational definition of "psychological maltreatment" that subsumes both psychologically abusive and psychologically neglectful caretaking behaviors. Each of these subtypes of maltreatment represents a clear deviation from the average expectable environment. However, even an issue as seemingly straightforward as identifying maltreatment subtypes can become unclear. It would be a mistake to assume that maltreatment always occurs in discrete subtypes. There is a high degree of comorbidity among maltreatment subtypes, indicating that many maltreated children experience more than one type of maltreatment (Cicchetti & Rizley, 1981; Egeland & Sroufe, 1981). The reality of the actual experience of many children is quite complicated, and this presents significant challenges for researchers and clinicians.

Beginning in 1974, as a component of the Child Abuse Prevention and Treatment Act (CAPTA) legislation, the U.S. Congress initiated the National Incidence Study of Child Abuse and Neglect (NIS-1). This survey collects information on child abuse and neglect from a representative sample of community-based professional and social service agencies in order to examine characteristics of child maltreatment, including those that may not have been reported to authorities. Beginning in 1986, the NIS studies obtained information on occurrences that endangered a child, as well as on incidents that inflicted actual demonstrable harm (USDHHS, 1996). According to the most recent National Incidence Study (NIS-3) (USDHHS, 1996), child maltreatment is defined as involving moderate harm from physical or sexual abuse and serious harm resulting from neglect. In 1993, NIS-3 estimated that 1,555,800 American children were abused or neglected according to the harm standard. Strikingly, NIS-3 also found that the rate of abuse and neglect in 1993 evidenced an increase of 67% compared to 1986 and a 149% increase since 1980. Figures such as these underscore the magnitude of the problem of child maltreatment. However, for research purposes, even greater clarity of children's actual experiences is necessary for a comprehensive understanding of the effects of maltreatment on development.

In order to more clearly operationalize the diverse experiences that constitute child maltreatment, investigators in our laboratory developed a nosology for classifying child maltreatment experiences (Barnett et al., 1993; Cicchetti & Barnett, 1991). This classification system contains operational definitions of the major subtypes of child maltreatment, rating scales for the severity of each maltreatment incident, an incorporation of the frequency and chronicity of the maltreatment acts, the identification of the perpetrator of each act, and the developmental period during which the maltreatment occurred (see Barnett et al.). This nosology has been adopted by a number of laboratories across the country and the initial reliability and validity studies that have been conducted have revealed sound psychometric properties for the classification system (Bolger, Patterson, & Kupersmidt, 1998; Manly, Cicchetti, & Barnett, 1994; Smith & Thornberry, 1995). The goal of such a detailed nosology is to provide as complete an account of each child's maltreatment experience as possible. By trying to quantify some of the major components of maltreatment, it may be possible to capture the more qualitative meaning of the experience for the child. This ultimately would provide researchers with a set of powerful independent variables in studies on the consequences of maltreatment. Utilization of the Barnett et al. nosological system in the investigations reported in this chapter enables comparisons to be drawn across studies.

Children who participated in the research reported in this chapter met legal definitions for child maltreatment. All children classified as maltreated were referred from the local Department of Social Services (DSS) for concerns related to child maltreatment and represented the group identified as maltreated. Because the majority of children receiving services related to maltreatment through the DSS are members of the lower socioeconomic status, comparison children were selected from the county lists of families receiving public assistance who resided in neighborhoods similar to those in which maltreated children lived. In order to obtain a comprehensive report of children's maltreatment experiences, as well as to verify the nonmaltreament status of comparison children, permission was obtained from both maltreating and comparison parents to check DSS records. Any comparison child whose family was found to have been investigated for child maltreatment was excluded from the study. DSS records were reviewed at six month intervals and any new information was incorporated into the characterization of our sample. In our experience, approximately 20% of children recruited as comparisons are actually found to be residing in a maltreating home. This fact underscores the extreme risk to which even nonmaltreated children participating in our studies are exposed. In accord with the impoverished status of the sample, children usually live in single-parent families. Approximately 60% of participants reside in minority families, and more boys than girls are typically included in the maltreated groups. These gender differences reflect the reality of more boys than girls being referred to DSS for services related to child maltreatment. In all investigations reported in this chapter, experimenters were unaware of maltreatment status and of experimental hypotheses.

An Ecological-Transactional Model of Child Maltreatment

Drawing upon the work of Bronfenbrenner (1979), Belsky (1980), Cicchetti and Rizley (1981) and Sameroff and Chandler (1975), Cicchetti and Lynch (1993) formulated an ecological-transactional developmental model that can be used to examine the way in which serious disturbances in caretaking environments, such as child maltreatment, impact individual development and adaptation. This model provides a broad and integrative framework for examining the processes and mechanisms that moderate or mediate the impact of child maltreatment on individual development and adaptation. Specifically, the Cicchetti and Lynch (1993) model suggests testable hypotheses to explain how forces from each level of the ecology, as well as an individual's current developmental organization, exert reciprocal influences on each other and shape the course of development.

According to Cicchetti and Lynch (1993) potentiating and compensatory risk factors associated with maltreatment are present at each level of the ecology. Risk factors within a given level of the ecology can influence outcomes and processes in surrounding levels of the environment. These constantly occurring transactions determine the amount of biological and psychological risk that the individual faces. At higher, more distal levels of the ecology, such as the *macrosystem* and the *exosystem*, potentiating factors increase the potential of conditions that support maltreatment. For example, cultural acceptance of corporal punishment and ideologies that provide justification for child maltreatment, domestic violence, war atrocities, and other forms of societal violence are features of the macrosystem that may increase the risk for maltreatment (Cicchetti, Toth, & Lynch, 1997; Staub, 1996). Potentiating factors also may be associated with characteristics of the exosystem. Structural characteristics of community organization and amount of community violence to which parents and children are exposed have been related to probabilities of child maltreatment, parenting practices, aggression, delinquency, and problems with peer relations (Coulton, Korbin, Su, & Chow, 1995; Drake & Pandey, 1996; Kupersmidt, Griesler, DeRosier, Patterson, & Davis, 1995; Lynch & Cicchetti, 1998a; Sampson & Laub, 1994; Tolan & Henry, 1996). Cumulative risk from the macro- and exosystems can negatively impact parents and their capacity to provide adequate parenting for their children (Cicchetti et al., 1997; Osofsky, 1995). Both chronic stressors and acute trauma can adversely affect parental discipline styles, emotional availability, and supervision of children (Punamaki, Quota, & El Sarraj, 1997; Sampson & Laub, 1994).

In contrast, compensatory factors decrease the potential of maltreatment eventuating (Coulton et al., 1995; Korbin, Coulton, Chard, Platt-Houston, & Su, 1998). For example, at the macrosystem level, a prosperous economy and low unemployment rate may decrease the risk for neglect; at the exosystem level active community and neighborhood programs may reduce isolation, thereby decreasing the potential for maltreatment.

Risk factors within the *microsystem* (i.e., the family) also contribute to the adaptiveness of family functioning, as well as to the presence or absence of maltreatment. Characteristics of the microsystem exert the most direct effects on children's development because it is the level of the ecology most proximal to the child.

An ecological-transactional perspective also can help to account for resilient outcomes. For example, compensatory factors include parental physical and mental health, adequate financial resources, low levels of community violence, marital harmony, and a child's adaptive developmental functioning prior to the experience of maltreatment. The presence of potentiating and compensatory factors at any level of the ecology, in dynamic transaction with the child's individual level of biological and psychological organization, may help to explain why some children display successful adaptation in the face of maltreatment and other disturbances in the caretaking environment. For any child, the influence exerted by specific potentiating and compensatory factors will vary. Moreover, outcome will be affected by the dynamic balance that exists between potentiating and compensatory factors. These potentiating factors can be relatively enduring (i.e., vulnerability factors) or more transient (i.e., challengers). Likewise, compensatory factors may be more long-term (i.e., protective factors) or transient (i.e., buffers). Developmental maladaptation is more likely to occur when vulnerability and challenger potentiating risk factors outweigh protective and buffering compensatory influences, whereas adaptation is more likely when the converse is present (Cicchetti, 1989; Cicchetti & Garmezy, 1993). Maladaptation and/or mental disorder are likely to be evidenced in those individuals where a pathological organization has evolved transactionally over the course of development and whose coping capacities and protective resources are unable to counter the influences of enduring vulnerabilities in conjunction with transient challengers (Cicchetti & Rizley, 1981).

In such a conceptualization of risk for maladaptive development and/or psychopathological outcome, it is important to keep in mind that risk factors do not *cause* maladaptation, but rather that they are indicators of a complex matrix of processes and mechanisms that impact on individual development (cf. Rutter, 1990). Potentiating and compensatory factors operate via their influence on competence or incompetence at progressive stages of development. Overall developmental outcome is affected not simply by the presence or absence of potentiating risk factors and compensatory influences but through the interplay that occurs between these factors and prior levels of adaptation (Cicchetti & Tucker, 1994; Sroufe, Egeland, & Kreutzer, 1990).

The manner in which children handle the challenges presented to them by societal, community, and family dysfunction is seen in their own *ontogenic* development. It is the particular pathway that individual development takes that results in ultimate adaptation or maladaptation. An ecological-transactional perspective depicts epigenesis as probabilistic in nature (cf. Gottlieb, 1992) and adopts an organizational approach on development. This organizational viewpoint portrays development as a series of qualitative reorganizations among and within biological and psychological systems as growth of the individual proceeds (Cicchetti & Schneider-Rosen, 1986; Sroufe, 1979). The analysis of this organization involves components at many levels, including the biological, behavioral, psychological, environmental, and societal levels. Processes within these domains are viewed as being in dynamic transaction across the life course and the individual assumes an increasingly active role in his or her own development over time. Through differentiation and hierarchic integration, continuity of functioning may be maintained over time, as prior patterns of adaptation (i.e., developmental history) are incorporated into successive reorganizations at subsequent periods of development. This organizational perspective implies that individuals are neither unaffected by earlier experiences nor immutably controlled by them. Change in developmental course is always possible as a result of new experiences and reorganizations and the individual's active self-organizing strivings for adaptation.

Across the developmental course, the evolving capacities of the individual and his or her active choices allow for new aspects of experience, both internal (i.e., biological) and external (i.e., environmental), to be coordinated in increasingly complex ways. At each developmental transition, the individual is confronted with specific developmental tasks that are central to that era. From infancy through adulthood, new developmental tasks (i.e., sensitive periods) emerge and are of primary importance during their particular stage of ascendance. However, despite subsequent developmental issues gaining greater salience at later points in development, each developmental task remains an issue of life span significance. The quality of the resolution of each stage-salient issues is coordinated, through the processes of differentiation and hierarchic integration, with the prior organization of developmental systems, and reorganization occurs, moving the individual forward in development. The quality of the resolution of each stage-salient issue primes the way subsequent developmental issues are likely to be negotiated. It is through their active role in the ontogenetic process that individuals begin to proceed down different developmental pathways.

For example, inadequate resolution of developmental challenges may result in a developmental delay or deviation in one of the biological or psychological systems. As a result, less than adequate integration within that domain will occur, and that poor within-domain integration will compromise adaptive integration across domains as hierarchical integration proceeds. Thus, incompetence in development may be viewed as a problematic integration of pathological structures. Over time, difficulty in the organization of one biological or psychological system may tend to promote difficulty with the way in which other systems are organized as hierarchical integration between separate systems occurs (cf. Hinde, 1992). The organization of the individual may then appear to consist of an amalgam of poorly integrated component systems.

While early incompetence tends to promote later incompetence because the individual arrives at successive developmental stages or transitions with less than optimal resources available for responding to the challenges of that period, this progression is probabilistic but not inevitable. Changes in the internal and external environment may lead to improvements in the ability of the individual to grapple with developmental challenges, resulting in a redirection in the developmental course. Thus, although historical factors canalize and constrain the adaptive process to some degree, plasticity is possible as a result of adaptive self-organization.

The ecological-transactional model has guided the development of investigations of maltreated children conducted within our laboratory. In this chapter, we focus on studies that have addressed developmental processes contributing to adaptive or maladaptive biological and psychological development in children who have been maltreated. We organize the discussion of these investigations within the various levels described in the ecological-transactional model.

Exosystem Level Influences on Developmental Outcome

As predicted by an ecological-transactional model, violence in the community, a characteristic of the exosystem, may be associated with an increased likelihood of domestic violence at home, a microsystem variable. There are significant positive correlations between children's reports of exposure to community violence and the level of spousal conflict in their homes (Richters & Martinez, 1993). Although it is not clear what the relationship between these two co-occurring forms of violence may be, it is possible that the stress and negative conditions associated with living in a violent community may cause heightened stress for some families that contributes to and potentiates an increased probability of violent responses to spousal conflict. For the children growing up in contexts where violence is occurring at multiple levels of the ecology, the risk for problems is great.

In a similar vein, community violence may be one of a number of exosystem factors that potentiate the occurrence of child maltreatment in the microsystem. A number of researchers have demonstrated links between exosystem variables such as neighborhood poverty, availability of social supports, population turnover, concentration of female-headed households, and proportion of children per adult resident with probabilities of child maltreatment (Coulton et al., 1995; Drake & Pandey, 1996; Garbarino & Gilliam, 1980; Korbin et al., 1998; Kupersmidt et al., 1995; Sampson & Laub, 1994). With regard to the impact of community violence on the occurrence of child maltreatment, it is possible that violence in communities acts as an enduring vulnerability factor increasing the risk for maltreatment at the level of the microsystem (Cicchetti & Lynch, 1993). More research is needed which examines both the relationship between community violence and child maltreatment and the enduring vulnerabilities and transient challengers that their co-occurrence create for children.

There has been extensive work demonstrating the serious consequences of child abuse and neglect on development and adaptation (see Cicchetti & Lynch, 1995). Moreover, histories of child maltreatment are associated with increased rates of behavior problems and psychopathology (Cicchetti & Toth, 1995), as well as with a higher prevalence of psychiatric symptoms and diagnoses. Maltreated children exhibit a greater incidence of attention deficit/hyperactivity disorder, oppositional defiant disorder, and post traumatic stress disorder (PTSD) than do nonmaltreated children (Famularo, Kinscherff, & Fenton, 1992). Maltreatment, especially physical and sexual abuse, also is related to a number of psychiatric complaints in childhood and adulthood, including panic disorders, anxiety disorders, depression, eating disorders, somatic complaints, dissociation, sexual dysfunction, borderline personality disorder, and traumatic stress reactions (for a review, see Cicchetti & Lynch, 1995).

However, research on the impact that community violence and maltreatment exert on children's mental health has not been conducted until recently. Lynch and Cicchetti (1998a) investigated children's exposure to community violence (an exosystem variable) and their history of child maltreatment (a microsystem variable) in the context of a summer day camp. The Lynch and Cicchetti investigation represents the first time that the joint effects of community violence and child maltreatment were examined in a single study. In keeping with the ecological-transactional model, Lynch and Cicchetti predicted that increased community violence occurring in the exosystem would be associated with the occurrence of higher rates of maltreatment in the microsystem. Further, they predicted that maltreatment and high levels of violence exposure would be associated with greater child maladaptation. Exposure to community violence was assessed based on children's reports on the Richters and Martinez (1993) Community Violence Survey. The questionnaire asks children to rate the frequency with which they have experienced, witnessed, or heard about various acts of violence in their community, such as shootings, stabbings, sexual assaults, drug deals, arrests by police, suicides, and murders.

Consistent with predictions from the ecological-transactional model, Lynch and Cicchetti (1998a) found that rates of maltreatment were higher among school-aged children who reported higher levels of violence in their community. This finding supports the notion that aspects of the exosystem are related to increased risk for problems in the microsystem. Specifically, community violence was associated with the rate of physical abuse and the severity of neglect. Children who reported higher exposure to violence in their neighborhoods were more likely than those from low reported-violence neighborhoods to have been physically abused. Although the severity of the physical abuse experiences of children from high- versus low-violence neighborhoods did not differ, the severity of neglect experiences did. Children who reported more violence in their community also were more severely neglected than children from communities where there was less reported violence.

Evidence also was obtained demonstrating how factors from different levels of the ecological context mutually shape individual development. Both child maltreatment and exposure to community violence were related to multiple indicators of children's adaptation. Maltreated children, in particular, manifested higher levels of externalizing and internalizing behavior problems as rated by camp counselors. A history of sexual abuse *per se* was associated with an increased probability of having clinically significant levels of externalizing behavior problems. Moreover, the severity of children's neglect experiences was related positively to their internalizing behaviors, traumatic stress reactions, and depressive symptomatology, and negatively to self-esteem. These findings suggest that in a context where children may be exposed to violence in the community, severe parental neglect may further contribute to behavioral and emotional maladaptation. Having parents fail to recognize and meet one's basic needs and/or deprive one of consistent access to external supports, as is frequently the case for neglected children, may be especially problematic for children growing up in stressful violent communities.

Exposure to high levels of community violence was associated with increased child reports of traumatic stress and depressive symptomatology and with lower self-esteem. Both victimization by violence and witnessing violence in the community were important elements of children's exosystem experiences. Increased amounts of violence *witnessed* in the community were reported by children with clinically high levels of externalizing behavior and depressive symptomatology. Children with clinically significant depressive symptomatology also reported having been personally *victimized* by more community violence than did children with less serious symptomatology. More generally, being directly victimized by violence in the community was related positively with traumatic stress and depressive symptomatology and negatively with self-esteem. However, when the effects of children's prior functioning and previous context were accounted for, victimization by community violence only was significantly related to self-reported traumatic stress.

As for the joint effect of maltreatment and community violence, the data indicate that there may be an additive effect of these two potentiating factors. Maltreated children from high-violence communities (indicating heightened proximal and distal risk) consistently exhibited worse functioning than nonmaltreated children from low-violence communities (signifying diminished proximal and distal risk). In contrast to predictions from the ecological-transactional model, however, exposure to community violence did not appear to moderate the overall effect of maltreatment on children's functioning. Lynch and Cicchetti (1998a) predicted that the proximal (microsystem) effects of child maltreatment would be moderated by the more distal (exosystem) effects of community violence. Such moderating influences would have been evident if, in addition to the group differences reported above, maltreated children from low-violence communities had displayed poorer functioning (as a result of their more proximal risk) than nonmaltreated children from high-violence communities (whose risk was more distal).

The findings presented in this study are consistent with research that has linked symptoms of post traumatic stress disorder to experiences of violence in the community and histories of maltreatment (see Pynoos, Steinberg, & Wraith, 1995 for a review). As children attempt to adjust to the traumatic and secondary stresses in their ecologies, they may exhibit proximal stress-related psychopathology in the form of PTSD, depression, anxiety disorders, conduct disorders, and a variety of other disturbances. In addition, impairment may be observed in the development of proximal issues associated with self-image, autonomy, and representations of self and others. The manner in which children ultimately respond to traumatic stress depends upon the severity of the trauma exposure, personality characteristics of the child, parental trauma-related distress, characteristics of the broader ecology, and the presence versus absence of additional stresses and adversities (see Pynoos et al.). Children such as those investigated in the Lynch and Cicchetti (1998a) study frequently have few supports in their environment to help them cope with the recurring (traumatic) stresses that they experience. Such contexts increase the probability of proximal stress-related psychopathology in these children.

Regarding self-perceptions, children in this study who were exposed to potentiating risk factors in the ecology frequently reported significantly lower self-esteem than those exposed to less risk. As seen in the work on PTSD, self-attributions and perceptions of self-efficacy can be negatively affected by environmental contexts filled with stress-related adversity. Growing up in chronically stressful contexts, such as those characterized by maltreatment and community violence, may contribute to feelings of learned helplessness and ineffectiveness in children. As a result, they may internalize negative attitudes about themselves that are expressed through low self-esteem. Increasingly, the contextual features that contribute to the formation of negative self-perceptions may start to influence children's more general representations of self and others. Significant figures such as their caregivers may come to be viewed by children as incapable of keeping them safe from the dangers present in their environment. Alternately, children may feel that they are unworthy of being kept safe. This mixture of affects and cognitions may contribute to the development of insecure relationships with caregivers among children who live in threatening environments. Empirical investigations are needed to understand the potential impact of environmental adversity on the quality of children's representations of self and others. Such research would contribute further to elucidating the effects of various ecological levels on children's functioning.

Microsystem Level Influences on Developmental Outcome

In our laboratory we have conducted an investigation that addresses the role of parenting on developmental outcome in maltreated children. In this study of microsystem-level regulation, Rogosch and Cicchetti (1994) examined the interface of family and peer relations through the study of child maltreatment. These investigators discovered that teachers, unaware of children's maltreatment status, consistently perceived maltreated children as evidencing greater disturbance in social functioning with peers than nonmaltreated children. Specifically, teachers evaluated maltreated children as less socially competent, as less socially accepted by their peers, and as displaying higher levels of behavioral disturbance, particularly externalizing problems. Classroom peers also distinguished maltreated children as more rejected or isolated by the peer group. Physically abused children showed the greatest differentiation from their nonmaltreated peers. Thus, evidence for continuity between disturbances in parent-child relationships and social adaptational difficulties in the peer group was established from the perspectives of both adults and peers.

A more refined view of the influence of maltreatment on social difficulties was obtained when different groups of children were examined based on their peer-perceived "profiles" of aggressive and withdrawn behavior. The combination of aggression and withdrawal was particularly important for determining which maltreated children were having the most social difficulty. In particular, maltreated children who were viewed by their peers as relatively high on both aggression and withdrawal evidenced substantially lower social effectiveness. Interestingly, maltreated and nonmaltreated children were not differentiated in terms of social effectiveness when they were only relatively high on aggression or on withdrawal. There also was a tendency among relatively highly aggressive children for more maltreated than nonmaltreated children to evidence high withdrawal. Accordingly, this combined pattern and its effects may become more readily apparent in the context of studying social development among children with highly dysfunctional parent-child relationships.

For the study sample, poor social effectiveness was predicted by maltreatment status as well as by the parenting dimensions of authoritarian control and limited autonomy promotion. However, the contribution of these forms of influence varied, depending on the profile of children's social behavior. Among those children who did not evidence the mixed aggressive-withdrawn pattern, authoritarian control and autonomy restriction contributed to social ineffectiveness, consistent with what would be predicted by processes of socialization (Maccoby & Martin, 1983). Maltreatment did not contribute additionally to prediction, suggesting that these parenting features may mediate the effect of maltreatment among children who exhibit more typical patterns of social behavior (i.e., only aggressive, only withdrawn, or neither). In contrast, among the children perceived as both aggressive and withdrawn, only maltreatment status contributed to predicting social effectiveness, and it did so to a substantial degree. Thus, for the children who evidenced the strongest deficits in social effectiveness, child maltreatment and not the other features of parenting, accounted for this difference.

An attachment theory perspective may be useful to account for the effects of maltreatment among the children who evidence the mixed aggressive and withdrawn presentation. Given the high prevalence of blending of resistance and avoidance in the attachment behaviors of maltreated infants and toddlers and patterns of disorganization and disorientation in those attachments (Carlson, Cicchetti, Barnett, & Braunwald, 1989), it is interesting to speculate on the blending of aggressiveness and withdrawal found among maltreated children. The possibility of more intense and frightening experiences in the parent-child relationship as a result of maltreatment may contribute to these intermingled patterns in that fearful and frightening behavior by caregivers has been associated with disorganized attachment behaviors (Main & Hesse, 1990). This pattern of intermingled behaviors may represent the continued operation of disorganized internal working (i.e., representational) models of relationships carried forward from the attachment relationship into new social encounters, resulting in disturbances in social adaptation. The aggressive-withdrawal strategy may be relied on protectively to diminish the anticipated negative aspects of interpersonal relations; termination of perceived interpersonal threats through the use of aggression may co-occur with withdrawal and isolation to avoid those threats.

The continuities in relationship disturbances from the family to the peer group at school indicate that maltreated children, particularly those who are aggressive and withdrawn, are in jeopardy of ongoing interpersonal adjustment problems. Parker and Asher (1987) have reviewed research supporting the connection between peer rejection and aggression and later maladjustment, particularly dropping out of school and criminality. The research reported here supports the role of family relationship disturbances as a source contributing to this pathway leading to later maladjustment. The continuity in relationship problems of maltreated children evolving in both the family and peer context also likely contributes to risk for forming later unstable marital relationships and repeating dysfunctional patterns of childrearing (Crittenden, Partridge, & Claussen, 1991; Howes & Cicchetti, 1993).

In addition to examining the effects of directly experiencing maltreatment within the family, researchers also have sought to understand the effects of domestic violence. Sternberg et al. (1993) examined the effects of domestic violence in Israeli children from low-income families. Specifically, child and maternal report of behavior problems were obtained on children who were victims of abuse, those who witnessed spousal violence, those who were victims as well as witnesses of violence, and a comparison group. Interestingly, witnessing spousal abuse did not affect children's reports of their adjustment as much as did being a victim of physical abuse or being a victim of and a witness to violence. In essence, the adjustment of children who witnessed domestic violence fell "in between" that of physically abused and nonabused children. With regard to maternal report, mothers reported more externalizing symptomatology in children who were witnesses only, as well as those who were physically abused and exposed to domestic violence (Sternberg et al, 1993).

It is clear that further investigations are needed on microsystemic influences on development in maltreated children. Moreover, the interpersonal difficulties evidenced in both family and peer relations and what they bode for future relationships call attention to the need for intervention services for maltreated children in order to prevent a developing course of failure in relationships and associated maladjustment. Additionally, further research is needed to elucidate the effects of witnessing domestic violence in the absence of actual child victimization.

Ontogenic Development

MALTREATMENT EXPERIENCES AND BRAIN PROCESSING

As neuroscientists analyze the neurodevelopmental process into fine molecular mechanisms, developmental psychopathologists, through their investigations of high-risk populations, including maltreated children, have the opportunity to rejuvenate the classical notions of environmental control of development. The mechanisms of neural plasticity cause the brain's anatomical differentiation to be dependent on stimulation from the environment. The role of nurture can now be reconceptualized. The traditional assumption was that the environment determines only the psychological residues of development, such as memories and habits, while brain anatomy matures on its fixed ontogenetic calendar. Environmental experience is now recognized as being critical to the differentiation of brain tissue itself (Cicchetti & Tucker, 1994; Eisenberg, 1995; Nelson & Bloom, 1997). Nature's potential can be realized only as it is enabled by nurture.

A number of neuroimaging investigations have demonstrated that adults who have experienced combat-related post traumatic stress disorder (PTSD) or adults who recollect having been sexually abused have reduced hippocampal volume (Bremner & Narayan, 1998; Gurvits et al., 1996; Stein, Koverola, Hanna, Torchia, & McClarty, 1997). Although prospective longitudinal assessments of the hippocampal structure of military personnel prior to the emergence of PTSD and prospective longitudinal studies of hippocampal volume prior to the experience of sexual abuse are needed in order to differentiate between the relative contributions of genetic and experiential processes to decreased hippocampal size, a plausible working hypothesis is that exposure to severe trauma can affect brain structure.

In keeping with the organizational perspective, wherein the study of multiple domains of psychological and biological systems are deemed necessary in order to have a comprehensive "whole child" portrayal of development, we believe that future neuroimaging studies must investigate the "whole brain." Thus, brain structures in addition to the hippocampus must be examined in traumatized children and adults (e.g., frontal lobes, corpus callosum, ventricles, etc.) in order to achieve a full understanding of the impact that social experiences such as maltreatment can exert on neurobiological development and functioning. Furthermore, because there may be sensitive periods for the effects of child maltreatment on brain development, investigators must strive to ascertain the age of onset, the developmental epochs during which maltreatment occurred, the perpetrator of the maltreatment, and the nature, severity and chronicity of the maltreatment experiences (Cicchetti & Barnett, 1991; Perry et al., 1995).

In our laboratory, we have conducted two experiments that have examined maltreated children's psychophysiological processing of emotional information (Pollak, Cicchetti, & Klorman, 1998). The goal of this research was to elucidate possible mechanisms through which the chronic stress experienced by children who have been maltreated could bring about problems in their processing of emotion stimuli.

The requirements of the experimental task were for children to recognize and respond to facial expressions of emotions. For all conditions, children were instructed to depress a hand-held button whenever they recognized the target facial expression (e.g., "angry," "happy," "fear"). This emotional expression, the "target," was only one of three emotions that were presented to the children. Across a variety of experimental conditions, children were required to attend to different facial expressions of emotion, and the probability of occurrence (rare or frequent) and task relevance (target or non-target) were manipulated (see Pollak et al., 1998).

In the first experiment, Pollak, Cicchetti, Klorman, and Brumaghim (1997) compared the event related potentials (ERPs) of a sample of school-aged maltreated children to a group of nonmaltreated children of comparable cognitive maturity and socioeconomic background. The ERP is an index of central nervous system functioning thought to reflect the underlying neurological processing of discrete stimuli (Hillyard & Picton, 1987). ERP's represent scalp-derived changes in brain electrical activity over time, obtained by averaging time-locked segments of the EEG that follow or precede the presentation of a stimulus. In this manner, ERPs allow for monitoring of neural activity associated with cognitive processing in real time (Donchin, Karis, Bashore, Coles, & Gratton, 1986).

Children were instructed to respond to either a happy or an angry face. Because the amplitude of the ERP is influenced by the probability of occurrence of the stimuli, both happy and angry faces appeared infrequently (i.e., on 25% of the trials), whereas the target neutral faces were displayed more frequently (i.e., on 50% of the trials). For both groups of children, there were few performance errors; thus, no distinctions could be made between emotion conditions (i.e., happy, angry, neutral) or between maltreated and nonmaltreated children with respect to accuracy or reaction time.

The ERPs of the nonmaltreated children were equivalent in both the happy and angry target conditions. The amplitude of the ERP was largest to the target stimuli, intermediate to the rare nontarget, and smallest to the frequent nontarget stimuli. In contrast, the ERPs of the maltreated children were larger in the angry than in the happy target conditions. This differential pattern of responding to emotion conditions suggests that, compared to nonmaltreated children, different patterns of information processing were being evoked depending upon the emotion to which the maltreated children were attending (Pollak et al., 1997).

In a subsequent experiment, Pollak, Klorman, Brumaghim, & Cicchetti (in press) compared the ERP responses of maltreated and nonmaltreated children to happy, angry, and fear facial expressions. This study was undertaken to determine the specificity of the relation between the ERP responses of the maltreated children and the nature of the eliciting stimuli. In particular, Pollak and colleagues were interested in whether the ERPs of maltreated children generalized to positive versus negative emotional valence, or were specific to displays of happiness versus anger. For example, negative emotions in addition to anger are frequently associated with maltreatment experiences (e.g., fear; see Gaensbauer & Hiatt, 1984; Hennessy, Rabideau, Cicchetti, & Cummings, 1994). Thus, it is important to ascertain whether maltreated children process all negative emotions similarly or whether each discrete emotion may convey its own unique information and be processed in a distinct fashion.

Pollak and colleagues (in press) found that, as was the case in the Pollak et al. (1997) study, nonmaltreated children displayed equivalent ERP amplitude responses to all of the target facial expressions of affect. However, the ERP amplitude responses of the maltreated children exceeded those of the nonmaltreated comparison children only in response to the angry target, but not to the fear or happy emotion expression as targets. These results suggest that there was specificity in maltreated children's differential processing of the emotional information (Pollak et al., in press).

In combination with the literature on the effects of maltreatment on psychological development, the findings of Pollak and colleagues (1997, 1998, in press) demonstrate that the socioemotional and behavioral difficulties observed in children who have been maltreated affect multiple biobehavioral systems (cf. Cicchetti, 1996). Specifically, the ERP data suggest that the experiences that maltreated children encountered during their development cause particular stimuli to become personally meaningful based, in part, upon the stored mental representations that have been associated with that stimulus over time. As such, prior experiences of maltreated children are reflected in these children's psychophysiological responses. It is hypothesized that the stresses associated with maltreatment may enhance the memory of salient stimuli in the environment (Pollak et al., 1998; Rieder & Cicchetti, 1989; Toth & Cicchetti, 1998). However, maltreatment experiences may affect the manner in which emotional information is processed by these children (cf. Rieder & Cicchetti, 1989; Rogosch, Cicchetti, & Aber, 1995). Conceivably, histories of maltreatment enhance the importance of negative emotional expressions—or reduce the significance of positive expressions—for these children (Fischer & Ayoub, 1994; Pollak et al., 1998; Rieder & Cicchetti, 1989).

In addition to the impact that maltreatment has on the selectivity of information attended to and encoded by maltreated children, the association of affect stimuli with traumatic experiences or memories also could alter the meaning imputed to the stimuli and the nature of the representations evoked by these memories (Cicchetti, 1991; Lynch & Cicchetti, 1998b; Pollak et al., 1998). Consequently, although such selectivity in responding may allow maltreated children to utilize behavioral responses that are adaptive to address the challenges presented by their environments (Cicchetti, 1991), they ultimately may prove to be maladaptive solutions when employed outside of the maltreating situation and may contribute to these children's social-cognitive difficulties (Dodge, Pettit, & Bates, 1990) and increased risk for behavior problems and psychopathology (Cicchetti, 1991; Pollak et al., 1997, 1998; Rogosch, Cicchetti & Aber, 1995).

Because the etiology of child maltreatment is multifaceted (Cicchetti & Lynch, 1993; Cicchetti & Rizley, 1981), it is highly likely that numerous neurobehavioral systems are affected by traumatic experiences. Thus, future research must strive for a more integrative understanding of the role of negative social experiences on brain-behavior relations. To this end, investigations that combine the tools of cognitive neuroscience, neuroimaging, and developmental psychology (see, e.g., Thatcher, Lyon, Rumsey, & Krasnegor, 1996; Toga & Mazziotta, 1996) must be conducted with traumatized children and adults. In particular, functional neuroimaging studies (fMRI), alone or in concert with the investigation of ERPs in various experimental paradigms, hold great promise for elucidating the organization of normal and abnormal brain development and functioning (see, e.g., Thatcher, Hallett, Zeffiro, John, & Huerta, 1994).

REPRESENTATIONS OF CAREGIVERS AS CONTRIBUTORS TO DEVELOPMENTAL OUTCOME

Children's representations of their relationships with their caregivers contribute to the development of the capacity for self-regulation and to the nature of subsequent outcomes. A number of investigations in our laboratory have examined the moderating impact of children's representations of their primary caregivers on various aspects of development.

Attachment and Self-Language Beeghly and Cicchetti (1994) conducted an investigation of the emergence of an internal state (IS) lexicon in maltreated youngsters. Evidence from both maternal interviews and direct observations of children's spontaneous language in the laboratory confirmed predictions that the IS lexicons of maltreated toddlers were significantly delayed, impoverished, and grammatically restricted, relative to demographically (i.e., low SES) and cognitively comparable (i.e., mental age matched) controls. Specifically, maltreated toddlers produced fewer IS words and fewer IS word types than their nonmaltreated counterparts, were more restricted in their ability to attribute IS to self and other agents, and were more context bound in their IS language use. These findings are consistent with more general deficits reported for maltreated toddlers' expressive language, which were described for this sample during maternal play contexts by Coster, Gersten, Beeghly, and Cicchetti (1989).

Notably, the group differences in children's IS language could not be explained entirely on the basis of differences in children's general linguistic maturity. Although individual differences in children's IS language were significantly related to their overall level of language maturity in both groups (a finding consistent with those reported for middle-class children), significant group differences in the content, attributional flexibility, and decontextualization of children's IS language were found even when the size of children's IS corpora and children's receptive abilities were controlled. Moreover, when moderating effects of the child's attachment relationship with the caregiver were considered, toddlers at the highest risk (maltreated and insecure) had the worst IS language profiles. Each of these aspects of IS language is discussed in turn below.

Distributions in the IS categories used by the low SES toddlers were roughly similar to those reported for middle-class children in the literature: Perception and volition words were used proportionately most frequently by both maltreated and nonmaltreated children, followed by words about feelings and affective states (Bretherton & Beeghly, 1982). In contrast, words for cognitive processes were rarely observed. Moreover, when cognitive terms were observed, they were used primarily in routines ("dunno") or to modulate assertions ("I think it'll fit") rather than as references to abstract mental states. These latter findings are consistent with prior research documenting the relatively late emergence of mental state terms in middle-class samples (e.g., Bretherton & Beeghly, 1982; Wellman, 1988).

Despite general distributional similarities in both the observed and reported data, significant main effects of maltreatment were found for particular IS categories in the laboratory data. Specifically, maltreated toddlers produced significantly fewer words denoting physiological feeling states (fatigue, hunger, thirst, illness, states of consciousness), negative affect (anger, sadness, disgust, fear), and obligation (permission, social or moral obligation). In contrast, no differences were observed for IS words more commonly produced to direct or guide behavior during task-oriented interactions, such as perception and volition.

Several possible explanations may be considered for the content differences observed for maltreated children. At a pragmatic level, maltreated children may have been trying to keep conversations with adults focused on the external and as "impersonal" as possible, an avoidant strategy that effectively minimizes intimate social interaction and, presumably, opportunities for further maltreatment or emotional injury. Characteristically, avoidant interactive styles during free play with mother (Coster et al., 1989) and during stressful conditions (e.g., separations, reunions) have been reported for maltreated toddlers (Alessandri, 1991, 1992; Crittenden, 1988).

On a more general level, differences in the amount and content of children's IS language may be explained in part by characteristics of the affective-linguistic environment reported for maltreating families (e.g., Silber, 1990; Wolfe, 1985), which appear to be inconsistent with those hypothesized to facilitate vocabulary growth (see Mervis, 1990; Snow, 1984, for reviews). This may be particularly true for the acquisition of terms for emotions and feeling states, because these words are thought to be acquired most readily during child-focused family discussions about emotions and negotiations of disputes and conflicting goals (Dunn & Brown, 1991). In contrast, the emotional climate of maltreating families has been characterized as highly disorganized, dysregulated, and noncontingent. Moreover, maltreating parents are reported to engage in maladaptive patterns of interactive behavior with their children that effectively preclude prolonged discussions about emotions (Howes & Cicchetti, 1993; Rogosch, Cicchetti, Shields, & Toth, 1995). In such a climate, maltreated children may have learned that it is unacceptable, threatening, or even dangerous to talk about feelings and emotions, particularly negative ones. Cicchetti and White (1990) hypothesized that the difficulties maltreated toddlers have expressing feelings in words may not only be a reflection of psychological intimidation by the caregiver, but also a manifestation of neuroanatomical and neurophysiological changes in brain structure and functioning that occur secondary to abuse or neglect.

A similar tendency to repress or deny negative feelings has been reported for older maltreated children. For example, Crittenden and DiLalla (1988) found that some insecurely attached, maltreated children showed a worrisome degree of "compulsive compliance"; that is, they did not express negative feelings overtly and were passively compliant with their mothers. Similarly, Vondra, Barnett, and Cicchetti (1989) found that maltreated school-age children were more likely to idealize their parents by exaggerating positive qualities and denying negative feelings or disturbances in the relationship (see also Lynch & Cicchetti, 1991).

Although possibly effective as a coping strategy during toddlerhood, a strategy of denying or repressing negative emotions may lead to a restricted or disorganized emotional lexicon and fewer dyadic exchanges about feeling states. Notably, these exchanges are thought to promote the acquisition of interpersonal regulatory skills and an increasingly differentiated self-other understanding (Bretherton, 1991; Cassidy, 1988). Ultimately, these communicative and regulatory problems could contribute to future communicative, cognitive, and socioemotional problems. Although direct links between IS language and regulatory skills of maltreated children have not been established, maltreatment has, in fact, been associated with significant problems in emotion regulation later in children (Rieder & Cicchetti, 1989; Shields & Cicchetti, 1997).

Additionally, a significant main effect of maltreatment on children's ability to attribute IS to self and other also was observed in both laboratory and maternal report data, even when controlling for the size of children's IS corpora. Specifically, maltreated toddlers were more restricted than MA-matched controls in their ability to use the same IS word for a variety of social agents, including self, other persons, toys, and photographs. To the extent that this linguistic ability reflects children's differentiating self and other understanding, this finding suggests that maltreated children may be more delayed in this domain than would be expected on the basis of their receptive language abilities.

Moreover, group differences in the correlational patterns of toddlers' linguistic abilities with self-other differentiation scores also were noted: Whereas nonmaltreated toddlers' ability to use IS words for self and other was significantly correlated with all general language indices [e.g., mean length of utterance (MLU), mean length of conversational episode (MLE), MA-equivalent from the Peabody Picture Vocabulary Test (PPVT-R)], maltreated toddlers' self-other differentiation scores were not significantly related to their discourse abilities (e.g., MLE, conversational relatedness). Interestingly, maltreated children's MLE scores were unrelated to their utterance complexity (MLU) and to every IS measure, whether observed or reported. These correlational differences suggest some degree of disorganization at the interface of maltreated children's self and socio-communicative systems (Cicchetti, 1991).

In keeping with prior research, heterogeneity was obtained in the functioning of the maltreated children in this study. Not all maltreated toddlers evidenced perturbations in self and socio-communicative development. Because Beeghly and Cicchetti (1994) concurrently assessed children's quality of attachment to their mothers, it was possible to ascertain whether quality of attachment moderated the impact of child maltreatment on child outcomes. Securely attached maltreated toddlers did not exhibit the dysfunctions revealed by the insecurely attached maltreated children. Children who were both maltreated and insecurely attached to their mothers showed more compromised IS language and conversational relatedness (MLE) than did a moderate risk (i.e., insecure nonmaltreated or secure maltreated toddlers) or a low-risk group (i.e., secure, nonmaltreated toddlers). Thus, secure attachment may be a protective factor ameliorating the link between maltreatment and self-system disturbances.

Relatedness, Symptomatology, Perceived Competence, and School Functioning In a further examination of the effects of children's representations of their mother's on children's functioning, Toth and Cicchetti (1996a) investigated the links among patterns of relatedness, depressive symptomatology, and perceived competence in school-age (i.e., 8 to 12 year old) maltreated children. The Relatedness Scales were administered individually to yield an assessment of the internal representational model that maltreated and nonmaltreated children have of their mothers. Theoretically, children's responses to these scales are viewed as consistent with attachment and self-system theory (Cicchetti, Toth, & Lynch, 1995). Lynch and Cicchetti (1991) found that maltreated children described more "confused" (i.e., insecure) and less "optimal" (i.e., secure) patterns of relatedness with a variety of individuals, including their mothers, teachers, peers, and best friends than did nonmaltreated comparison children. Although the assessment of these patterns of relatedness cannot be equated with attachment *per se*, the fact that maltreated children evidence a preponderance of insecure attachment relationships in infancy and toddlerhood and that nonoptimal relationship patterns are present in school-age maltreated children suggests the presence of a maladaptive pathway from insecure attachment in the early years to the development of negative representational models of relationship figures in later childhood.

The Relatedness Scales have two subscales that measure children's feelings of relatedness to specific others: Emotional Quality and Psychological Proximity Seeking. Emotional quality refers to the positive and negative emotions that children report with regard to a specific relationship figure. For example, "When I'm with my mother, I feel loved," reflects positive emotional quality. The Psychological Proximity Seeking subscale contains items that tap the degree to which children wish they were psychologically closer to their relationship partner. For example, "I wish my mother understood me better," is considered to reflect high psychological proximity seeking. In general, the more positive the quality of emotion that a child reports, the less the child reports needing to feel psychologically closer to that individual. Thus, if a child reports feeling loved by the mother, one would not expect the child to report the need to be better understood by the mother.

Individual patterns of relatedness are obtained by examining the configuration of each child's scores on both the Emotional Quality and Psychological Proximity Seeking dimensions of relatedness for a particular relationship figure. Normative work conducted by Lynch and Cicchetti (1991, 1997) has yielded five prototypical patterns of relatedness, including the following: (1) *optimal*—higher than average levels of positive emotion and lower than average amounts of proximity seeking, reflective of feeling secure and satisfied with the degree of closeness; (2) *adequate*—average levels of emotional quality and proximity seeking; (3) *deprived*—lower than average levels of emotional quality but higher than average amounts of proximity seeking, reflective of wanting to feel closer to the relationship figure despite describing the relationship as characterized by feelings of negativity and insecurity; (4) *disengaged*—lower than average levels of emotional quality and lower than average proximity seeking, reflecting negative feelings toward the relationship figure and the lack of desire to be closer; and (5) *confused*—high levels of emotional quality in conjunction with high amounts of proximity seeking, reflecting the need for more psychological proximity despite feeling emotionally positive and secure with the relationship figure.

Optimal and adequate patterns of relatedness are considered to be similar to "secure" attachment relationships, whereas nonoptimal relatedness patterns (i.e., deprived, disengaged, and confused) are conceptualized to be similar to "insecure" relationships (see Cicchetti et al., 1995; Lynch & Cicchetti, 1997). Within the insecure categorization, deprived and disengaged patterns are considered to be similar to anxious-ambivalent (Type C) and anxious-avoidant (Type A) attachments, respectively, whereas the confused pattern is consistent with atypical attachments (i.e., Type A/C—see Crittenden, 1988— and Type D—see Main & Solomon, 1990).

Toth and Cicchetti (1996a) found that when compared with nonmaltreated children, maltreated children exhibit lower perceived competence in the areas of scholastic competence, social acceptance, and behavioral conduct. When examining subtypes of maltreatment, children who had experienced sexual abuse were more likely to report depressive symptomatology and impaired behavioral conduct than were nonmaltreated children. Although differences on symptomatology did emerge between maltreated and nonmaltreated children, these findings were due largely to the children who had been sexually abused.

The role of relationship history in buffering or exacerbating the emergence of maladaptation was examined more elaborately by using relatedness as an attachment—like construct. In investigating the nature of the link between maltreatment status and relatedness to mother, patterns of relatedness emerged as a significant variable that was contributing to depressive symptomatology and impaired perceptions of social acceptance. Interestingly, children with confused patterns of relatedness evidenced the highest level of depressive symptomatology, whereas impaired social acceptance was present in children reporting disengaged-deprived patterns of relatedness. The findings with respect to confused patterns are compatible with the "over-bright" characterization of children with atypical attachment organizations (Crittenden & DiLalla, 1988; Main & Solomon, 1990). Specifically, Toth and Cicchetti (1996a) suggest that children who evidenced confused patterns of relatedness may present similar "over-bright" presentations that lead them to be accepted by peers, although they continue to report high levels of depressive symptomatology. In contrast, the impaired social acceptance reported by children with disengaged-deprived patterns of relatedness is consistent with the peer difficulties and social withdrawal frequently noted among children having insecure-avoidant and insecure-ambivalent attachment relationships with their primary caregiver (Rubin, Hymel, Mills, & Rose-Krasnor, 1991).

In examining maltreatment subtype, sexually abused children reported depressive symptomatology in a range consistent with mild depression, unlike the nonclinically significant symptom level endorsed by all other children. The sexually abused children also reported lower competence on behavioral conduct. When factoring in patterns of relatedness, sexually abused children with nonoptimal patterns of relatedness evidenced extremely elevated levels of depressive symptomatology that were consistent with depression considered to be of clinical significance. This contrasted markedly with the nonclinical level of symptomatology endorsed by sexually abused children who reported optimal-adequate relatedness to mother. Additionally, sexually abused children with confused patterns of relatedness reported extremely elevated levels of depressive symptomatology, compared with other sexually abused children. Thus, the present findings provide an interesting view on the sequelae of childhood sexual abuse and may be helpful in accounting for the varied outcomes that have been described in childhood victims of sexual abuse (Kendall-Tackett et al., 1993). Outcome for these children is likely to be a function of the perpetrator of abuse and of the protection and support or lack thereof that the sexually abused child perceives from his or her primary caregiver. Issues such as whether abuse is perpetrated by a family member, friend, or unknown perpetrator also are likely to impact on the sequelae associated with sexual abuse, with more distant relationships likely to exert a less deleterious effect, especially if family support is available to the child.

To further elucidate the nature of the link between maltreatment status and patterns of relatedness, a composite of maltreatment status and patterns of relatedness was developed and examined for various relationship figures (i.e., mothers, teachers, peers, best friend). These analyses provided support for the hypothesis that differences between maltreated children with and without optimal-adequate patterns of relatedness would emerge. Specifically, maltreated children with confused patterns of relatedness with mother reported more depressed symptomatology than maltreated children with optimal-adequate relatedness to mother. Other relationship figures did not reveal these differences among maltreated children, although some interesting differences emerged among nonmaltreated children with different patterns of relatedness to their best friend. Nonmaltreated children with optimal-adequate relatedness to best friend reported less depressive symptomatology than nonmaltreated children with disengaged-deprived patterns of relatedness to best friend.

In a prospective longitudinal study, Toth and Cicchetti (1996b) examined the role of children's representations of attachment relationships with their mother in affecting school adaptation in maltreated and nonmaltreated children between the ages of 7 and 12 years. Toth and Cicchetti's (1996b) hypotheses that a secure (i.e., optimal/adequate) pattern of relatedness with mother would foster positive school adaptation, whereas an insecure (i.e., non-optimal) relationship would contribute to maladaptive functioning were partially confirmed. Nonmaltreated children who reported secure patterns of relatedness to mother exhibited less externalizing symptomatology, more ego-resilience, and fewer school record risk factors (e.g., attendance problems, grade retention, suspensions, poor performance on standardized tests, failing 50% of subjects) than did maltreated children who reported insecure patterns of relatedness. Within the nonmaltreated group of children, optimal/adequate patterns of relatedness exerted a positive effect on school functioning. Interestingly, for maltreated children this was true only with respect to school record data. However, for teacher-rated externalizing symptomatology and social acceptance, maltreated children with nonoptimal patterns of relatedness to mother were rated as evidencing more positive adaptation than were maltreated children with optimal/adequate patterns of relatedness.

The finding that maltreated children with nonoptimal patterns of relatedness to mother were rated as more adaptive by their teachers than were maltreated children with optimal patterns of relatedness may be accounted for by the "compulsive compliant" attachment organization discussed previously (cf. Crittenden & DiLalla, 1988). The fact that teachers rated the behavior of the maltreated children with nonoptimal patterns of relatedness as being more prosocial, while actual school record data did not verify this positive report, suggests that the compliance observed by teachers does not fully capture the actual functioning of these children. Thus, although unexpected, the relatedness patterns and functioning exhibited by the maltreated children in this investigation are understandable within an attachment theory model and they supplement our knowledge in an important way.

The investigation by Toth and Cicchetti (1996b) is important in elucidating the impact of the home environment on children's adaptation to school. In this study, the security that a child experienced in relation to his or her mother was related to how well the child functioned in the school setting. Because a range of outcomes was measured, including behavior problems, social relations, ego resilience, and a composite of school record data associated with school failure, a comprehensive portrayal of functioning was obtained. For all areas examined, the quality of relatedness to mother in interaction with maltreatment status significantly impacted on adaptation in school. This short-term longitudinal study confirmed that children's representations of their mothers were associated with their performance in school a year later. This suggests that a child's representation of his or her caregiver affected adaptation outside of the child's home.

Relatedness and Memory In a further examination of caregiver influences on individual development, Lynch and Cicchetti (1998b) examined the links among trauma, mental representation, and memory in a sample of 8 to 13-year-old maltreated and nonmaltreated children. These investigators charted the divergent pathways emanating from experiences of trauma (i.e., community violence, an exosystem variable, and child maltreatment, a microsystem variable) and how other domains of functioning may influence the effect of trauma on the memory of children.

Based on children's history of interaction with their primary caregiver, representational models are thought to reflect children's feelings of security with others and their perceptions of the world as a safe place. Representational models also are believed to be involved in selectively guiding the attention of individuals to attachment-relevant information in organizing this information about the world, self, and others in ways that allow the individual to make forecasts about what to expect in the future (Bowlby, 1980; Bretherton, 1990; Main, Kaplan, & Cassidy, 1985). Attachment theory suggests that it is adaptive to have representational models that aid in the processing and interpreting of interpersonal information because they can provide psychological protection for the individual (Bowlby, 1980). For example, children who regularly have their bids for support rejected by their caregivers may develop cognitive strategies that reduce attention to and memory for attachment-related stimuli, thus minimizing these children's likelihood of experiencing subsequent rejection (Main, 1990).

Representational models may influence the processing of social information in a variety of ways. Although the literature occasionally is contradictory, most of the research suggests that individuals attend to and remember information that is consistent with their representational model or "interpersonal schema" (Belsky, Spritz, & Crnic, 1996; Kirsh & Cassidy, 1997). Representational models are believed to guide the processing of new information in ways that allow these interpersonal schemas to be confirmed and maintained (Fiske & Taylor, 1991). For example, in a study of 7 to 12 year olds, Rudolph, Hammen, and Burge (1995) used an incidental recall task in which they presented children with a list of positive and negative attribute words. They found that children's biased memory for positive mother-referent stimulus words was related to their positive representations of their mothers' acceptance and support. In addition to recall, children's deployment of attention (which influences the way in which information is encoded in memory) also may be guided by the nature of mental representations. Rieder and Cicchetti (1989) have found that maltreated children, who generally have insecure attachments, display ready cognitive assimilation of aggressive stimuli. However, as discussed earlier, maltreated children's resulting hypervigilance for aggressive stimuli may have deleterious effects on their information processing in non-threatening conditions. Based on findings such as these, Lynch and Cicchetti (1998b) hypothesized that early attachment experiences and their resulting representational models appear to contribute to biases in attention and memory.

Lynch and Cicchetti (1998b) proposed that the representational models of children who have been traumatized by parental maltreatment and community violence would affect information processing and memory in ways that are consistent with schemas associated with feelings of insecurity. If this is the case, then should one expect to find consistent main effects of trauma on children's memory? Or rather is it more likely that there may be multiple pathways leading from experiences of trauma to different outcomes in memory?

With these questions in mind, Lynch and Cicchetti (1998b) examined the links among trauma, representational models of caregivers using the Relatedness Scales described above, and children's memory for mother-referent attribute words using the incidental recall task of Rudolph et al. (1995). Lynch and Cicchetti (1998b) hypothesized that the security of children's representational models would moderate the effects of trauma on memory for mother-relevant information in the incidental recall task.

Because schema-congruent information is most likely processed (i.e., encoded and retrieved) more efficiently than schema-incongruent information (Rudolph et al., 1995), Lynch and Cicchetti (1998b) anticipated that children with representations of caregivers that reflected feelings of security would demonstrate better recall for positive attributes about their caregivers than children with insecure models. Furthermore, Lynch and Cicchetti (1998b) predicted that traumatized children with insecure models would recall higher proportions of negative attributes about caregivers than other children, and nontraumatized children with secure models would recall higher proportions of positive attributes. The Lynch and Cicchetti (1998b) study represents the first investigation that has examined the joint impact of child maltreatment and victimization by community violence on children's memory performance.

Forty-four adjectives describing positive attributes (e.g., loving, patient, kind) and negative attributes (e.g., strict, mean, bad) were presented verbally one at a time while the child was shown a card on which each individual word was typed. Children were presented each word under one of two different encoding conditions presented in randomized order. After children were presented with each word, they were asked either (a) Does the word describe your mom? (i.e., mother-referent encoding), or (b) Does the word have big letters? (i.e., structural encoding). Each question was asked for half of the adjectives, and two previously developed versions of the task were administered randomly to children in order to counterbalance the encoding question asked about each word. After completing the ratings and without prior warning, children were asked to recall as many words as possible. The adjectives were divided into four groups of 11 words: *positive mother-referent, negative mother-referent, positive structural*, and *negative structural*.

Lynch and Cicchetti (1998b) found that the security of children's patterns of relatedness moderates the effect of maltreatment and victimization by community violence on the recall of mother attribute words, thereby providing evidence that there are individual developmental pathways shaping memory performance in children who have experienced trauma. Not all children who had experienced trauma exhibited the same ability to process and retrieve words that described positive and negative attributes about their mothers. Performance of traumatized versus non-traumatized children on the incidental recall task was moderated by the security of children's mental representations of maternal caregivers. Somewhat paradoxically, among maltreated children, those who reported *optimal* (i.e., secure) patterns of relatedness demonstrated the greatest memory bias for negative mother-referent stimuli (i.e., by recalling a higher proportion of no-rated positive attribute words than did maltreated children with insecure patterns). One might assume that children with secure patterns of relatedness, even if they had been maltreated, would be less biased toward negative references about mothers than insecure children would be. However, this was not the case. With regard to victimization, among children who were victimized by high levels of violence, those who reported *non-optimal* (i.e., insecure) patterns of relatedness demonstrated a larger memory bias for negative mother-referent stimuli than those with secure patterns.

Two different processes appear to be operating in these interactions. In the case of children who were maltreated, those with secure patterns of relatedness may be more receptive than insecure children to acknowledging that their maltreating caregivers do not possess certain positive attributes. Such openness would be consistent with prior research indicating that secure children are more able than insecure children to discuss and recall both positive and negative interpersonal material (Beeghly & Cicchetti, 1994; Farrar, Fasig, & Welch-Ross, 1997; Kirsh & Cassidy, 1997). As a result, even though some maltreated children in this investigation reported feeling secure with their caregivers, they were able to openly acknowledge that their caregivers lacked certain positive attributes. This open admission that their caregivers were imperfect is congruent with their representational models, and therefore their recall of these words was facilitated (Bowlby, 1980; Kirsh & Cassidy, 1997; Rudolph et al., 1995). For children who have been victimized by high levels of community violence, their recall for no-rated positive mother attribute words is increased if they also report an insecure pattern of relatedness with their maternal caregiver. In contrast to the data regarding maltreatment-related trauma, there appears to be an additive effect of victimization by community violence and insecurity of mental representation on the recall of negative mother-referent stimuli. Insecure children who have been victimized by violence in their community appear to have highly negative mental representations of their mothers, as indicated by their high recall rate of no-rated positive attribute words.

Children's memory for mother-referent attribute words also was influenced by an interaction between histories of child maltreatment and victimization by community violence. Nonmaltreated, nonvictimized children recalled a lower proportion of negative stimuli about their mothers (i.e., no-rated positive attribute words) than any other children, indicating that these stimulus words were not congruent with their schemas of maternal caregivers. Conversely, nonmaltreated children who had been victimized by high levels of violence and maltreated children who had been less victimized recalled relatively high proportions of these no-rated positive attribute words. Such a pattern of recall suggests that these children's maternal representations have a negative valence. Surprisingly, children who experienced the greatest amount of trauma, namely maltreated children who also reported being victimized by high levels of community violence, recalled relatively few of these negative mother-referent stimulus words. It is possible that the children who experienced multiple forms of trauma lack organized and coherent schemas of their caregivers. Such disruptions in the formation of maternal schema might be expected as these children come to terms with the reality that the person from whom they are evolutionarily programmed to seek help, namely their primary caregiver (Bowlby, 1969; Cicchetti & Lynch, 1995), cannot keep them safe from traumatic experiences. Disorganized or incoherent representations could result in either impairments or distortions in the recall of mother-referent stimuli because children would lack an organized schema to facilitate the processing, encoding, and retrieval of such information.

Additionally, consistent with the expectation that experiences of trauma would be associated with alterations and biases in attention and memory, Lynch and Cicchetti (1998b) found differences among traumatized and non-traumatized children in how they processed material on the incidental recall tasks. When presented with a mother-referent encoding cue, maltreated children tended to rate a lower number of positive attribute words in the affirmative, indicating that they thought that fewer of these words described their caregivers than did nonmaltreated children. Likewise, children who had been victimized by high levels of community violence indicated that more of the negative attribute words described their mother than children victimized by less violence did. These differences, associated with experiences of trauma, may indicate a selective bias in how children attended to and processed mother attribute words. Such encoding biases may be related to differences in how these children ultimately retrieve and recall mother attribute words.

Not surprisingly, children's feelings and patterns of relatedness predicted their ratings of mother-attribute words as well. Regardless of trauma status, children with optimal patterns of relatedness rated the highest number of positive attribute words as describing their mothers, whereas children with deprived patterns endorsed the greatest number of negative attribute words with respect to their mother. These findings are consistent with claims that representational models selectively guide attention to and processing of social information (in this case, mother attribute words). Interestingly, the main effect of patterns of relatedness disappears when it comes to the *recall* of mother-referent words. Instead, children's memory for mother-referent words indicates that security of mental representation interacts with experiences of trauma in influencing recall.

In summary, research from our laboratory has converged to demonstrate that from toddlerhood through school-age, children who have experienced maltreatment are at considerable risk for insecure attachment relationships with their caregiver. Importantly, however, is the fact that not all maltreated children develop insecure attachment relationships and that a positive attachment with a caregiver can mediate or moderate the adverse sequelae of maltreatment. Additionally, the Lynch and Cicchetti (1998b) and Toth and Cicchetti (1996b) investigations further demonstrate that insecure attachments may not operate as straightforwardly as might be expected and that, depending on the domain of development being investigated, an insecure relationship may, in fact, result in some positive aftermath (e.g., the ability to accurately evaluate the caregiver). Finally, issues related to the broader community in which children reside may exacerbate or moderate the sequelae of maltreatment.

EMOTION PROCESSES AS CONTRIBUTORS TO DEVELOPMENTAL OUTCOME

In addition to children's representations of their caregivers, research in our laboratory has examined emotion regulatory processes as moderators and mediators of developmental outcomes in maltreated children. In a prospective longitudinal study, Rogosch, Cicchetti, and Aber (1995) investigated the linkages among a history of child maltreatment, early deviations in cognitive/affective processes, and difficulties in peer relations in a sample of maltreated and nonmaltreated school-aged children. On average, children were first studied when they were six years of age and then two years later when they were approximately eight years of age. During the laboratory visits at age six, assessments of affect understanding and cognitive control functioning were conducted. During the subsequent two year longitudinal follow-up, peers and teachers provided assessments of peer relations in the school setting.

Consistent with prior investigations (cf. Mueller & Silverman, 1989), maltreated children evidenced problematic peer relations.

From the perspective of both peers and teachers, maltreated children were deficient in terms of the social competence they exhibited in interactions with their agemates. Further, maltreated children were found to be perceived as exhibiting more undercontrolled and aggressive social behavior, a form of social maladaptation that is replete with risk for long-term adaptational failure (Parker & Asher, 1987). Physically abused children also were shown to be more likely to be socially avoided, isolated, or rejected by their peers than were nonmaltreated children. These findings are particularly noteworthy given the high-risk nature of the entire sample. The comparison children in this investigation were drawn from the lowest socioeconomic strata; thus, they, too, were exposed to multiple forms of social adversity that would be posited to pose challenges to the success of their social adaptation. Nevertheless, above and beyond this common social adversity, the maltreated children were more deficient in their ability to engage in successful peer relations.

In addition, the findings expand upon formulations regarding the social cognitive and affective processes involved in successful peer relations. In terms of cognitive control functioning (Santostefano, 1978, 1985), the *leveling/sharpening* cognitive control was shown to relate to higher levels of socially effective, competent peer relations. Leveling/sharpening concerns the manner in which the individual maintains images of past information and compares these images with present perceptions. This cognitive control ranges from constructing global images that are fused with present perceptions so that changes in information are not readily noticed, to constructing articulate images that are distinguished from present perceptions so that similarities and differences between past and present information are noticed. Greater maturity in this cognitive control, as indicated by maintaining more differentiated, articulate perceptions of past and current external stimuli and detecting nuances and differences in perceptual stimuli more accurately and readily, was related to greater social success. Such abilities may be related to greater facility in detecting and interpreting variations in the changing social field and guiding one's social interactions in accord with those differentiated perceptions. It should be noted that these relations were obtained while controlling for intelligence level, indicating that this cognitive control function was related to social competence in a manner not accounted for by mere differences in intellectual abilities. In contrast, greater difficulty in socially effective peer relations was found for lower levels of this cognitive control. Children who were more diffuse in their perceptions (not maintaining distinct and differentiated perceptions of past and current stimuli) and who were more delayed in their abilities to detect subtle differences were found to be more deficient in their social functioning with peers. These findings are similar to those of Dodge et al. (1990) in that aggressive children had more difficulty in attending to and perceiving relevant social cues. Socially ineffective children may, by tending to turn away from the diversity of external stimuli and perhaps being out of sync with current realities of social situations, encounter greater difficulty in engaging and interacting successfully with peers in an ever changing and multifaceted social environment.

In contrast to the work of Dodge et al. (1990), the findings of Rogosch, Cicchetti, and Aber (1995) demonstrated that leveling/sharpening was related to social effectiveness rather than to aggressiveness per se. In fact, the leveling/sharpening cognitive control measure was not found to predict higher levels of undercontrolled, externalizing, and aggressive behavior. Further, these results were obtained with the nonaggressive stimuli. The leveling/sharpening test with the aggressive stimuli was not found to predict either social effectiveness or behavioral dysregulation. These findings suggest that distortions in attributions related to aggressive situations may not tell the complete picture; differences in social cognitive processes in more general, nonaggressive contexts also are important for social success with peers.

Emotion processes also were found to be related to social functioning with peers. In particular, greater understanding of appropriate negative affect in frustrating interpersonal situations predicted lower levels of aggressive and undercontrolled behavior with peers, or conversely, difficulties in accurately understanding expected emotional reactions involving sadness and anger were related to later behavioral dysregulation. Children who are more uncertain about when negative affect is appropriately expressed and who have difficulty inferring how others would be likely to feel in frustrating situations appear to have difficulty controlling their own expression of negative affect, as indicated by higher levels of externalizing behavior.

The longitudinal relations among these cognitive/affective processes and later social functioning also must be considered. Although the study is limited because assessments of concurrent relations of these processes and social adaptation were not obtained, it is noteworthy that earlier deficiencies in these processes assessed in a developmental laboratory presaged later social dysfunction as assessed by peers and teachers in an elementary school context. Whether these social-cognitive and affective divergences continue to operate in current social interactions is uncertain. Nevertheless, their earlier presence suggests that they may have been influential in guiding the course and development of interactions with peers as these children progressed through the early school years. Additionally, another limitation of the study involves only an initial determination of maltreatment history without continued reassessments of possible ongoing maltreatment. If more knowledge of continued and concurrent maltreatment experiences were available, more specificity about the historical and contemporary effects of maltreatment could be delineated.

Nevertheless, the findings of Rogosch, Cicchetti, & Aber (1995) illustrate that these distortions in cognitive/affective processes are more likely to develop in the context of families with a history of maltreatment. The often volatile, confusing, inconsistent, and threatening character of relationships with parents experienced by maltreated children poses serious hazards to these children's abilities to make sense of interpersonal situations and emotional reactions in themselves and others. Findings from the cognitive control assessments indicate that maltreated children maintain more immature, diffuse perceptions of external stimuli. These children may be retreating from active engagement with the world around them in efforts to maintain internal security (Aber & Allen, 1987). Similarly, the difficulty in understanding appropriate negative affect is likely to develop for maltreated children because of the serious distortions in the emotional reactions they experience from their parents (Rogosch, Cicchetti, Shields, & Toth, 1995). Given such distortions, maltreated children are likely not only to have developed aberrations in the regulation of their own emotions but also to have a divergent understanding of the typical emotional reactions of others. Attachment theory posits that representational models of self and other develop in the context of the attachment relationship with the primary caregiver, and that these representational models are used to guide later expectations in other relationships. Given the insecure and disorganized attachment organizations prominent among maltreated infants and children (Carlson et al., 1989), the cognitive control delays and difficulties in understanding appropriate affective reactions among maltreated children may be an outgrowth of their representational models formulated in their attachment relationships with maltreating caregivers (cf. Rieder & Cicchetti, 1989).

Rogosch, Cicchetti, and Aber (1995) conducted tests of a mediational model linking a history of child maltreatment to deficits in cognitive/affective processes, to later difficulties in peer social functioning. These mediational tests received support. Such tests are critical for demonstrating the pathways of how maltreatment leads to later social dysfunction.

In terms of negative affect understanding explaining the relation between maltreatment and social effectiveness, despite all preliminary tests of predictive relations among these three domains being supported, the mediational model was not substantiated. In this case, the apparent association between negative affect understanding and social effectiveness appeared to be accounted for by both of these constructs being predicted by child maltreatment. In contrast, leveling/sharpening did evidence a role in mediating this link, although the effect was only partially mediated as maltreatment continued to exert an independent effect on later social effectiveness. Other processes not measured in this investigation (e.g., attachment, emotion expression and regulation) may further assist in explaining the relationship.

Finally, negative affect understanding was shown to mediate the relationship between child maltreatment and behavioral dysregulation, as well as to mediate the relationship of physical abuse to later peer rejection. Thus, this model supports the view that child maltreatment contributes to difficulty in accurately inferring emotional reactions in others, which in turn results in problematic peer relations. A similar model has been articulated for a nonrisk sample, linking parental emotional expressiveness to children's emotion understanding and social acceptance with peers (Cassidy, Parke, Butkovsky, & Braungart, 1992).

Although not predicted, two different pathways leading from maltreatment to the quality of functioning with peers were evident in the results. Rather than both cognitive/affective measures predicting various peer outcomes, the leveling/sharpening cognitive control was more distinctly involved in contributing to later social effectiveness with peers, whereas negative affect understanding was more strongly related to problems in behavioral control and aggressiveness and to peer rejection among physically abused children. These findings suggest that maltreatment has diverse effects on processes of child adaptation, and that not all maltreated children respond in the same manner. Differences in the quality of how developmental challenges are negotiated among maltreated children may result in different forms of difficulty in later attempts to negotiate relationships with peers.

The longitudinal relations among the constructs in this investigation also are important, as we see troubled parent-child relationships leading to an emerging aberration in the organization of cognitive and affective processes, which later results in social dysfunction. The findings are consistent with the organizational/transactional perspective on development (Cicchetti, 1989; Cicchetti & Rizley, 1981; Sroufe, 1979) and illustrate how difficulties negotiating prior developmental tasks contribute to later difficulties as new developmental challenges are confronted.

More generally, these results also help to place problematic peer relations in the context of earlier developmental deviations arising out of severe relationship dysfunction between parent and child (cf. Cicchetti, Lynch, Shonk, & Manly, 1992). This relationship disturbance is particularly troublesome because we see how relationship problems become extended to new relationships outside of the family. The finding of negative affect understanding mediating the relationship between physical abuse and later avoidance and rejection by peers is particularly striking in this respect. This continuity of relationship pathology across different types of relationships is of major concern. Many maltreating parents, with their own history of being maltreated in childhood, also experience substantial problems in relationships with spouses and other adults (Crittenden et al., 1991; Howes & Cicchetti, 1993). In concert with the findings of Rogosch, Cicchetti, and Aber (1995), maltreated children would appear to be at risk for continued problems in negotiating successful relationships as new interpersonal contexts are encountered.

Shields, Cicchetti, and Ryan (1994) investigated developmental processes that place maltreated children at risk for impaired peer relationships. These investigators assessed the influence of both behavioral and emotional regulation on social competence in 8 to 12 year old maltreated and nonmaltreated children. Observations by counselors and research assistants were conducted during a summer day camp, an ecologically valid context in which to study children's social interactions.

Maltreated school-age children were found to be less socially competent than economically disadvantaged comparison children, according to assessments by both counselors and independent observers. Additionally, in maltreated children this attenuated social competence was co-incident to self-regulatory deficits. Specifically, maltreated children were more likely to evidence behavioral dysregulation, most often in the form of internalizing difficulties, as assessed by both the CBCL-TRF (Achenbach, 1991) and independent observers' ratings of behavior during semistructured free-play sessions.

Impaired self-regulation also was expressed as emotional dysregulation among maltreated children. This investigation was unique in its focus on emotional processes in older at-risk children, which were assessed via observations of spontaneous affective expressions in naturalistic social settings. Maltreated grade-schoolers' interactions during play with peers more often reflected maladaptive patterns of emotion regulation, characterized by inflexible and situationally inappropriate affective displays. Because similar processes have been witnessed among maltreated toddlers and preschoolers, this study suggests that these emotional deficits may be enduring, placing maltreated children at ongoing risk for maladaptation during the grade school years, as well.

Of special import was the finding that self-regulatory deficits mediated the effects of maltreatment on children's social competence. When behavioral dysregulation composite scores, representing internalizing and externalizing difficulties, were entered into a regression equation predicting children's peer competencies, each accounted for a unique amount of the variance in peer competence. Furthermore, these behavioral regulation composite variables rendered maltreatment an insignificant predictor of social competence. In demonstrating that behavioral regulation appears to mediate in part maltreatment's effects on peer competence, this study delineates important developmental processes that place maltreated children at risk for disruptions in interpersonal relationships.

Contrary to alternate models that suggest that emotion influences children's competence primarily via its ability to motivate discrete social behaviors, analyses of children's interactions during semistructured free-play periods demonstrated that emotional processes predicted a unique amount of the variance in peer competence, over and above the effects of behavior. Similarly, social behaviors, in the form of prosocial acts and aggression, remained significant predictors of social competence when controlling for the effects of emotion, with aggression playing an especially important role among maltreated children. As an organizational perspective would suggest, although emotional and behavioral self-regulatory processes are interrelated, each appears to represent a distinct developmental system that differentially and individually affects children's competence.

In a subsequent investigation also conducted in a summer day camp, Shields and Cicchetti (1998) examined the interplay among emotion, attention, and aggression in a sample of 6 to 12-year-old maltreated and nonmaltreated children. A central focus of this study was to explore mechanisms of maltreatment's deleterious effects on behavioral and emotional dysregulation.

In this naturalistic day camp setting, Shields and Cicchetti (1998) found that maltreated children were more verbally and physically assaultive, with physical abuse placing children at special risk for aggression. Maltreated children also were more likely to show the distractibility, overactivity, and poor concentration characteristic of children who experience deficits in attention modulation. Physically and sexually abused children also displayed attention disturbances suggestive of subclinical or nonpathological dissociation, including daydreaming, blank stares, and confusion. Deficits in emotion regulation also were evident, in that maltreated children were less likely to show adaptive regulation and more likely to display emotional lability/negativity and contextually inappropriate emotion expressions. These findings are especially compelling, given the conservative nature of this research design, in that the impoverished nonmaltreated comparison subjects also were at a substantial degree of developmental risk. Such pervasive deficits in maltreated children's regulatory capacities are cause for special concern, as the ability to modulate behavior, attention, and emotion underlie children's adaptive functioning in a number of key domains—including self-development, academic achievement, and interpersonal relationships (Cicchetti, 1989).

This study also expanded upon earlier work by investigating mechanisms of the effects of maltreatment in general, and of physical abuse in particular. Whereas other factors (including social cognition and insecure attachments) only partially mediate maltreatment's effect on aggression (Dodge, Pettit, Bates, & Valente, 1995), emotion dysregulation appears to be a key mediating mechanism whereby abuse subverts children's behavioral regulation. Consistent with the literature on reactive aggression (Coie & Dodge, 1998), maltreatment appears to foster mood lability and anger reactivity, which in turn provokes aggressive responding. It is important to note, however, that angry reactivity was not the only emotional process associated with aggression, as contextually inappropriate displays of both positive and negative affect also mediated maltreatment's effects. Therefore, research on children's emotions should take care to consider a wide array of regulatory processes, rather than focusing exclusively on negative mood, when attempting to understand the role of emotion in behavioral dysregulation and social maladjustment.

Shields and Cicchetti (1998) also demonstrated that impaired capacities for attention modulation contribute to emotion dysregulation in at-risk children. These findings were consistent with research among normative populations, which has highlighted attention modulation as a primary regulatory process. Specifically, attention deficits mediated maltreatment's effects on emotional lability/negativity, inappropriate affect, and attenuated emotion regulation. Attention processes that suggest subclinical or nonpathological dissociation (e.g., daydreams, confusion, and blank stares) also contributed to maltreated children's deficits in emotion regulation. Thus, maltreatment's effects on attention appear to be complex, in that abuse seems to potentiate disruptions in attention that result in both a relative detachment from and unawareness of one's surroundings, as well as in a hyper-attunement and reactivity to the social surround. Together, these deficits appear to compromise maltreated children's ability to regulate behavior and affect in social settings.

Given attention's critical role in emotional and behavioral dysregulation, future research would do well to more fully examine how maltreatment exerts a negative effect on children's attention modulation. Research has suggested that maltreated children develop highly attuned vigilance systems (Posner & Raichle, 1994) in response to their continual exposure to extreme environmental stress (Rieder &

Cicchetti, 1989). With this hypervigilance, maltreated children show distractibility, heightened arousal, and attention and information-processing biases towards cues that may signal danger or threat. Although this vigilance may help children maintain their safety in un-predictable and dangerous environments (Cicchetti, Toth, & Lynch, 1995; Crittenden & Ainsworth, 1989), it also may interfere with the strategic shifting and focusing of attention away from distressing cues and thoughts in the service of affect regulation (Rieder & Cicchetti, 1989; Rogosch, Cicchetti, & Aber, 1995).

Such highly attuned vigilance systems could fuel emotional arousal, especially when representations of others as threatening and of the world as unsafe color maltreated children's understanding of their experiences (Derryberry & Reed, 1994, 1996). Angry reactivity would be a likely response among individuals who fear victimization and exploitation, as functionalist perspectives on emotion highlight the important self-protective function of anger (Campos, Mumme, Kermoian, & Campos, 1994). Because maltreated children tend to per-ceive threat in even neutral or friendly situations, they may evidence a self-defensive reactivity that is consistent with their experiences and expectations but inappropriate to the context at hand (Dodge et al., 1995; Rogosch, Cicchetti, & Aber, 1995). In this way, attention processes may interact with negative representations and maladap-tive social information processing to foster emotional negativity and reactivity among maltreated children; this emotion dysregulation, in turn, seems to provoke reactive aggression by children with histories of physical abuse.

In summary, investigations of school-age children conducted in our laboratory reveal that emotion regulatory abilities may medi-ate the link between maltreatment experiences and developmental outcomes. Difficulties with emotion regulation have been shown to adversely affect children's peer relations and to contribute to the emergence of behavior problems and psychopathology. Moreover, an organizational perspective on development suggests that, in the absence of adaptive self-organization, positive experiences, and/or intervention, these difficulties are likely to continue across the life-course, resulting in future difficulties in the relationship arena and in overall functioning.

Resilience

In accord with our interest in the processes and pathways that contribute to developmental outcome, we next direct our attention toward investigations of resilience. The fact that some children manifest adaptive functioning despite experiences of extreme adversity helps to elucidate the contributors to varied outcome in maltreated children. Moreover, identification of those factors that are related to resilience possess important implications for informing prevention and intervention efforts for maltreated children.

As Masten and Coatsworth (1998) have articulated, the identification of resilience implies the presence of two requirements: a) exposure to significant threat or severe adversity; and b) the achievement of positive adaptation despite the experience of these major assaults on the developmental process. Thus, resilience is conceptualized as a phenomenon reflecting both competence and adversity, and not as a static personality trait or personal attribute of the individual. Resilience is a dynamic process and occurs in transaction with intra- and extra-organismic forces (Egeland, Carlson, & Sroufe, 1993; Cicchetti et al., 1993). Thus, discovering the processes whereby individuals initiate their self-striving tendencies (cf. Waddington, 1957) when confronted with acute and chronic adverse experiences will shed important light on how dynamic and active self-organizing strivings exert a critical role in determining whether an individual will traverse on an adaptive or a maladaptive developmental pathway (Cicchetti & Rogosch, 1996; Cicchetti & Tucker, 1994; Egeland et al.).

The roots of empirical work on resilience can be traced back to prior research in diverse areas, including investigations of individuals with schizophrenia and their offspring, studies of the effects of persistent poverty, and work on coping with acute and chronic stressors (Cicchetti & Garmezy, 1993). Through elucidating the processes that contribute to competent adaptation despite the presence of adversity, research on resilience can enhance the understanding of pathways to both normal development and psychopathology. Furthermore, research on the processes leading to resilient outcomes offers great promise as an avenue for facilitating the development of prevention and intervention studies (Cicchetti & Toth, 1992; Toth & Cicchetti, 1999). Through the examination of the proximal and distal processes and mechanisms that contribute to positive adaptation in situations that more typically eventuate in maladaptation, researchers and clinicians will be better prepared to devise ways of promoting competent outcomes in high-risk populations.

To date there have been few studies that have focused on illuminating the processes that bring about competent functioning in maltreated children (see, e.g., Egeland & Farber, 1987; Herrenkohl, Herrenkohl, & Egolf, 1994; Moran & Eckenrode, 1992). In our laboratory, we have conducted two studies on the pathways to resilient functioning in maltreated 8 to 13 year old school-age children. The first investigation was cross-sectional (Cicchetti et al., 1993), whereas the second was longitudinal in nature (Cicchetti & Rogosch, 1997). In both samples, maltreated and nonmaltreated children were at jeopardy for maladaptation because of a variety of risk factors, including (a) limited maternal education, (b) single parenting, (c) relationship instability, (d) unskilled occupational status of the head of the household, (e) family unemployment, (f) dependency on the state for subsistence as reflected in the receipt of financial aid, and (g) disadvantaged minority status. The presence of these cumulative risk factors has been shown to be related to a variety of difficulties in childhood, ranging from psychiatric disorders (Rutter, 1979), to the development of subsequent criminality (Kolvin, Miller, Fleeting, & Kolvin, 1988), to compromised socioemotional and cognitive development (Sameroff, Seifer, Barocas, Zax, & Greenspan, 1987; Seifer, Sameroff, Baldwin, & Baldwin, 1992).

In addition to the aforementioned chronic familial adversities and extreme psychosocial risks, approximately 62% of the children in each sample had experienced severe enough parent-child relationship disturbances to warrant the determination of child maltreatment by government officials. As such, these children were confronted with the presence of a major stressor that has been consistently linked with maladaptive developmental outcomes (Cicchetti & Toth, 1995).

Thus, both of the investigations in our laboratory differ from many published studies in the area of resilience. For example, in general population studies, some individuals have undergone more stressful experiences than others. As a result, high levels of risk constructs, such as severe stress, are characteristic of only a small subgroup of the sample, with most subjects experiencing minimal risk. Furthermore, in studies of the adaptation of the offspring of parents with psychiatric disorders, there is considerable variability in the forms of intrafamilial adversity to which these children are exposed, including the degree to which there are actual disturbances in parent-child relations (Downey & Coyne, 1990; Richters & Weintraub, 1990). Moreover, these offspring actually vary to an unknown degree on whether or not they have a genetic vulnerability to the disorder being investigated (see Cicchetti & Aber, 1986; Garmezy & Streitman, 1974). In contrast, all of the children in our studies experienced substantial and chronic psychosocial adversity, and the definition of the special risk group of interest, the maltreated children, necessitated that severe dysfunction in the parent-child relationship was additionally present.

In these investigations, both conducted in a summer day camp setting, we built upon the tradition of studies on resilience by examining functioning in a number of areas that are important for the adaptation of school-age children. Because children identified as resilient do not necessarily function equally well in all contexts and in all developmental domains (Kaufman, Cook, Arny, Jones, & Pittinsky, 1994; Luthar, 1991, 1993), we assessed areas of strength and vulnerability, included multiple measures of the constructs that were investigated, employed explicit operational definitions of competence, examined separate areas of functioning, and utilized multiple raters and informants. Moreover, school records served as a face valid index of the children's functioning in a setting outside of the summer camp.

Because we were especially interested in discovering the processes by which competent adaptation could occur in the face of multiple stressors, we examined a number of personal child resources that have been found to be compensators or moderators of adaptation in prior high-risk studies: (a) intelligence, (b) self-esteem, and, (c) ego-control and ego-resiliency. Maltreated children as a group were shown to evidence lower overall competence when compared to their nonmaltreated counterparts. In particular, over 43% of the maltreated children, compared to approximately 26% of the nonmaltreated comparisons, displayed either zero or one resilient self-striving. However, there was an equal proportion of maltreated and nonmaltreated children who demonstrated high levels of competence as determined by their performance on the composite index of adaptive functioning developed by the investigators. Interestingly, the pathways to resilient adaptation were different for the maltreated and nonmaltreated high functioning children with respect to self-esteem, ego-control, and ego-resiliency.

Block and Block (1980) argued that if individuals are to be adaptively attuned to their environments, then they must be able to monitor and modulate their impulses, feelings, and desires. In their words, ego-control is the "threshold or operating characteristics of an individual with regard to the expression or containment" (p. 43) of these impulses. Accordingly, ego-overcontrol is denoted by an excessive boundary impermeability whereby such individuals are made uneasy by ambiguity and inconsistency. Ego-undercontrol, in contrast, is characterized by excessive boundary permeability, resulting in inadequate modulation of feelings and impulses. An individual's ability to alter characteristic levels of boundary permeability-impermeability is central to the construct of ego-resiliency, which refers to the ability to modify ego-control, in either direction, as a function of the demand characteristics of the environment. In the investigation of Cicchetti et al. (1993), ego-resiliency, ego overcontrol, and positive self-esteem were found to predict competence in maltreated children, whereas ego-resiliency and positive self-esteem predicted adaptive functioning in the high-risk comparison children.

In a subsequent investigation, Cicchetti and Rogosch (1997) conducted a short-term longitudinal study of a new sample of maltreated and nonmaltreated school-age children. The dynamic nature of resilience necessitates that children from high-risk backgrounds who are functioning at high levels of adaptation despite their experiences with adversity must be examined over time in order to ascertain whether they remain resilient, drop off yet recover their adaptive functioning, decline, or manifest an unstable functioning profile. If resilience is a possible outcome of experiencing chronic familial adversities, such as is the case for maltreated children, then this must be shown in the context of longitudinal research.

Cicchetti and Rogosch (1997) employed a very similar measurement strategy as had been utilized in the study by Cicchetti and colleagues (1993). The only measures and constructs added to the longitudinal study were assessments of the nature of children's self-reported relatedness with their primary caregiver and counselors' ratings of the quality of their relationships with children in their group at camp. Cicchetti and Rogosch chose to augment their battery with relationship measures because numerous empirical investigations and anecdotal clinical reports attest to the protective function that a secure or emotionally sensitive relationship can confer on children experiencing adversity (Masten & Coatsworth, 1995, 1998; Werner, 1995).

Children were assessed annually for three consecutive years in the camp setting. Importantly, the decision to employ a similar measurement strategy across the two studies allowed for a built-in potential replication of the findings obtained in the initial study by Cicchetti and colleagues (1993). We know of no other empirical investigations in the area of resilience that have assessed whether or not the findings noted in one study continued to be upheld in another comparable sample. If preventive interventions are to be developed based on the results from studies of resilient maltreated children, then it is essential that investigators be certain that the purported predictors of resilience are generalizable and durable.

Consistent with the extant literature on the correlates and consequences of child maltreatment (Cicchetti & Lynch, 1995; Cicchetti & Toth, 1995; Malinosky-Rummell & Hansen, 1993), maltreated children exhibited greater deficits than nonmaltreated children on six of the seven indicators of adaptive functioning. Moreover, many of these deficits were found to persist across two or three consecutive years of assessment. Further, across each of the three years, maltreated children manifested a lower level of competent functioning than did the nonmaltreated comparisons. Additionally, the continuity of maladaptive functioning exhibited by maltreated children across the three years of this investigation was substantial. Taken together, these results underscore the deleterious impact that maltreatment experiences have on competent functioning and attest to the nontransient nature of their influence.

With respect to the differential impact that maltreatment subtypes exert on adaptation, sexually abused, physically abused, and emotionally maltreated children exhibited lower competence on the adaptive functioning composite than did either the neglected or the nonmaltreated children, neither of whom differed from one another. However, there was no relation found between number of maltreatment subtypes experienced and the adaptive functioning composite.

Cicchetti and Rogosch (1997) identified six pattern groups based on an analysis of their three-year adaptive functioning composite for the maltreated and nonmaltreated children. These groups were operationalized as *low, medium, high, improve, decline,* and *unstable* with respect to the number of resilient self-indicators exhibited in each of the three consecutive years of assessment. For each of the three years of assessment the following criteria were used: 1) children in the *low* group had zero or one (out of seven possible) resilient self-strivings on the adaptive functioning composite; children in the *medium* group had scores of two to four; and children in the *high* group had scores of five or higher. Moreover, children in the *improve* group displayed an increased level of adaptive functioning over time; in contrast, children in the *decline* group were those whose level of functioning decreased over time, and children in the *unstable* group were those whose level of functioning fluctuated over time.

In terms of placement in the three-year pattern groups, a greater percentage of maltreated children (40.6%) than nonmaltreated (20%) children were found in the low group. Strikingly, 9.8% of the maltreated children compared to only 1.3% of the nonmaltreated children displayed zero competence indicators—that is, an absence of resilient strivings across the three-year assessment period. Moreover, there was a higher percentage of nonmaltreated (10.0%) than maltreated (1.5%) children in the *high* group. Furthermore, 35% of the nonmaltreated children had ever achieved membership in the *high* group, whereas only 9.8% of maltreated children had done so.

In accord with findings in the resilience literature, depending on how resilience is conceptualized, the number of children so designated varies (Luthar, 1991; Luthar, Cicchetti, & Becker, in press). Nonetheless, fewer maltreated than nonmaltreated children can be considered resilient, regardless of the definition employed. For example, if membership in the high functioning three-year adaptive pattern group is operationalized as resilience, then 10.0% ($n = 8$) of the nonmaltreated children, compared to 1.5% ($n = 2$) of the maltreated children are resilient. Further, if the high and improve pattern groups are defined as resilient, then 26.3% ($n = 21$) of the nonmaltreated and 12.0% ($n = 16$) of the maltreated children meet this criterion. Finally, if a more broad definition of resilience is employed in which membership in the high, improve, or medium group constitutes competent functioning in the face of adversity, then 61.3% ($n = 49$) of the nonmaltreated and 37.6% ($n = 50$) of the maltreated children qualify as resilient. Thus, although each operational definition yields some number of resilient maltreated children, far fewer are found in the more stringent (i.e., high; high plus improve) definitions.

A great deal of stability in resilient and nonresilient functioning of children was demonstrated across the three years of assessment. Of special concern is the consistently poor functioning of the "low competent" group, comprised predominantly of maltreated children. Along these same lines, the not insignificant percentage of maltreated children who exhibited no resilient strivings across the longitudinal assessments is cause for great concern. Because self-righting tendencies are characteristics inherent to all living organisms, the consistent absence of such strivings over time in 10% of the maltreated children examined is extremely aberrant and alarming.

An inspection of the factors that contributed to membership in the low functioning group reveals a number of characteristics that conspire against the development of these normal resilient self-strivings in some of the nonmaltreated children. Specifically, lower ego resilience and a greater difficulty in forming positive relationships with nonparental adults (i.e., camp counselors) both differentiated children in the low group from those in all other groups. Moreover, increased ego undercontrol discriminated children in the low group from all groups except the decline and unstable groups.

As in the initial study conducted by Cicchetti and colleagues (1993), Cicchetti and Rogosch (1997) compared the predictors of resilient functioning in maltreated and nonmaltreated children. For the maltreated group, three factors accounted for 69% of the variance in the three-year period of adaptive functioning: ego-resiliency, ego-overcontrol, and positive self-esteem. In contrast, for the nonmaltreated children, relationship factors (i.e., perceived emotional availability of the mother and positive relationships with camp counselors) played a prominent role in the prediction of adaptive functioning, in addition to ego resiliency. Thus, although virtually identical amounts of the variance were accounted for in predicting competent functioning, different characteristics distinguished resilient maltreated and nonmaltreated children. Stated differently, it appears that relationship factors may be more critical to resilient outcomes in nonmaltreated disadvantaged children, whereas personality characteristics and self-system processes may be more important for resilient maltreated children.

Given the poor quality of attachment relationships that are characteristic of maltreated children and their caregivers (Cicchetti et al., 1995), it makes sense that maltreated children might not emphasize relationships as they embark upon pathways to resilient functioning. Earlier we noted that Toth and Cicchetti (1996b) found that maltreated children who reported optimal/adequate (i.e., secure) relationships with their mothers did not attain competence in their overall school functioning. The results of Cicchetti and Rogosch's (1997) longitudinal investigation suggest that self-reliance and self-confidence, in concert with interpersonal reserve, may bode well for the development of resilient adaptation in maltreated children. Clearly, pulling back from conflict in the family and detaching from high-intensity affect in the family can help one escape abuse or achieve competent adaptation. Moreover, the findings attesting to the importance of reliance upon the self highlight the role that children play in actively constructing their outcomes and in influencing their ultimate adaptation.

Given our current focus on pathways to competent outcomes, it is instructive to inquire how maltreated children were able to develop ego-control, ego-resiliency, and positive self-esteem while experiencing such adverse circumstances. Stated differently, is there evidence that maltreated children traverse different pathways in their strivings for competent adaptation? Clearly, maltreated children have not experienced the good-quality caregiving and secure attachment relationships with their caregivers that Block and Block (1980) identified as antecedent conditions of ego-resiliency in an economically advantaged sample of children. Maltreated children, though capable of developing good-quality relationships with nonparental adults such as their teachers, have more difficulty connecting positively with alternate caregivers than do nonmaltreated children (Lynch & Cicchetti, 1992). Moreover, maltreated children lack the maternal support and additional family characteristics found to antedate the development of ego-control. Similarly, maltreated children also are unlikely to experience warm, nurturant, and mirroring aspects in parent-child relationships, features that are central to positive self-regard (Harter, 1983). Discovering the processes by which maltreated children develop adaptive personality organizations and self-esteem despite their aversive family experiences is a central challenge for understanding resilience in development.

In future research, it also will be critical to examine the question of whether employing alternative or less commonly utilized pathways to achieving competent adaptation is successful in contributing to children remaining resilient over time or whether the utilization of

such alternate pathways renders children more vulnerable to mani-
festing later maladaptation. Likewise, because resilience is an ongoing and dynamic developmental construct, it should not be expected
that maltreated children who are functioning adaptively will do so
at all future assessment periods. In addition to attaining competence
in the face of adversity, recovery of function also can shed light on
developmental organization in maltreated children (cf. Masten et
al., 1990; Skuse, 1984). Thus, it will be as important to discern the
processes underlying recovery of function as it is to discover the
mechanisms that contribute either to ongoing resilient adaptation
or to a decline from such functioning. Elucidating issues such as
these will have important implications for service development and
provision to this vulnerable population.

Implications for Prevention and Intervention

The research reviewed in this chapter is useful in elucidating the
varied processes to adaptive and maladaptive developmental outcomes in children who have been maltreated. Moreover, the fact that
maltreatment exerts its influence at various levels of the ecology
highlights the importance of intervening at all components of the
ecologies of children who have been maltreated. Therefore, in our
discussion of the implications of research conducted in our laboratory
for prevention and intervention efforts, we organize our presentation
in accord with the distal and proximal ecologies addressed by the Cicchetti and Lynch (1993) model. We then conclude by addressing the
implications of resilience research for prevention and intervention.

INTERVENTIONS AT THE EXOSYSTEM LEVEL

An important implication of the Lynch and Cicchetti (1998a) investigation of community violence and child maltreatment is the
criticality of intervening in the lives of children growing up in the
context of "socially toxic environments" (cf. Garbarino, 1995). Not
only did Lynch and Cicchetti find that rates of maltreatment are
higher among children who reported high levels of community violence but also that maltreatment and community violence may exert
an additive negative effect on children's functioning. The gravity of
these findings are underscored by recent government statistics that
reveal increasing numbers of children being victimized by violent

crime (Federal Interagency Forum on Child and Family Statistics, 1997) and rising rates of child maltreatment (USDHHS, 1996). Because child maltreatment and community violence influence and transact with individual functioning to result in sustained adversity and disturbances in development, interventions must be targeted at these areas. Community based interventions must be directed at the contextual adversity that children from impoverished neighborhoods are likely to encounter. The schools offer a valuable resource that can be brought to bear in the amelioration of the sequelae associated with exposure to violence. Perhaps more importantly, the schools can help to promote psychological wellness and competence in children before maladaptive processes associated with residing in a pernicious community have emerged (Cowen et al., 1996).

Findings such as those of Lynch and Cicchetti (1998a) emphasize the need to move beyond mental disorder-focused modes of intervention to broad scale prevention efforts. As a society, we must grapple with the fact that increasing numbers of our nation's children are residing in poverty. Exposure to violence, either as a witness or as a victim, affects even our youngest children. Therefore, rather than trying to combat the effects of such exposure, we also must find ways of minimizing these influences in society. Although research may be helpful in informing us about the consequences of exposure to violence, the entire exosystem (e.g., churches, schools, neighborhood centers, etc.) must be marshalled to adequately deal with the pervasive influences that may compromise the development of children.

INTERVENTIONS AT THE MICROSYSTEM LEVEL

Research conducted at the level of the microsystem, as illustrated by Rogosch and Cicchetti's (1994) examination of the mediational role of parenting on peer relations, highlights the importance of fostering positive parenting in order to facilitate healthy child development. Preventive programs in the community that can be directed at improving parenting emerge as one possible avenue for intervention. Typically, such programs are geared toward promoting competence and sensitivity in parents and improving coping with stressful living conditions (Wolfe, 1993). The earlier that such programs are initiated, the better. In fact, Daro (1993) discusses the utility gained when hospitals provide parenting education programs for expectant parents. The community-based provision of preventive services, including self-help groups, crisis intervention, and in-home parent aid services also may be useful in reducing the incidence of problematic parenting and maltreatment, resulting in a decreased need for more intensive intervention services after maltreatment has emerged (Wekerle & Wolfe, 1993).

Overall, interventions with families must be sensitive to variations in family organization, structure, roles, and patterns of relating that are influenced by cultural, racial, and ethnic diversity (Sternberg, 1993; Wilson & Saft, 1993). Differences in parenting may be better adapted to the needs and realities of certain cultural nuances. Consequently, effective interventions must consider cultural perspectives and incorporate knowledge of this diversity into intervention approaches in order to ensure that a given intervention is acceptable to and consistent with relevant cultural orientations and preferences of the families being served (Slaughter, 1988).

In addition to interventions that are directed at improving parenting, the findings of Rogosch and Cicchetti (1994) highlight the importance of fostering positive peer relations in children who are at risk as a function of malignant microsystemic influences. The use of peers in promoting positive social interactions emerges as a potentially useful intervention strategy. Evaluation studies have converged to support the efficacy of employing more well-functioning agemates to improve the peer interactions of less competent children (Fantuzzo, Coolahan, & Weiss, 1997; Selman, Schultz, & Yeates, 1991). The utilization of interventions designed to help maltreated children more accurately read the cues and intents of peers also is likely to be helpful in fostering positive relationships.

INTERVENTIONS AT THE ONTOGENIC LEVEL

Research on the sequelae of maltreatment conveys the negative and often lifelong effects of child abuse and neglect on individual development. In the absence of intervention, victims of maltreatment typically evidence difficulties in multiple domains of development. Additionally, the negative caregiving histories of maltreated children increase the probability of maltreatment continuing to contribute to maladaptive relationships, often resulting in the cross-generational perpetuation of maltreatment.

Increasingly, interventions for maltreated children that are informed by developmental theory are being advocated (Cicchetti & Toth, 1992; Erickson, Korfmacher & Egeland, 1992; Finkelhor & Kendall-Tackett, 1997; Toth & Cicchetti, 1993; Toth & Cicchetti, 1999). By attending to the manner in which children negotiate critical issues of development, clinicians may assist parents in understanding their children's behavior and in promoting parenting approaches that are consistent with attaining an optimal resolution of the developmental challenges of a given period (Cicchetti, Toth, & Bush, 1988).

Although interventions for maltreated children that target the biological consequences of abuse and neglect are necessarily in their infancy due to the paucity of studies elucidating the impact of abuse and neglect on neurobiological growth and functioning, nonetheless efforts need to be directed toward understanding the possible effects of intervention on biological processes. In fact, although speculative, it may be that interventions can actually improve maltreated children's processing of information through the re-organization of brain structure and function. It will be important that future evaluations of interventions for maltreated children incorporate assessments of biological as well as psychological functioning in order to ascertain whether intervention can result in positive modifications of brain processing.

In moving into the arena of interventions that can address the psychological sequelae of child maltreatment, the arena of attachment relationships assumes importance. The results of the Lynch and Cicchetti (1998b) investigation of trauma and memory highlight the need for interventions that address attachment relationships. Lynch and Cicchetti provide evidence for divergent pathways to outcome from experiences of trauma. These points of divergence appear to be associated with differences in the security of children's mental representations. Based on their pattern of responding to and recalling mother attribute words, maltreated children with secure patterns of relatedness may be more open to acknowledging the absence of certain positive attributes in their caregivers. Conversely, children who have been victimized by community violence but who report a secure pattern of relatedness appear to retain more positive schemas of their caregivers. In either case, the openness or positivity of these particular traumatized children's schemas of maternal caregivers may act as a protective mechanism that facilitates more adaptive developmental outcomes. Representational models influence social information processing by guiding attentional processes (Kirsh & Cassidy, 1997; Rudolph et al., 1995). For secure children, this may allow them to attend to interpersonal information more flexibly, resulting in increased relationship success. If children who have been traumatized can develop and maintain representational models that are open to new experience and to re-working prior relationship histories, then the likelihood that they will experience successful interpersonal relationships and more positive overall adaptation is increased. Traumatized children with insecure representational models may be more likely to experience traumatic stress reactions, in part because they may be less able to engage in successful and supportive interpersonal relationships. Thus, this study, as well as others reported in this chapter that reveal interpersonal difficulties in family and peer relations, call attention to the need for intervention services directed toward the representational models of maltreated children in order to prevent the development of a course of failure in relationships and maladjustment.

In addition to the importance of facilitating the development of accurate representational models that can be applied to specific relationship figures, work reported in this chapter underscores the role that emotion regulation exerts on functioning (Rogosch, Cicchetti, & Aber, 1995; Shields & Cicchetti, 1998; Shields et al., 1994). Parents can again be effective in helping to prevent the emergence of behavior problems and deficits in emotional regulation. For example, Greenberg, Kusche, and Speltz (1991) propose that parents provide a warm, supportive presence, facilitate child recognition and mediation of affective states, and involve children in interactions that support planning and anticipation of future events. Because such parenting characteristics are unlikely to be present in maltreating families, the implementation of preventive interventions in families at risk for maltreatment are recommended. Moreover, child-focused interventions that utilize cognitive behavioral techniques to foster increased regulatory abilities are suggested for children who have been maltreated. It is urged that strategies such as these be employed even prior to the emergence of clinically-significant symptomatology in order to prevent more severe dysfunction.

RESILIENCE AND INTERVENTION

Empirical research on the processes contributing to resilient outcomes enables practitioners to view knowledge of developmental change, both within the child, as well as in distal (e.g., culture or community) and proximal ecologies (e.g., family), as unique opportunities for promoting positive adaptation in adverse situations (Cicchetti, 1993; Toth & Cicchetti, 1999). For example, Cicchetti and Rogosch's (1997) finding that personality resources and self-confidence were major predictors of resilient adaptation in maltreated children suggests that preventive interventions should focus on enhancing self-system processes such as autonomy, mastery, and self-determination in these youngsters (cf. Ryan, Deci, & Grolnick, 1995).

Furthermore, an understanding that resilience is a dynamic developmental process can be brought to bear in helping those who achieve resilient outcomes to retain their competent functioning. As Luthar (1991) and Werner (1995) have discussed, individuals who appear to be "stress-resistant" may experience inner distress. Because such covert reactions to stress are often difficult to detect, it is essential that practitioners pay attention to the dynamic nature of resilient status and to the ongoing stress that may be engendered by the coexistence of emotional pain with manifest competence. Consequently, resilient children may glean substantial long-term benefits through periodic "booster" sessions in which the extent of underlying distress is explored, and further interventions offered if needed. Moreover, even in the absence of inner distress, children may move in and out of competent functioning at varied periods of development. Thus, we strongly advocate a preventive approach whereby psychological wellness is fostered rather than intervening only after psychopathology has emerged (cf. Cowen, 1994).

Conclusion

In this chapter, we utilized an ecological-transactional model to conceptualize research on the effects of child maltreatment on child development. There is no doubt that child maltreatment is an enormous problem that exerts a toll not only on its victims, but also on society more broadly. In a recent National Institute of Justice report (Miller, Cohen, & Wiersema, 1996), the costs and consequences of child abuse were estimated at $56 billion dollars annually. The cost estimate included direct costs (e.g., medical, lost earnings, public programs for victims, etc.), as well as indirect costs (e.g., pain, diminished quality of life). In the last 20 years, significant progress has occurred with respect to understanding the deleterious effects of maltreatment. Unfortunately, fewer advances have been made with respect to preventing the occurrence of maltreatment or developing effective treatments that have been empirically evaluated and that are widely available.

The research presented in this chapter elucidates some of the malignant effects of child physical and sexual abuse, as well as child neglect. Child maltreatment affects children's successful resolution of stage-salient issues, not just at a single period of development, but across the life span. Importantly, the research reported in this chapter also highlights some of the diversity in process and outcome associated with child maltreatment and conveys the complexity encountered when conducting research on this critical societal problem. A number of avenues for further research emerge from the work reported herein. It is no longer advisable to conduct investigations that focus solely on uncovering main effects associated with child maltreatment because such simplistic approaches are likely to garner results that do not convey accurately the realities of child maltreatment. The development and implementation of comprehensive, longitudinal investigations of child maltreatment and its co-occurring risk factors are critical if these scientific findings are to be appropriately applied to the formulation and evaluation of prevention and intervention strategies for vulnerable children and families.

If additional resources are to be made available to combat child maltreatment, then professionals must become advocates for these children and families. As mental health services become increasingly regulated by monetary considerations, information must be made available that elucidates the costs of failing to provide treatment and the value associated with intervening preventively before significant mental disorders emerge. Toward this goal, treatments developed specifically for maltreated children must be evaluated empirically and the effectiveness of interventions must be assessed over time. Additionally, when an intervention is shown to be effective, this knowledge must be transported into community arenas where the majority of children are seen and not restricted to federally-funded, university-based clinics (cf. Weisz, Weiss, & Donenberg, 1992). Despite the availability of increased knowledge regarding the importance of intervening with maltreated children, far too few professionals receive adequate training in this area and far too many vulnerable youngsters are failing to receive needed services.

References

Aber, J. L., & Allen, J. P. (1987). The effects of maltreatment on young children's socioemotional development: An attachment theory perspective. *Developmental Psychology, 23,* 406–414.

Aber, J. L., & Cicchetti, D. (1984). Socioemotional development in maltreated children: An empirical and theoretical analysis. In H. Fitzgerald, B. Lester, & M. Yogman (Eds.), *Theory and research in behavioral pediatrics, Vol. II* (pp. 147–205). New York: Plenum Press.

Aber, J. L., & Zigler, E. (1981). Developmental considerations in the definition of child maltreatment. *New Directions for Child Development, 11,* 1–29.

Achenbach, T. M. (1991). *Manual for the Child Behavior Checklist and 1991 Profile.* Burlington VT: University of Vermont, Department of Psychiatry.

Alessandri, S. M. (1991). Play and social behavior in maltreated preschoolers. *Development and Psychopathology, 3,* 191–205.

Alessandri, S. M. (1992). Mother-child interactional correlates of maltreated and nonmaltreated children's play behavior. *Development and Psychopathology, 4,* 257–270.

Barnett, D., Manly, J. T., & Cicchetti, D. (1993). Defining child maltreatment: The interface between policy and research. In D. Cicchetti & S. L. Toth (Eds.), *Child abuse, child development, and social policy* (pp. 7–73). Norwood NJ: Ablex.

Beeghly, M., & Cicchetti, D. (1994). Child maltreatment, attachment and the self system: Emergence of an internal state lexicon in toddlers at high social risk. *Development and Psychopathology, 6,* 5–30.

Belsky, J. (1980). Child maltreatment: An ecological integration. *American Psychologist, 35,* 320–335.

Belsky, J., Spritz, B., & Crnic, K. (1996). Infant attachment security and affective-cognitive information processing at age three. *Psychological Science, 7,* 111–114.

Block, J. H., & Block, J. (1980). The role of ego-control and ego-resilience in the organization of behavior. In W. A. Collins (Ed.), *Minnesota Symposia on Child Psychology: Vol. 13. Development of cognition, affect, and social relations* (pp. 39–101). Hillsdale NJ: Erlbaum.

Bolger, K., Patterson, C., & Kupersmidt, J. (1998). Peer relationships and self-esteem among children who have been maltreated. *Child Development, 69,* 1171–1197.

Bowlby, J. (1969). *Attachment and loss. Vol. I: Attachment.* New York: Basic Books.

148

MOTIVATION AND CHILD MALTREATMENT

Bowlby, J. (1980). *Attachment and loss: Loss, sadness, and depression*. New York: Basic Books.

Bremner, J. D., & Narayan, M. (1998). The effects of stress on memory and the hippocampus throughout the life cycle: Implications for childhood development and aging. *Development and Psychopathology, 10*, 871–885.

Bretherton, I. (1990). Open communication and internal working models: Their role in the development of attachment relationships. In R. Thompson (Ed.), *Nebraska Symposium on Motivation: Vol. 36. Socioemotional development* (pp. 57–113). Lincoln: University of Nebraska Press.

Bretherton, I. (1991). Pouring new wine into old bottles: The social self as internal working model. In M. Gunnar & L. A. Sroufe (Eds.), *Minnesota Symposia on Child Psychology: Vol. 23. Self processes and development.* (pp. 1–41). Hillsdale NJ: Erlbaum.

Bretherton, I., & Beeghly, M. (1982). Talking about internal states: The acquisition of an explicit theory of mind. *Developmental Psychology, 18*, 906–921.

Bronfenbrenner, U. (1979). *The ecology of human development: Experiments by nature and design*. Cambridge MA: Harvard University Press.

Campos, J. J., Mumme, D., Kermoian, R., & Campos, R. G. (1994). A functionalist perspective on the nature of emotion. In N. A. Fox (Ed.), The development of emotion regulation: Biological and behavioral considerations. *Monographs of the Society for Research in Child Development, 59*(2–3), (Serial No. 240, pp. 284–300).

Carlson, V., Cicchetti, D., Barnett, D., & Braunwald, K. (1989). Finding order in disorganization: Lessons from research on maltreated infants' attachments to their caregivers. In D. Cicchetti & V. Carlson (Eds.), *Child maltreatment: Theory and research on the causes and consequences of child abuse and neglect* (pp. 494–528). New York: Cambridge University Press.

Cassidy, J. (1988). Child-mother attachment and the self in six-year-olds. *Child Development, 59*, 121–134.

Cassidy, J., Parke, R. D., Butkovsky, L., & Braungart, J. M. (1992). Family- peer connections: The roles of emotional expressiveness within the family and children's understanding of emotions. *Child Development, 63*, 603–618.

Cicchetti, D. (1989). How research on child maltreatment has informed the study of child development: Perspectives from developmental psychopathology. In D. Cicchetti and V. Carlson (Eds.), *Child maltreatment: Theory and research on the causes and consequences of child abuse and neglect.* (pp. 377–431). New York: Cambridge University Press.

Cicchetti, D. (1991). Fractures in the crystal: Developmental Psychopathology and the emergence of the self. *Developmental Review, 11*, 271–287.

Cicchetti, D. (1993). Developmental Psychopathology: Reactions, Reflections, Projections. *Developmental Review, 13*, 471–502.

Cicchetti, D. (1996). Child maltreatment: Implications for developmental theory and research. *Human Development, 39*, 18–39.

Cicchetti, D., & Aber, J. L. (1986). Early precursors to later depression: An organizational perspective. In L. Lipsitt and C. Rovee-Collier (Eds.), *Advances in infancy, Vol. 4* (pp. 87–137). Norwood NJ: Ablex.

Cicchetti, D., & Barnett, D. (1991). Toward the development of a scientific nosology of child maltreatment. In W. Grove & D. Cicchetti (Eds.), *Thinking clearly about psychology: Essays in honor of Paul E. Meehl. Vol. 2: Personality and psychopathology* (pp. 346–377). Minneapolis: University of Minnesota Press.

Cicchetti, D., & Carlson, V. (Eds.). (1989). *Child maltreatment: Theory and research on the causes and consequences of child abuse and neglect*. New York: Cambridge University Press.

Cicchetti, D., & Garmezy, N. (Eds.). (1993). Special Issue: Milestones in the development of resilience. *Development and Psychopathology, 5*, 497–774.

Cicchetti, D., & Lynch, M. (1993). Toward an ecological/transactional model of community violence and child maltreatment: Consequences for children's development. *Psychiatry, 56*, 96–118.

Cicchetti, D., & Lynch, M. (1995). Failures in the expectable environment and their impact on individual development: The case of child maltreatment. In D. Cicchetti & D. J. Cohen (Eds.), *Developmental Psychopathology. Vol. 2: Risk, disorder, and adaptation* (pp. 32–71). New York: Wiley.

Cicchetti, D., Lynch, M., Shonk, S., & Manly, J. T. (1992). An organizational perspective on peer relations in maltreated children. In R. D. Parke and G. W. Ladd (Eds.), *Family-peer relationships: Modes of linkage.* (pp. 345–383). Hillsdale NJ: Erlbaum.

Cicchetti, D., & Manly, J. T. (1990). A personal perspective on conducting research with maltreating families: Problems and solutions. In G. Brody & I. Sigel (Eds.), *Methods of family research. Volume 2: Families at risk* (pp. 87–133). Hillsdale NJ: Erlbaum.

Cicchetti, D., & Rizley, R. (1981). Developmental perspectives on the etiology, intergenerational transmission and sequelae of child maltreatment. *New Directions for Child Development, 11*, 32–59.

Cicchetti, D., & Rogosch, F. (1996). Equifinality and multifinality in developmental psychopathology. *Development and Psychopathology, 8*, 597–600.

Cicchetti, D., & Rogosch, F. A. (1997). The role of self-organization in the promotion of resilience in maltreated children. *Development and Psychopathology, 9*, 797–815.

Cicchetti, D., Rogosch, F., Lynch, M., & Holt, K. (1993). Resilience in maltreated children: Processes leading to adaptive outcome. *Development and Psychopathology, 5*, 629–647.

Cicchetti, D., & Schneider-Rosen, K. (1986). An organizational approach to childhood depression. In M. Rutter, C. Izard, & P. Read (Eds.), *Depression in young people, clinical and developmental perspectives* (pp. 71–134). New York: Guilford.

Cicchetti, D., & Toth, S. L. (1992). The role of developmental theory in prevention and intervention. *Development and Psychopathology, 4*, 489–493.

Cicchetti, D., & Toth, S. L. (Eds.). (1993). *Child abuse, child development, and social policy*. Norwood NJ: Ablex.

Cicchetti, D., & Toth, S. L. (1995). A developmental psychopathology perspective on child abuse and neglect. *Journal of the American Academy of Child and Adolescent Psychiatry, 34*, 541–565.

Cicchetti, D., & Toth, S. L. (1997). Transactional ecological systems in developmental psychopathology. In S. S. Luthar, J. Burack, D. Cicchetti, & J. Weisz (Eds.), *Developmental psychopathology: Perspectives on risk and disorder* (pp. 317–349). New York: Cambridge University Press.

Cicchetti, D., Toth, S. L., & Bush, M. (1988). Developmental psychopathology and incompetence in childhood: Suggestions for intervention. In B. Lahey & A. Kazdin (Eds.), *Advances in Clinical Child Psychology* (pp. 1–71). New York: Plenum Press.

Cicchetti, D., Toth, S. L., & Lynch, M. (1995). Bowlby's dream comes full circle: The application of attachment theory to risk and psychopathology. *Advances in Clinical Child Psychology, 17*, 1–75.

Cicchetti, D., Toth, S. L., & Lynch, M. (1997). Child maltreatment as an illustration of the effects of war on development. In D. Cicchetti & S. L. Toth (Eds.), *Rochester symposium on developmental psychopathology. Vol. VIII. Trauma: Perspectives on theory, research and intervention* (pp. 227–262). Rochester NY: University of Rochester Press.

Cicchetti, D., & Tucker, D. (1994). Development and self-regulatory structures of the mind. *Development and Psychopathology, 6*, 533–549.

Cicchetti, D., & White, J. (1990). Emotion and developmental psychopathology. In N. L. Stein, B. L. Leventhal, & T. Trabasso (Eds.), *Psychological and biological approaches to emotion* (pp. 359–382). Hillsdale NJ: Erlbaum.

Coie, J. D., & Dodge, K. A. (1998). Aggression and antisocial behavior. In W. Damon (Ed.), *Handbook of Child Psychology. Vol. 3: Social, emotional, and personality development* (pp. 779–862). New York: Wiley.

Coster, W. J., Gersten, M. S., Beeghly, M., & Cicchetti, D. (1989). Communicative functioning in maltreated toddlers. *Developmental Psychology, 25*, 1020–1029.

Coulton, C., Korbin, J., Su, M., & Chow, J. (1995). Community level factors and child maltreatment rates. *Child Development, 66*, 1262–1276.

Cowen, E. L. (1994). The enhancement of psychological wellness: Challenges and opportunities. *American Journal of Community Psychology, 22*, 149–179.

Cowen, E., Hightower, A. D., Pedro-Carroll, J. L., Work, W. C., Wyman, P. A., & Haffey, W. G. (1996). *School-based prevention for children at risk: The Primary Mental Health Project*. Washington DC: American Psychological Association.

Crittenden, P. M. (1988). Relationships at risk. In J. Belsky & T. Nezworski (Eds.), *Clinical implications of attachment theory* (pp. 136–174). Hillsdale NJ: Erlbaum .

Crittenden, P. M., & Ainsworth, M. D. S. (1989). Attachment and child abuse.

In D. Cicchetti and V. Carlson (Eds.), *Child maltreatment: Theory and research on the causes and consequences of child abuse and neglect* (pp. 432–463). New York: Cambridge University Press.

Crittenden, P. M., & DiLalla, D. (1988). Compulsive compliance: The development of an inhibitory coping strategy in infancy. *Journal of Abnormal Child Psychology, 16*, 585–599.

Crittenden, P. M., Partridge, M. F., & Claussen, A. H. (1991). Family patterns of relationship in normative and dysfunctional families. *Development and Psychopathology, 3*, 491–512.

Daro, D. (1993). Child maltreatment research: Implications for program design. In D. Cicchetti & S. L. Toth (Eds.), *Child abuse, child development and social policy* (pp. 331–367). Norwood NJ: Ablex.

Derryberry, D., & Reed, M. A. (1994). Temperament and the self-organization of personality. *Development and Psychopathology, 6*, 653–676.

Derryberry, D., & Reed, M. A. (1996). Regulatory processes and the development of cognitive representations. *Development and Psychopathology, 8*, 215–234.

Dodge, K., Pettit, G. S., & Bates, J. E. (1990). Mechanisms in the cycle of violence. *Science, 250*, 1678–1683.

Dodge, K. A., Pettit, G. S., & Bates, J. E. (1997). How the experience of early physical abuse leads children to become chronically aggressive. In D. Cicchetti & S. L. Toth (Eds.), *Rochester symposium on developmental psychopathology. Vol. VIII. Trauma: Perspectives on theory, research and intervention* (pp. 263–288). Rochester NY: University of Rochester Press.

Dodge, K. A., Pettit, G. S., Bates, J. E., & Valente, E. (1995). Social information-processing patterns partially mediate the effect of early physical abuse on later conduct problems. *Journal of Abnormal Psychology, 104*, 632–643.

Donchin, E., Karis, D., Bashore, T., Coles, M., & Gratton, G. (1986). Cognitive psychophysiology and human information processing. In M. Coles, E. Donchin, & S. Porges (Eds.), *Psychophysiology* (pp. 244–267). New York: Guilford.

Downey, G., & Coyne, J. C. (1990). Children of depressed parents: An integrative review. *Psychological Bulletin, 108*, 50–76.

Drake, B., & Pandey, D. (1996). Understanding the relationship between neighborhood poverty and specific types of child maltreatment. *Child Abuse and Neglect, 20*, 1003–1018.

Dunn, J., & Brown, J. (1991). Relationships, talk about feelings, and the development of affect regulation in early childhood. In J. Garber & K. A. Dodge (Eds.), *The development of emotion regulation and dysregulation* (pp. 89–108). New York: Cambridge University Press.

Egeland, B. (1997). Mediators of the effects of child maltreatment on developmental adaptation in adolescence. In D. Cicchetti and S. L. Toth (Eds.), *Rochester symposium on developmental psychopathology. Vol. VIII. Trauma: Perspectives on theory, research and intervention* (pp. 403–434). Rochester NY: University of Rochester Press.

152

MOTIVATION AND CHILD MALTREATMENT

Egeland, B., Carlson, E., & Sroufe, L. A. (1993). Resilience as process. *Development and Psychopathology, 5*, 517–528.

Egeland, B., & Farber, E. (1987). Invulnerability among abused and neglected children. In E. J. Anthony & B. Cohler (Eds.), *The Invulnerable Child* (pp. 253–288). New York: Guilford.

Egeland, B., & Sroufe, L. A. (1981). Developmental sequelae of maltreatment in infancy. *New directions for child development, 11*, 77–92.

Eisenberg, L. (1995). The social construction of the human brain. *American Journal of Psychiatry, 152*, 1563–1575.

Emery, R. & Laumann-Billings, L. (1998). An overview of the nature, causes, and consequences of abusive family relationships: Toward differentiating maltreatment and violence. *American Psychologist, 53*, 121–135.

Erickson, M. F., Korfmacher, J., & Egeland, B. (1992). Attachments past and present: Implications for therapeutic intervention with mother-infant dyads. *Development and Psychopathology, 4*, 495–507.

Famularo, R., Kinscherff, R., & Fenton, T. (1992). Psychiatric diagnoses of maltreated children: Preliminary findings. *Journal of the American Academy of Child and Adolescent Psychiatry, 31*, 863–867.

Fantuzzo, J., Coolahan, K. C., & Weiss, A. D. (1997). Resiliency partnership-directed intervention: Enhancing the social competencies of preschool victims of physical abuse by developing peer resources and community strengths. In D. Cicchetti and S. L. Toth (Eds.), *Rochester symposium on developmental psychopathology. Vol. VIII. Trauma: Perspectives on theory, research and intervention* (pp. 463–489). Rochester NY: University of Rochester Press.

Farrar, M. J., Fasig, L. G., & Welch-Ross, M. K. (1997). Attachment and emotion in autobiographical memory development. *Journal of Experimental Child Psychology, 67*, 389–408.

Federal Interagency Forum on Child and Family Statistics (1997). *America's children: Key national indicators of well-being*. Washington DC.

Finkelhor, D., & Kendall-Tackett, K. (1997). A developmental perspective on the childhood impact of crime, abuse, and violent victimization. In D. Cicchetti & S. L. Toth (Eds.), *Rochester symposium on developmental psychopathology. Vol. VIII. Trauma: Perspectives on theory, research and intervention* (pp. 1–32). Rochester NY: University of Rochester Press.

Fischer, K. W., & Ayoub, C. (1994). Affective splitting and dissociation in normal and maltreated children: Developmental pathways for self in relationships. In D. Cicchetti & S. L. Toth (Eds.), *Rochester Symposium on Development and Psychopathology: Vol. 5: Disorders and dysfunctions of the self* (pp. 149–222). Rochester NY: University of Rochester Press.

Fiske, S. T., & Taylor, S. E. (1991). *Social cognition*. New York: McGraw-Hill.

Gaensbauer, T. J., & Hiatt, S. (1984). Facial communication of emotion in early infancy. In N. Fox & R. Davidson (Eds.), *The psychopathology of affective development* (pp. 207–230). Hillsdale NJ: Erlbaum.

Garbarino, J. (1995). *Raising children in a socially toxic environment: Childhood in the 1990s*. San Francisco: Jossey-Bass.

Garbarino, J., & Gilliam, G. (1980). *Understanding abusive families*. Lexington MA: Lexington Books.

Garmezy, N., & Streitman, S. (1974). Children at risk: The search for antecedents to schizophrenia. Part I: Conceptual models and research methods. *Schizophrenia Bulletin, 8*, 14–90.

Gottlieb, G. (1992). *Individual development and evolution: The genesis of novel behavior*. New York: Oxford University Press.

Greenberg, M. T., Kusche, C. A., & Speltz, M. (1991). Emotional regulation, self-control, and psychopathology: The role of relationships in early childhood. In D. Cicchetti & S. L. Toth (Eds.), *Rochester Symposium on Developmental Psychopathology. Vol. 2: Internalizing and externalizing expressions of dysfunction* (pp. 21–55). Hillsdale NJ; Erlbaum.

Gurvits, T. V., Shenton, M. E., Hokama, H., Ohta, H., Lasko, N. B., Gilbertson, M., Orr, S. P., Kikinis, R., Jolesz, F. A., McCarley, R. W., & Pitman, R. K. (1996). Magnetic resonance imaging study of hippocampal volume in chronic, combat-related posttraumatic stress disorder. *Biological Psychiatry, 40*, 1091–1099.

Harter, S. (1983). Developmental perspectives on the self-system. In P. H. Mussen (Series Ed.) & E. M. Hetherington (Vol. Ed.), *Handbook of child psychology: Vol. 4. Socialization, personality, and social development* (4th ed., pp. 275–385). New York: Wiley.

Hennessy, K. D., Rabideau, G. J., Cicchetti, D., & Cummings, E. M. (1994). Responses of physically abused and nonabused children to different forms of interadult anger. *Child Development, 65*, 815–828.

Herrenkohl, E. C., Herrenkohl, R., & Egolf, M. (1994). Resilient early school-age children from maltreating homes: Outcomes in late adolescence. *American Journal of Orthopsychiatry, 64*, 301–309.

Hillyard, S., & Picton, T. (1987). Electrophysiology of cognition. In V. Mountcastle (Ed.), *Handbook of Physiology, Vol. V: High Functions of the Brain* (pp. 519–583). Bethesda MD: American Physiological Society.

Hinde, R. (1992). Developmental psychology in the context of other behavioral sciences. *Developmental Psychology, 28*, 1018–1029.

Howes, P., & Cicchetti, D. (1993). A family/relational perspective on maltreating families: Parallel processes across systems and social policy implications. In D. Cicchetti & S. L. Toth (Eds.), *Child abuse, child development, and social policy* (pp. 249–300). Norwood NJ: Ablex.

Juvenile Justice Standards Project (1977). *Standards relating to child abuse and neglect*. Cambridge MA: Ballinger.

Kaufman, J., Cook, A., Arny, L., Jones, B., & Pittinsky, T. (1994). Problems defining resiliency: Illustrations from the study of maltreated children. *Development and Psychopathology, 6*, 215–229.

Kendall-Tackett, K. A., Williams, L. M., & Finkelhor, D. (1993). Impact of sexual abuse on children: A review and synthesis of recent empirical studies. *Psychological Bulletin, 113*, 164–180.

Kirsh, S., & Cassidy, J. (1997). Preschoolers' attention to and memory for attachment-relevant information. *Child Development, 68*, 1143–1153.

Kitzman, H., Olds, D., Henderson, C., Hanks, C., Cole, R., Tatelbaum, R., McConnochie, K., Sidora, K., Luckey, D., Shaver, D., Engelhardt, K., James, D., & Barnard, K. (1997). Effect of prenatal and infancy home visitation by nurses for pregnancy outcomes, childhood inquiries, and repeated childbearing: A randomized controlled trial. *Journal of the American Medical Association, 278*, 644–652.

Kolvin, I., Miller, F., Fleeting, M., & Kolvin, P. (1988). Risk and protective factors for offending with particular reference to deprivation. In M. Rutter (Ed.), *Studies of psychosocial risk: The power of longitudinal data* (pp. 77–95). New York: Cambridge University Press.

Korbin, J. E., Coulton, C. J., Chard, S., Platt-Houston, C., & Su, M. (1998). Impoverishment and child maltreatment in African-American and European-American neighborhoods. *Development and Psychopathology, 10*, 215–233.

Kupersmidt, J. B., Griesler, P. C., DeRosier, M. E., Patterson, C. J., & Davis, P. W. (1995). Childhood aggression and peer relations in the context of family and neighborhood factors. *Child Development, 66*, 360–375.

Luthar, S. S. (1991). Vulnerability and resilience: A study of high-risk adolescents. *Child Development, 62*, 600–616.

Luthar, S. S. (1993). Annotation: Methodological and conceptual issues in the study of resilience. *Journal of Child Psychology and Psychiatry, 34*, 441–453.

Luthar, S. S., Cicchetti, D., & Becker, B. (in press). The construct of resilience: A critical evaluation and guidelines for future work. *Child Development*.

Lynch, M., & Cicchetti, D. (1991). Patterns of relatedness in maltreated and nonmaltreated children: Connections among multiple representational models. *Development and Psychopathology, 3*, 207–226.

Lynch, M., & Cicchetti, D. (1992). Maltreated children's reports of relatedness to their teachers. *New Directions for Child Development, 57*, 81–107.

Lynch, M., & Cicchetti, D. (1997). Children's relationships with adults and peers: An examination of elementary and junior high school students. *Journal of School Psychology, 35*, 81–99.

Lynch, M., & Cicchetti, D. (1998a). An ecological-transactional analysis of children and contexts: The longitudinal interplay among child maltreatment, community violence, and children's symptomatology. *Development and Psychopathology, 10*(2), 235–257.

Lynch, M., & Cicchetti, D., (1998b). Trauma, mental representation, and the organization of memory for mother-referent material. *Development and Psychopathology, 10*(4), 739–759.

Maccoby, E. E., & Martin, J. A. (1983). Socialization in the context of the family: Parent-child interaction. In P. Mussen (Ed.) & E. M. Hetherington (Vol. Ed.), *Handbook of child psychology, Vol. 4. Socialization, personality, and social development* (4th ed., pp. 1–102). New York: Wiley.

Main, M. (1990). Cross-cultural studies of attachment organization: Recent studies, changing methodologies, and the concept of conditional strategies. *Human Development, 33*, 48–61.

Main, M., & Hesse, E. (1990). Parents' unresolved traumatic experiences are related to infant disorganized attachment status: Is frightened and/or frightening parental behavior the linking mechanism? In M. Greenberg, D. Cicchetti & E. M. Cummings (Eds.), *Attachment in the preschool years* pp. 161–182). Chicago: University of Chicago Press.

Main, M., Kaplan, N., & Cassidy, J. C. (1985). Security in infancy, childhood and adulthood: A move to the level of representation. In I. Bretherton & E. Waters (Eds.), *Growing points of attachment theory and research: Monographs of the Society for Research in Child Development, 50*(1–2), (Serial No. 209, pp. 66–104).

Main, M., & Solomon, J. (1990). Procedures for identifying infants as disorganized/disoriented during the Ainsworth Strange Situation. In M. Greenberg, D. Cicchetti, & E. M. Cummings (Eds.), *Attachment during the preschool years* (pp. 121–160). Chicago: University of Chicago Press.

Malinosky-Rummell, R., & Hansen, D. J. (1993). Long-term consequences of childhood physical abuse. *Psychological Bulletin, 114*, 68–79.

Manly, J. T., Cicchetti, D., & Barnett, D. (1994). The impact of subtype, frequency, chronicity and severity of child maltreatment on social competence and behavior problems. *Development and Psychopathology, 6*, 121–143.

Masten, A. S., Best, K., & Garmezy, N. (1990). Resilience and development: Contributions from the study of children who overcome adversity. *Development and Psychopathology, 2*, 425–444.

Masten, A. S., & Coatsworth, J. D. (1995). Competence, resilience, and psychopathology. In D. Cicchetti and D. J. Cohen (Eds.), *Developmental Psychopathology. Vol. 1: Risk, disorder, and adaptation* (pp. 715–752). New York: Wiley.

Masten, A. S., & Coatsworth, D., (1998). The development of competence in favorable and unfavorable environments: Lessons from research on successful children. *American Psychologist, 53*, 205–220.

McGee, R. A., & Wolfe, D. A. (1991). Between a rock and a hard place: Where do we go from here in defining psychological maltreatment? *Development and Psychopathology, 3*, 119–124.

Melton, G., & Flood, M. (1994). Research policy and child maltreatment: Developing the scientific foundation for effective protection of children. *Child Abuse and Neglect, 18*(Suppl. 1), 1–28.

Mervis, C. B. (1990). Early lexical development of children with Down syndrome. In D. Cicchetti & M. Beeghly (Eds.), *Children with Down syndrome: A developmental perspective* (pp. 252–301). New York: Cambridge.

Miller, T. R., Cohen, M. A., & Wiersema, B. (1996). *Victim costs and consequences: A new look.* Washington DC: National Institute of Justice.

Moran, P. B., & Eckenrode, J. (1992). Protective personality characteristics among adolescent victims of maltreatment. *Child Abuse and Neglect, 16*, 743–754.

Mueller, E., & Silverman, N. (1989). Peer relations in maltreated children. In D. Cicchetti and V. Carlson (Eds.), *Child maltreatment: Theory and research on the causes and consequences of child abuse and neglect* (pp. 529–578). New York: Cambridge University Press.

National Research Council (1993). *Understanding child abuse and neglect*. Washington DC: National Academy Press.

Nelson, C. A., & Bloom, F. E. (1997). Child development and neuroscience. *Child Development, 68,* 970–987.

Olds, D., Eckenrode, J., Henderson, C., Kitzman, H., Powers, J., Cole, R., Sidora, K., Morris, P., Pettit, L., & Luckey, D. (1997). Long-term effects of home visitation on maternal life course and child abuse and neglect. Fifteen-year follow-up of a randomized trial. *Journal of the American Medical Association, 278,* 637–643.

Osofsky, J. (1995). The effects of exposure to violence on young children. *American Psychologist, 50,* 782–788.

Parker, J. G., & Asher, S. R. (1987). Peer acceptance and later personal adjustment: Are low-accepted children "at risk"? *Psychological Bulletin, 102,* 357–389.

Perry, B., Pollard, R., Blakley, T., Baker, W., & Vigilante, D. (1995). Childhood trauma, the neurobiology of adaptation, and "Use-Dependent" development of the brain: How "states" become "traits." *Infant Mental Health Journal, 16,* 271–291.

Pollak, S., Cicchetti, D., & Klorman, R. (1998). Stress, memory, and emotion: Developmental considerations from the study of child maltreatment. *Development and Psychopathology, 10,* 811–828.

Pollak, S., Cicchetti, D., Klorman, R., & Brumaghim, J. (1997). Cognitive brain event-related potential and emotion processing in maltreated children. *Child Development, 5,* 773–787.

Pollak, S., Klorman, R., Brumaghim, J. & Cicchetti, D. (in press). P3b reflects maltreated children's reactions to facial displays of emotion. *Psychophysiology.*

Posner, M. I., & Raichle, M. E. (1994). *Images of mind.* New York: Scientific American Books.

Post, R., Weiss, S. R. B., Smith, M., Zhang, L. X., Xing, G., Osuch, E., & McCann, U. (1998). Neural plasticity and emotional memory. *Development and Psychopathology, 10,* 829–855.

Punamaki, R. L., Quota, S., & El Sarraj, E. (1997). Models of traumatic experiences and children's psychological adjustment: The roles of perceived parenting and the children's own resources and activity. *Child Development, 68,* 718–728.

Pynoos, R., Steinberg, A., & Wraith, R. (1995). A developmental Model for childhood traumatic stress. In D. Cicchetti & D. Cohen (Eds.), *Developmental psychopathology: Risk, disorder, and adaptation* (pp. 72–95). New York: Wiley.

Richters, J. E., & Martinez, P. (1993). The NIMH community violence project: I. Children as victims and witnesses to violence. *Psychiatry, 56,* 7–21.

Richters, J., & Weintraub, S. (1990). Beyond diathesis: Toward an understanding of high risk environments. In J. Rolf, A. S. Masten, D. Cicchetti, K. H. Nuechterlein, & S. Weintraub (Eds.), *Risk and protective factors in the development of psychopathology* (pp. 67–96). New York: Cambridge University Press.

Rieder, C., & Cicchetti, D. (1989). Organizational perspective on cognitive control functioning and cognitive-affective balance in maltreated children. *Developmental Psychology, 25,* 382–393.

Rogosch, F., & Cicchetti, D. (1994). Illustrating the interface of family and peer relations through the study of child maltreatment. *Social Development, 3,* 291–308.

Rogosch, F., Cicchetti, D., & Aber, J. L. (1995). The role of child maltreatment in early deviations in cognitive and affective processing abilities and later peer relationship problems. *Development and Psychopathology, 7,* 591–609.

Rogosch, F., Cicchetti, D., Shields, A., & Toth, S. L. (1995). Facets of parenting disturbance in child maltreatment. In M. H. Bornstein (Ed.), *Handbook of parenting: Vol. 4* (pp. 127–159). Hillsdale NJ: Erlbaum.

Rubin, K., Hymel, S., Mills, R., & Rose-Krasnor, L. (1991). Conceptualizing different developmental pathways to and from social isolation in childhood. In D. Cicchetti & S. L. Toth (Eds.), *Rochester symposium on developmental psychopathology, Vol. 2: Internalizing and externalizing expressions of dysfunction* (pp. 91–122). Hillsdale NJ: Erlbaum.

Rudolph, K. D., Hammen, C., & Burge, D. (1995). Cognitive representations of self, family, and peers in school-age children: Links with social competence and sociometric status. *Child Development, 66,* 1385–1402.

Rutter, M., (1979). Protective factors in children's responses to stress and disadvantage. In M. W. Kent & J. E. Rolf (Eds.), *Primary prevention of psychopathology: Vol. 3. Social competence in children* (pp. 49–74). Hanover NH: University Press of New England.

Rutter, M. (1990). Psychosocial resilience and protective mechanisms. In J. Rolf, A. S., Masten, D. Cicchetti, K. H. Nuechterlein, & S. Weintraub (Eds.), *Risk and protective factors in the development of psychopathology* (pp. 181–214). New York: Cambridge University Press.

Ryan, R. M., Deci, E. L., & Grolnick, W. S. (1995). Autonomy, relatedness, and the self: Their relation to development and psychopathology. In D. Cicchetti & D. J. Cohen (Eds.), *Developmental Psychopathology. Vol. 1: Theory and methods.* (pp. 618–658). New York: Wiley.

Sameroff, A., & Chandler, M. (1975). Reproductive risk and the continuum of caretaking casualty. In F. Horowitz (Ed.), *Review of child development research. Vol. 4* (pp. 187–244). Chicago: University of Chicago Press.

Sameroff, A. J., Seifer, R., Barocas, R., Zax, M., & Greenspan, S. (1987). Intelligence quotient scores of 4-year-old children: Social environmental risk factors. *Pediatrics, 79,* 343–350.

Sampson, R. J., & Laub, J. H. (1994). Urban poverty and the family context of delinquency: A new look at structure and process in a classic study. *Child Development, 65,* 523–540.

158

MOTIVATION AND CHILD MALTREATMENT

Santostefano, S. (1978). *A bio-developmental approach to clinical child psychology.* New York: Wiley.

Santostefano, S. (1985). *Cognitive control therapy with children and adolescents.* Elmsford NY: Pergamon Press.

Seifer, R., Sameroff, A., Baldwin, C., & Baldwin, A. (1992). Child and family factors that ameliorate risk between 4 and 13 years of age. *Journal of the American Academy of Child and Adolescent Psychiatry, 31,* 893–903.

Selman, R. L., Schultz, L. H., & Yeates, K. O. (1991). Interpersonal understanding and action: A development and psychopathology perspective on research and prevention. In D. Cicchetti and S. L. Toth (Eds.), *Rochester Symposium on Developmental Psychopathology. Vol. 3: Models and integrations* (pp. 289–329). Rochester NY: University of Rochester Press.

Shields, A., & Cicchetti, D. (1997). Emotion regulation among school-age children: the development and validation of a new criterion Q-sort scale. *Developmental Psychology, 33,* 906–916.

Shields, A., & Cicchetti, D. (1998). Reactive aggression among maltreated children: The contributions of attention and emotion dysregulation. *Journal of Clinical Child Psychology, 27,* 381–395.

Shields, A., Cicchetti, D., & Ryan, R. (1994). The development of emotional and behavioral self regulation and social competence among maltreated school-age children. *Development and Psychopathology, 6,* 57–75.

Silber, S. (1990). Conflict negotiation in child abusing and nonabusing families. *Journal of Family Psychology, 3,* 368–384.

Skuse, D. (1984). Extreme deprivation in early childhood—II. Theoretical issues and a comparative review. *Journal of Child Psychology and Psychiatry, 31,* 893–903.

Slaughter, D. (1988). Programs for racially and ethnically diverse American families: Some critical issues. In H. Weiss & F. Jacobs (Eds.), *Evaluating family programs* (pp. 461–476). New York: Aldine.

Smith, C. A., & Thornberry, T. (1995). The relationship between child maltreatment and adolescent involvement in delinquency. *Criminology, 33,* 451–481.

Snow, C. E. (1984). Parent-child interaction and the development of communicative ability. In R. L. Schielelbusch & L. Pickar (Eds.), *The acquisition of communicative competence* (pp. 69–107). Baltimore MD: University Park Press.

Sroufe, L. A. (1979). The coherence of individual development: Early care, attachment, and subsequent developmental issues. *American Psychologist, 34,* 834–841.

Sroufe, L. A., Egeland, B., & Kreutzer, T. (1990). The fate of early experience following developmental change: Longitudinal approaches to individual adaptation in childhood. *Child Development, 61,* 1363–1373.

Staub, E., (1996). Cultural-societal roots of violence: The examples of genocidal violence and of contemporary youth violence in the United States. *American Psychologist, 51,* 117–132.

Stein, M. B., Koverola, C., Hanna, C., Torchia, M. G., & McClarty, B. (1997). Hippocampal volume in women victimized by childhood sexual abuse. *Psychological Medicine, 27*, 951–959.

Sternberg, K. J. (1993). Child maltreatment: Implications for policy from cross-cultural research. In D. Cicchetti & S. L. Toth (Eds.), *Child abuse, child development and social policy* (pp. 191–211). Norwood NJ: Ablex.

Sternberg, K. J., Lamb, M. E., Greenbaum, C., Cicchetti, D., Dawud, S., Manela Cortes, R., Krispin, O., & Lorey, F. (1993). Effects of domestic violence on children's behavior problems and depression. *Developmental Psychology, 29*, 44–52.

Thatcher, R., Hallett, M., Zeffiro, T., John, E. R., & Huerta, M. (Eds.), (1994). *Functional neuroimaging: Technical foundations.* San Diego: Academic Press.

Thatcher, R., Lyon, G., Rumsey, J., & Krasnegor, N. (Eds.). (1996). *Developmental neuroimaging: Mapping the development of brain and behavior.* San Diego: Academic Press.

Thompson, R. A. (1995). *Preventing child maltreatment through social support: A critical analysis.* Thousand Oaks CA: Sage.

Thompson, R. A., & Wilcox, B. (1995). Child maltreatment research: Federal support and policy issues. *American Psychologist, 50*, 789–793.

Toga, A., & Mazziotta, J. (Eds.). (1996). *Brain mapping: The methods.* San Diego: Academic Press.

Tolan, P. H., & Henry, D. (1996). Patterns of psychopathology among urban poor children. *Journal of Consulting and Clinical Psychology, 64*, 1094–1099.

Toth, S. L., & Cicchetti, D. (1993). Child maltreatment: Where do we go from here in our treatment of victims? In D. Cicchetti & S. L. Toth (Eds.), *Child abuse, child development, and social policy* (pp. 399–438). Norwood NJ: Ablex.

Toth, S. L., & Cicchetti, D. (1996a). Patterns of relatedness and depressive symptomatology in maltreated children. *Journal of Consulting and Clinical Psychology, 64*, 1094–1099.

Toth, S. L., & Cicchetti, D. (1996b). The impact of relatedness with mother on school functioning in maltreated youngsters. *Journal of School Psychology, 3*, 247–266.

Toth, S. L., & Cicchetti, D. (1998). Remembering, forgetting, and the effects of trauma on memory: A developmental psychopathology perspective. *Development and Psychopathology, 10*(4), 589–605.

Toth, S. L., & Cicchetti, D. (1999). Developmental Psychopathology and child psychotherapy. In S. Russ & T. Ollendick (Eds.), *Handbook of psychotherapies with children and families* (pp. 15–44). New York: Plenum Press.

Trickett, P., & McBride-Chang, C. (1995). The developmental impact of different types of child abuse and neglect. *Developmental Review, 15*, 311–337.

United States Department of Health and Human Services (USDHHS), National Center on Child Abuse and Neglect (1996). *Child abuse and neglect case-level data 1993.* Washington DC: US Government Printing Office.

Vondra, J., Barnett, D., & Cicchetti, D. (1989). Perceived and actual competence among maltreated and comparison school children. *Development and Psychopathology, 1*, 237–255.

Waddington, C. H. (1957). *The strategy of the genes*. London: Allen & Unwin.

Weisz, J. R., Weiss, B., & Donenberg, G. R. (1992). The lab versus the clinic: Effects of child and adolescent psychotherapy. *American Psychologist, 47*, 1578–1585.

Wekerle, C., & Wolfe, D. A. (1993). Prevention of child physical abuse and neglect: Promising new directions. *Clinical Psychology Review, 13*, 501–540.

Wellman, H. M. (1988). First steps in the child's theorizing about mind. In J. W. Astington, P. L., Harris & D. R. Olson (Eds.), *Developing theories of mind* (pp. 64–92). New York: Cambridge University Press.

Werner, E. E. (1995). Resilience in development. *Current Directions in Psychological Science, 3*, 81–85.

Wilson, M. N., & Saft, E. W. (1993). Child maltreatment in the African-American community. In D. Cicchetti & S. L. Toth (Eds.), *Child abuse, child development and social policy* (pp. 213–247). Norwood NJ: Ablex.

Wolfe, D. A. (1985). Child abusive parents: An empirical review and analysis. *Psychological Bulletin, 97*, 462–482.

Wolfe, D. A. (1993). Child abuse intervention research: Implications for policy. In D. Cicchetti & S. L. Toth (Eds.), *Child abuse, child development and social policy*. (pp. 369–397). Norwood NJ: Ablex.

Wolfe, D. A., & Wekerle, C. (1997). Pathways to violence in teen dating relationships. In D. Cicchetti & S. L. Toth (Eds.), *Rochester symposium on developmental psychopathology. Vol. VIII. Trauma: Perspectives on theory, research and intervention* (pp. 1–32). Rochester NY: University of Rochester Press.

Zuravin, S. J. (1991). Research definitions of child abuse and neglect: current problems. In R. Starr & D. A. Wolfe (Eds.), *The effects of child abuse and neglect: Issues and research* (pp. 100–128). New York: Guilford.

Child Abuse Prevention: New Directions and Challenges

Deborah A. Daro

The Chapin Hall Center for Children
University of Chicago

Child abuse is not a new phenomenon. Since the first parent-child dyad, adult caretakers have struggled with the demands presented by their children (de Mause, 1974; TenBensel, Rheinberger, & Radbill, 1997). In an effort to meet these demands, parents have drawn on the modeling they experienced with their own parents and extended family members, the availability of support and advice from friends, and assistance provided by local services and related resources. Over the past 30 years, prevention advocates have designed and implemented hundreds of interventions to resolve a parent's lack of knowledge and skills, to create extended networks of formal support, and to alter normative and societal standards for child rearing and education. Whether one talks about the family support movement, the early childhood movement, or child abuse prevention, these and similar efforts have created a plethora of programs that have, in the eyes of many, significantly improved the conditions for children (Daro, 1988; Schorr & Schorr, 1985; Willis, Holden, & Rosenberg, 1992)

Not all families, however, have equal access to or benefit from early intervention efforts so not all children are being helped (Daro, 1993; USDHHS, 1990). On balance the majority of prevention programs target and successfully serve parents who recognize their limitations. Far fewer resources exist for families who may not know they need assistance or, if they recognize their shortcomings, do not know how to access help. These families are generally not good at applying a theoretical concept to their own child's behavior or adjusting a technique to suit their child's continued development. Parents may be unable, or unwilling, to integrate the social, emotional, and cognitive competencies needed for healthy parenting.

In addition to leaving many families underserved, current prevention services often fail to achieve their desired outcomes (Daro & Cohn, 1988; Gutterman, 1997). Despite early and thoughtful interventions, many recipients will indeed mistreat their children or remain unable to provide the consistent nurturing and supervision necessary for their child's safe and full development. Dramatic changes in family structure, community cohesiveness, and public social welfare and health care delivery have further expanded the gap between what parents need to safely rear their children and what society can offer. Collectively, these service failures and environmental challenges have resulted in continued high annual rates of child abuse reports, child abuse fatalities and serious injury and acts of violence involving young children (Chalk & King, 1998; Sedlak & Broadhurst, 1996).

Limitations in the existing prevention system call for new thinking in how prevention efforts are crafted and presented to potential participants. Specifically, these reflections suggest that future prevention efforts need to be built upon three key principals. First, such efforts need to offer community planners flexible, empirically based criteria for "building" their own prevention programs. Simply adopting predetermined, monolithic intervention strategies has not produced a steady expansion of high quality, effective interventions (Brookings Institute, 1998; Schorr, 1997). Replication efforts need to include a specific planning phase in which local stakeholders (e.g., potential participants, local service providers, funders, the general public, etc.) assess the scope of maltreatment in their community, identify local human and social service resources, and craft a service delivery system in keeping with local realities.

Second, intensive efforts for those families facing the greatest challenges need to be nested within a more broadly defined network of support services. Successfully engaging and retaining those parents facing the greatest challenges will not result from more stringent efforts to identify and serve only these parents. Until systems are established which normalize the parent support process by assessing and meeting the needs of all new parents, prevention efforts will continue to struggle with issues of stigmatization and deficit-directed imagery.

Finally, prevention programs need to focus not merely on changing individual behaviors but also on using these services as a springboard for systemic reforms in health and social service institutions. Moving programs from isolated demonstration efforts to full-scale system reform is not at all self-evident. While many private and public agencies have engaged in efforts to alter the way major institutions interface with families, few consistent success stories exist (Kagan, 1996; Schorr, 1997; St. Pierre, Layzer, Goodson, & Bernstein, 1997). Developing such success stories is essential.

Collectively, these three concepts form the foundation for creating a prevention approach with the breadth, depth, and quality necessary for maximizing the nurturing potential of both families and communities. This paper is about how these principals come together in the design and implementation of a national initiative to prevent child abuse and other negative outcomes for children. Healthy Families America (HFA) grew out of a recognition that prevention had left the most vulnerable of families behind. It saw that although prevention advocates had generated a plethora of programs, many of these efforts had short shelf lives. Those that survived over time changed focus and intent in response to shifts in funding sources and staff interests. Also, few communities had the service profile necessary to achieve notable change in high-risk families. These failures placed an ever-greater burden on an already overburdened child welfare system. Many families were entering CPS systems because the informal and voluntary services they needed were either unavailable or insufficient to protect children (Besharov, 1986, 1990; National Association of Public Child Welfare Administrators [NAPCWA], 1988). In short, child welfare advocates had been far more successful in crafting programs than they had been in weaving these programs together into coherent and effective systems.

The paper begins by briefly outlining HFA's theory of change and its specific goals and objectives. The paper then summarizes the rationale and structure of HFA's approach for replicating intensive home visitation services and the lessons that have been realized from the initiative's early experiences. Third, the paper examines the inherent dilemma between primary and secondary prevention efforts, and highlights the way in which HFA model hopes to disengage from this dilemma by nesting secondary efforts within a universal system of support. Finally, the paper explores how HFA and similar large-scale prevention efforts can be used to foster significant and lasting changes in health care and child welfare delivery systems.

Healthy Families America: A New Course for Prevention

Central to the development of HFA was the realization that the prior conceptual framework, which governed child abuse prevention efforts, was seriously flawed. Initially, the vast majority of work in this field assumed that the diversified causal factors associated with maltreatment required an equally diversified response system. Community service planners were encouraged to adopt a broad continuum of services to prevent child abuse, each of which was viewed as equally necessary and equally efficacious (Cohn, 1986; Daro, 1988; Helfer, 1982). While promoting this continuum of prevention services was understandable, even logical, it missed an important aspect underlying the theories of maltreatment: child maltreatment arises from both the individual contribution of many causal factors and the combined impacts of these factors on parents' abilities to care for their children. Enhancing one's parental capacity required prevention providers to understand how a diverse array of chronic and acute circumstances might influence a parent's perception of their children, their role as parents and their willingness to change. A prevention imagery that merely suggested a diverse array of service options without also offering explicit strategies on how to integrate these efforts across disciplines and intent proved disappointing to prevention advocates.

In response to this disappointment, the HFA initiative shifted the prevention paradigm from the horizontal to the vertical. It assumes that not all prevention efforts are equal in importance or impact, but rather that prevention efforts are best planned and delivered in a more orderly way, beginning with a strong foundation of support for every mother and child, available when a child is born or a woman is pregnant. Subsequent prevention services such as parent support groups, early childhood education programs, parenting education options, or family counseling services are then integrated into this universal base of support, as necessary, in response to emerging

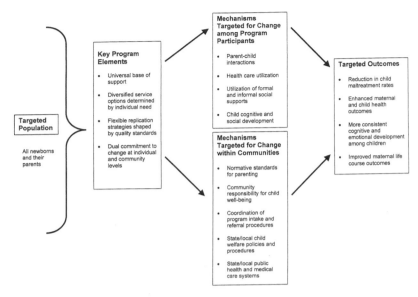

Figure 1. Healthy Families America: Theory of change

needs presented by the growing child or the evolving parent-child relationship.

A key component of this universal foundation is developing strategies that alter both individual parent-child relationships and community systems of support. HFA's theory of change, as described in Figure 1, therefore seeks to expand the availability of high quality, intensive home visitation services, and to create community-wide commitment for these and other services that promote a supportive atmosphere for all new parents. With respect to its efforts to alter individual parenting behaviors, HFA efforts must produce stronger relationships and a sense of mutual reciprocity among families in a given community. Families must come to view HFA not merely as a source of assistance for themselves but also as an opportunity to offer help and guidance to other new parents in their community. Further, to provide adequate assistance to all new parents, HFA efforts must move beyond direct efforts to families and begin to serve as a catalyst for reshaping existing child welfare and health care efforts and improving coordination among other prevention and family support initiatives. To improve individual parental capacity and provide a more supportive environment for parents, the HFA approach suggests effective prevention initiatives require universal availability, diversified levels of support, flexible replication procedures, and a greater integration across multiple service systems and economic sectors. The organizing principal for prevention becomes not the avoidance of a particular set of social dilemmas (e.g., child abuse, substance abuse, juvenile crime, etc.) but rather the establishment of the familial and community conditions conducive to optimal child development.

This vision of prevention efforts has been shaped by several realities:

The most consistent outcomes within the family support field have been realized by programs which have targeted their efforts to new parents during pregnancy or at the time they give birth ((Karoly et al., 1998; Olds & Kitzman, 1993; Ramey & Ramey, 1998).

Emerging research on brain development has underscored the unique and powerful opportunities for cognitive and emotional development presented in a child's first few years of life (Cowan, 1979; Epstein, 1979; Purves, 1994; Schore, 1994).

The potential exists to reach virtually all new parents by the time their children are born due to the high percentage of children delivered in medical facilities and the growing percentage of women in all income groups accessing prenatal care (Forum on Child and Family Statistics, 1997).

Despite our best efforts, child abuse remains a major public health threat to children. Three million children are reported every year as potential victims of maltreatment and at least three children a day, most of whom are under the age of five, die as a result of abuse or neglect (Wang and Daro, 1998).

HFA sought to address many of these limitations by creating a system of support more responsive to emerging political and familial realities than past prevention efforts. Established in 1992 by the National Committee to Prevent Child Abuse with initial financial support from Ronald McDonald House Charities, HFA seeks to establish the infrastructure for a universal system of support for all new parents and to provide high quality, intensive home visitation services efforts for those families facing the greatest challenges. Central to the HFA concept is the systematic, universal assessment of all new parents in a given geographic region to determine their capacity to adequately care for their newborn. The ultimate goal of this process would be to insure that parents had access to needed services, with those facing the greatest challenges being provided the most intensive service options.

To effectively meet the needs of families facing the greatest difficulties, HFA planners drew on the experiences of many in the early childhood and family support fields. These efforts underscored the importance of developing a home visitation component which provided direct services to both the parent and the child, identified multiple and diverse target outcomes, and had sufficient intensity and duration to allow for the development of a strong relationship between provider and participant (Daro, 1988; Kagan, Powell, Weissbournd, & Zigler, 1987; USDHHS, 1991; Weiss & Jacobs, 1988). In addition to providing the building blocks for the program's structure, these data also underscored the importance of nesting HFA's intensive home visitation efforts within the context of a universal system of support. HFA is not about creating 50, 100, or even 1,000 new individual home visitation programs. Rather, the initiative seeks to create the political will to develop and sustain a system of support such that all new parents have the resources they need to care for their children.

How are HFA's design and development different from what prevention advocates have undertaken in the past? Three features distinguish this effort from its predecessors. First, HFA proponents started from a vision of what they wanted to accomplish not what they sought to avoid. While preventing child abuse is certainly of central importance to this effort, equal emphasis is placed on the program achieving a broad array of positive outcomes or conditions for children and their parents. Full immunization and access to health care services, stronger parent-child interactions, more consistent, positive parenting skills, expanded use of informal and formal supports, and higher likelihood for arriving at school ready to learn are among the outcome goals commonly articulated by HFA sites nationwide (Mitchel-Bond & Cohn-Donnelly, 1993).

Second, HFA was conceived as a system built upon partnerships not individual ownership. From the outset, emphasis was placed on creating linkages at both the national and local levels to encourage the joint utilization of resources. The enormity of the goal required that partnerships be built across disciplines as well as economic sectors. While significant public, institutional funding is critical to the sustainability of this effort, private investments are equally essential for establishing an adequate financial base for long-term viability. Private investment also is needed to generate the broad political and normative support central to effecting meaningful systemic change. In promoting this type of shared ownership, HFA planners did not endorse dismantling existing programs in order to create a pool of resources for a new HFA site. Instead the initiative promoted the HFA framework as a way to combine local resources in a new, more efficient manner.

Finally, HFA program development is not a replication of a single model but rather the construction of a local program and overall support system based upon a set of core principles rooted in empirical research and clinical practice. Each community is given substantial flexibility to create the programs and partnerships best suited to its needs within the framework of those elements believed to offer the greatest potential for success. While careful attention is paid to achieving these elements, the HFA approach also emphasizes flexibility at the state and community level. All HFA sites seek compatibility with local needs and existing resources; reflect planning and collaboration among key local public and private agencies and interests; minimize the duplication of effort and maximize the use of scare public resources; and reflect a commitment to empirical research in developing and refining its efforts.

A useful hallmark of the HFA process has been the identification of clear operating goals and objectives that cut across a wide range of functional areas. Current goals include the following:

to ensure that the public knows that HFA is an effective way to prevent child abuse and to mobilize grassroots support for HFA program sites; to ensure HFA's viability by dramatically increasing ongoing funding;
to ensure that all parts of the country can offer in-depth training and quality controls necessary for effective program development and service delivery;
to enhance national, state, and community capacity to build upon and expand existing service networks; and
to produce new insights on the most effective approaches to supporting new parents, as well as how to best achieve the HFA vision within different communities.

These multiple foci—concentrating on the public, professional, legislative and research communities—has created multiple sources of input and influence. Rather than developing the service model or system in isolation from local realities, HFA advocates concentrate on gleaning from a number of sources current best thinking on how to design, promote and deliver the most effective family support services. Collectively these efforts have realized remarkable progress. In 1998 an estimated 33,000 families were enrolled in intensive home visitation services offered by over 300 HFA programs located in 38 states and the District of Columbia. Overall, 53,500 new parents were assessed and provided information on various educational, health and support services (Daro & Winje, 1999). While HFA is not a panacea for all that ails America, it is a promising example of how prevention efforts will need to be structured in the future if they hope to maximize their impacts on families, communities, and social institutions.

Creating Flexible Frameworks

The prevention field is replete with examples of interventions that have achieved notable success with specific target populations. Evidence can be found which supports the efficacy of home visitation services as well as, among others, group-based educational programs, self-help groups, family resource centers, crisis intervention services and respite care nurseries (Daro, 1996; Kagan et al., 1987; Willis et al., 1992). In the past, those interested in establishing a prevention program in their communities would simply seek out these models and attempt to replicate them as perfectly as possible. To their disappointment, such replications often failed to produce the anticipated outcomes due to differences in community context, parental value, or staff expectations and skills (St. Pierre et al., 1997).

The limitations of rigid replication schemes suggest the need for more flexible methods. This is particularly true in the case of child abuse prevention services where values and community standards of care have a powerful impact on what parents view as abusive behaviors and on the acceptance of early intervention and supportive services. In response to this dilemma, HFA's intensive service component was designed around a system of twelve critical elements rather than as a highly specified program model. While allowing flexibility and local decision-making in tailoring services to a community's parent population and service network, the HFA system requires all home visitation programs which adopt the name "HFA" to adhere to these elements.

HFA's 12 critical elements or standards were based upon an extensive review of the family support and early intervention literature. These reviews focused on identifying those service features most commonly associated with positive participant outcomes. Promising programs were compared to determine if they shared any common features in terms of participant characteristics, duration and intensity, or staff qualifications (Daro, 1991). In addition to empirical research, the process also drew upon general theories of parent-child interaction, human development and child maltreatment to suggest ways in which programs could improve their abilities to alter participant attitudes, behaviors, and skills (Bowlby, 1969; Bronfenbrenner, 1979; Steele, 1987).

As indicated in Figure 2, these 12 elements cover 3 broad aspects of program development: service initiation or how families are identified for and engaged in services; service content or how programs are structured; and provider selection and training or how programs are staffed. This section summarizes the empirical base underlying the establishment of these elements and the lessons being learned by HFA planners through the application of these elements in program development.

SERVICE INITIATION

To maximize the impacts of prevention services, the field has long supported the notion of early intervention. Strong theoretical and empirical arguments exist for initiating parenting support services at the time a child is born or early in the mother's pregnancy. Most important is the belief that such early initiation of services facilitates the development of a secure, positive attachment between the parent and child, a cornerstone for later development (Bowlby, 1969; 1973; 1980). Recently, particular attention has been paid to the impact of early attachment on patterns of brain development. "Infants thrive on one-to-one interactions with parents. Sensitive, nurturing parenting is thought to provide infants with a sense of basic trust that allows them to feel confident in exploring the world and forming positive relationships with other children and adults" (Carnegie, 1994, p. 5).

Figure 2. Critical elements for establishing HFA home visitation programs

Service Initiation

- Prevention services need to be initiated prenatally or at the time a baby is born.
- In order to ensure the efficient allocation of resources, programs need to implement a standardized process of assessing the needs of all new parents in their target community.
- Services need to be offered on a voluntary basis and use positive, persistent outreach efforts to build family trust in accepting services.

Service Content

- Services for those families facing the greatest challenges need to be intensive (at least once a week) with well-defined criteria for increasing or decreasing the service intensity.
- Services must be made available to families for an extended period (three to five years) in order to achieve lasting behavioral change.
- Services should be culturally competent such that the staff understands, acknowledges and respects cultural differences among participants; materials used should reflect the cultural, linguistic, racial and ethnic diversity of the population served.
- Services should be comprehensive, focusing on supporting the parent as well as supporting parent-child interaction and child development.
- At a minimum, all families should be linked to a medical provider to assure timely immunizations and well-child care. Depending upon the family's needs, they also may be linked to additional services such as school readiness programs; child care; job training programs; financial, food and housing assistance programs; family support centers; substance abuse treatment programs; and domestic violence shelters.
- Staff should have limited caseloads to assure that home visitors have an adequate amount of time to spend with each family to meet its varying needs and to plan for future activities.

Service Provider Selection and Training

- Service providers will be selected based upon their ability to demonstrate a combination of the requisite personal characteristics

172

MOTIVATION AND CHILD MALTREATMENT

(e.g., being nonjudgmental, empathic, compassionate, possessing the ability to establish a trusting relationship) and knowledge base as represented by a specific academic degree or employment portfolio.

• All service providers must receive intensive, didactic training specific to their roles within the HFA service structure as defined by the critical elements and related standards of best practice.

• Program staff should receive ongoing, effective supervision so that they are able to assist families in realizing their service objectives and protect themselves from stress-related burnout.

By initiating services at birth or earlier, HFA interventions are in a position to help shape the quality of these early interactions.

While disagreement exists as to how soon these attachments are solidified or how fluid they are over time, there is little disagreement that facilitating early, positive interaction between an infant and her parents is a productive vehicle for improving a child's developmental outcomes. Indeed, early intervention efforts have been found to produce significant and substantial impacts on parenting behavior and child health and well being (Daro, 1993; Gutterman, 1997; Karoly et al., 1998; Ramey & Ramey, 1998).

In addition to recognizing the importance of initiating services early, the uneven performance of prevention efforts in terms of their ability to accurately target and engage those families most in need suggested that HFA efforts would have to pay greater attention to crafting participant enrollment strategies. Rather than enrolling only those families who request assistance, HFA's universal assessment process (i.e., systematically examining the parental capacity and strengths of all those giving birth in a particular hospital or geographic area) determines the need for service among a broader, and often more resistant, target population. Enrollment in prevention services is no longer solely contingent upon a parent's ability to identify and access services on their own. Rather, the HFA approach offers the potential to bring prevention services into the homes of those most in need. While services continue to be offered on a voluntary basis, HFA personnel make a concerted effort to provide those families facing the greatest challenges with multiple opportunities to receive home visitation services. Indeed, several examples were noted in the literature which suggested that this type of persistence in providing prevention services did result in successfully engaging a more at-risk population than had previously enrolled in prevention services (Daro, Jones, & McCurdy, 1993; Olds & Kitzman, 1993).

Lessons Learned Regarding Service Initiation Early HFA program experiences have underscored the importance of initiating services at birth or sooner. Several assessments of HFA program operations suggests that those programs initiating contact with mothers in their first or second trimester have greater success in engaging families in intensive services than those who delay first contact until the time of birth (Daro and Harding, 1999). Consequently, HFA program managers are expanding their partnerships with pre-natal clinics rather than predominately relying upon assessing new parents in the hospital at the time of birth.

In contrast, early evidence on the success of aggressive outreach methods has been somewhat disappointing. While HFA outreach methods are resulting in a greater percentage of high-risk families being identified and offered service, these methods are not as successful as had been hoped in engaging those at highest risk. Even after months of repeated attempts to engage families in intensive services, HFA evaluators are finding that somewhere between 20 and 30% of those families targeted for service fail to utilize the program. These retention rates are comparable to other early intervention programs that have targeted similar populations and, therefore, may not indicate a unique performance difficulty (Gueron & Pauly, 1991; Johnson & Walker, 1991; Quint, Polit, Bos, & Cave, 1994; St. Pierre et al., 1995). They do, however, raise serious questions about the ability of voluntary efforts to provide sufficient coverage of the at-risk population such that measurable change in aggregate indicators of distress is achieved. Further, research presented in the following section has found that a significant percentage of families who presented no indication of stress at the time they gave birth, faced significant parenting challenges by the time their children were six and twelve months of age. Current HFA assessment procedures are not only failing to engage a sufficient percentage of those they target, they apparently also are excluding from services families in need of assistance. Collectively, these experiences suggest the need to reform HFA enrollment procedures. They also underscore the importance of nesting these efforts in a broader array of services designed to provide some support to all new parents. Strategies for accomplishing this change are discussed in the following section on universal access.

SERVICE CONTENT

The past 15 years have seen a tremendous growth in the number and quality of evaluative efforts in the family support field (Daro, 1988; Halpern, 1984; Weiss & Jacobs, 1988). Although this research is far from perfect (Azar, 1988; Howing, Wodarski, Kurtz, & Gaudin, 1989), they did offer HFA planners useful guidelines in articulating a home visitation program profile more likely to produce positive outcomes. Useful guidance was found in the areas of program duration, intensity, and sensitivity to unique cultural differences.

While short term interventions have achieved certain gains with program participants, it is widely thought that achieving lasting behavioral changes with parents facing multiple challenges requires extended interventions (Daro, 1988; Ramey & Ramey, 1998; Schorr, 1997). A number of the most promising home-based as well as center-based programs provide services for one to two years (Ellwood, 1988; Lutzker & Rice 1984, 1987; Olds, Henderson, Chamberline, & Tatelbaum, 1986). Further, at least three longitudinal studies suggest not only that comprehensive parenting services provided over two years produce initial gains but also that these gains are strengthened over time. (Olds et al., 1997; Seitz, Rosenbaum, & Apfel, 1985; Wiedner, Poisson, Lourie, & Greenspan, 1988). Areas showing improvement include parenting skills, parent-child relationships, educational achievement, employment rates, and economic well being (Daro, 1993; Karoly et al., 1998; Ramey & Ramey, 1998).

Maximizing the impacts of HFA services also requires that home visiting be seen not merely as a direct service but as a gateway to myriad other therapeutic, remedial, and supportive services (Daro, 1988; National Vaccine Advisory Committee, 1991; Olds & Kitsman, 1993). At a minimum, early intervention efforts targeting families at greater risk need to adopt an integrated view of the parenting process (Belsky & Vondra, 1990: Sameroff & Chandler, 1975; Sandler, 1979). Specifically, preventing child abuse requires that service providers seek gains in at least three areas—the parent's development as both person and parent; the child's cognitive, emotional, and social development;

and the positive and strong development of the parent-child relationship. Services essential to enhancing parental capacity include knowledge and skills in the areas of child development, discipline, and child management. Beyond focusing on the parenting process, home visitors have the opportunity to connect program participants to such personal and basic services as food, housing, educational assistance, job training, and health care. Because no single program can directly provide this broad continuum of service, achieving this diversification relies upon the ability of each HFA program site to cultivate partnerships with a variety of local services. This strategy requires program managers to reach across disciplines, drawing on the expertise and resources found in both public institutions such as educational, health, welfare and economic development, as well as private, community-based service agencies.

Beyond the duration and scope of an intervention, success is also influenced by the provider-participant ratio. Limited caseloads offer the potential for direct service providers to be more responsive to each program participant (Edelwich & Brodsky, 1980; Frankel, 1988; Leeds, 1984). Such responsiveness is particularly essential when one is working with multi-problem families in which new service needs may emerge without advance warning. Simply put, limited caseloads allow home visitors to spend more time with each family. This additional time encourages the development of strong relationships between home visitors and the families receiving services, a relationship that is essential for high quality intervention (Berlin, O'Neal & Brooks-Gunn, 1998; Brazelton, 1992; Wasik, Bryant, & Lyons, 1990).

Finally, the battle for culturally competent social services is long-standing in this country, particularly when services seek to change behaviors as personal and culturally determined as parenting. Efforts to provide services to children and families that are sensitive and responsive to their needs and adaptive strengths have their roots in the late 1800's (Specht & Courtney, 1994; Wasik et al., 1990). The "friendly visitor" programs established by the Charity Organization Societies (COS) during this period were designed to provide not charity but rather an individual who would establish a relationship with families. While these early visitors were rarely from the same culture or socio-economic group as the program's recipients, pioneers in this field such as Mary Richmond and Jane Addams believed that an important part of solving an individual's problem lay in understanding the person and his or her situation (Specht & Courtney). The success of the settlement house was due, at least in part, to the fact that service providers appreciated the families' "indigenous language and cultures, specifically their behavioral norms, rituals, and routines, that is, their agreed-upon shared ways of behaving within constituted family and community groups" (Slaughter-Defoe, 1993, p.175).

Achieving a culturally competent service system requires service providers and agency administrators to acknowledge that cultural differences as well as similarities exist within the population and that such differences are value free. The process requires practitioners to be aware of the cultures represented among their caseload, to understand the basic parameters of these cultures, and to recognize that cultural diversity will affect a family's participation in service delivery (Anderson & Fenichel, 1989). Under this conceptualization, the systematic application of protocols governing appropriate parent-child interaction or standards of child care, for example, stand in sharp contrast to a service delivery system which encourages providers to place the information provided to a participant within the context of the participant's cultural perceptions of appropriate parent-child interactions.

Lessons Learned Regarding Service Content HFA programs have embraced the philosophical and programmatic features outlined in this set of critical elements. Unlike the diversity observed in the manner in which programs are identifying and engaging participants, HFA providers are consistently offering home visits in an intensive manner; responding to the cultural realities present among their target populations; providing a variety of modeling and direct service options to parents in order to enhance their ability to better meet their own needs and those of their children; and offering service referrals for the full range of health, social, educational and economic needs facing the families with whom they work. On balance caseloads have remained limited, even if this has meant that individual programs have had to close intakes for a period of time in order to avoid staff overload.

The critical planning question facing the HFA initiative, however, is not whether programs follow these critical elements but rather if these elements are necessary to achieve the array of outcomes targeted by HFA services. On this point, available data is less clear.

With respect to duration, a sizable percentage of program participants are leaving the program within one year of enrollment. This pattern raises questions as to the optimal service period. While some parents may indeed require consistent intervention for three to five years, others may have their needs adequately addressed in a six to twelve month time period. Also, programs are reporting that some number of families exit and reenter the program based upon their evolving needs or desire for assistance. Greater attention should be paid to the potential implications of these "revolving door" users on the program's overall intent. If the program is utilized in this manner, does it evolve into more of a crisis management intervention rather than an intervention truly able to empower families to move toward self-sufficiency and competent decision making? On the other hand, the crisis nature of the target population suggests that ongoing access may be a necessary condition for ensuring a child's safety or a parent's ability to meet their parenting responsibilities. Some families simply may never be secure enough to manage without access to external support, however temporal. Rather than establish an absolute ideal duration period, HFA interventions may need to balance optimal duration against participant characteristics and program goals.

Second, much remains to be learned in the area of cultural competence. The absence of significant empirical research on service impacts for families from different racial and cultural backgrounds limits the discussion of best practice standards with these populations (Cross, Bazron, Dennis & Isaacs, 1989; Garbarino, Cohn & Ebota, 1982; Mann, 1990). While practitioners most certainly need to be cognizant of the differences in family life and parenting responsibilities among people of color, it remains unclear if such differences demand unique intervention systems. For example, a recent evaluation of child abuse prevention services targeting adolescent parents found no significant differences in outcomes by the participant's race. Afro-American and White teens responded equally well (and equally poorly) to the various interventions tested. Age (i.e., 16 years of age or under and over 16) and the initial point of service delivery (i.e., pregnant or post-birth) were far more accurate predictors of participant outcomes than race (Daro et al., 1993). Even though these findings are far from conclusive, they suggest that the relationship between cultural competency and program outcomes require further study. Creating culturally sensitive or relevant programming may not require the development of unique interventions. Achieving this standard may rest in refining the service delivery process in ways not yet defined in the literature.

Third, HFA's intensive home visitation programs appear best at strengthening parent-child interactions (Daro & Harding, 1999 Daro, McCurdy, & Harding, 1998). Less solid evidence of progress is found in the areas of enhancing social support and improving a child's developmental outcomes. In part, the absence of significant gains in these areas might reflect the limited time period during which these programs have worked with families. Altering a child's developmental trajectory or solidifying social networks may well require multiple years of directed intervention. On the other hand, home visitation, in and of itself, may not be the most effective strategy to accomplish a broad array of outcomes. While working with parents within their home may offer an excellent method to improve parent-child interactions, other goals may require that participants be referred to other interventions and service delivery systems.

SERVICE PROVIDER SELECTION AND TRAINING

The ultimate success of a personalized intervention such as home visitation hinges upon the direct service provider's capabilities. These individuals are, in the minds of many recipients, the program itself. In a comprehensive evaluation of prevention services in the Greater Philadelphia area, relationships with specific service providers were the most frequently cited benefit of service enrollment (Daro et al., 1993). To the extent HFA hopes to provide the framework for a new universal system of support for new parents, ensuring the hiring of highly qualified personnel and the ongoing training and supervision of this work force is paramount.

Research regarding the critical characteristics of direct service personnel consistently identifies the most effective provider as one who posses the knowledge and interpersonal skills necessary to successfully engage families in the intervention as well as to assist families in mastering a core set of skills (Halpern & Larner, 1987; Wasik, 1993). For example, providers identified as having the greatest success in engaging families and altering parental practices have the following characteristics: an active interest in new ideas; an active interest in people and an ability to engage people socially; an ability to accept people's life situations without prejudging them; an ability to relate to a family's experiences without becoming enmeshed in the family's problem cycles; and relative stability in his or her own personal life (Halpern & Larner; Wasik, 1993). These characteristics appear particularly essential in working with teenage parents. An analysis of provider attitudes in at least one teen parent program found that a staff member's expectations played a significant role in the extent to which material was accurately presented to the teen and the extent to which the teen responded in a positive manner (Musick, Bernstein, Percansky & Stott, 1987).

In addition to having knowledge and an interpersonal skill set that prepares them for their role, HFA home visitors also must receive formal training to develop the knowledge and skills necessary to assure compliance with all aspects of the program's critical elements. Research on child abuse prevention efforts and other home visitation models suggests a variety of appropriate staff training objectives. For example, Wasik (1993) recommends that home visitor training programs cover six areas: history of home visiting, philosophy of home visiting, knowledge and skills of the helping process, knowledge of families and children, knowledge and skills specific to programs, and knowledge and skills specific to communities. This array of skills underscores the importance of offering providers a context for understanding the potential and limitations of the intervention. By offering providers background on the history of home visitation and its commitment to personalized interventions, home visitors are better able to apply their skills to a diverse array of circumstances.

Supervision of direct service personnel is a recommended practice in all disciplines. At a minimum, regular supervision ensures that best practice standards are being accurately implemented and that direct service personnel receive the support they need to avoid frustration and burnout. Further, the emotional intensity of home visitation services and the fact that such services are provided in isolation makes supervision in the case of HFA programs particularly critical (Wasik et al., 1990). Supervision in these cases becomes a way of ensuring that staff and program participants establish and sustain a mutually satisfying relationship in which families receive the support and direction they desire and program staff maintain a sense of accomplishment.

Lessons Learned Regarding Provider Selection and Training Insuring comprehensive training opportunities has been a critical component of the HFA initiative. HFA national staff have sponsored nine "train the trainer" institutes, providing local sites with more than 45 individuals to provide guidance to HFA program managers and direct service personnel. In addition, HFA, through its national partners, has created an even greater pool of resources for local sites, thereby expanding the topics and approaches available to programs as they seek to find the training methods best suited to their staff and participant characteristics. This type of flexibility is essential if HFA is to provide the range of choices necessary to meet the diverse needs of its growing network of providers.

While expanding the range of training options available for program staff is an important feature of HFA's development, equally important is ensuring that the training offered program managers and direct service personnel is of the highest quality and adheres to the principals outlined in the program's critical elements. To this end, several challenges face national planners. These issues include:

rigorous review of the underlying values of staff with respect to the target population, particularly when the target population is engaged in an activity some may view as inappropriate (e.g. teen parents, substance abusing parents, etc.);

initial and ongoing training of staff with respect to program goals and objectives;

ongoing staff supervision and support, allowing staff multiple opportunities to raise issues surrounding the delivery of service; and

continuous reassessment to ensure that the staffing pattern selected for a given program represents the most viable solution given personnel skills and participant needs.

The next generation of direct service training will be less focused on the transfer of specific information and more focused on assisting staff in adapting a given body of knowledge to a family's specific needs. This concept is far more difficult but essential if the HFA commitment to allowing flexibility in service implementation is to succeed. To maximize their impacts with program participants, home visitors will need to be skilled in adopting visit protocols to reflect a parent's specific needs and abilities. In the absence of this skill, it seems unlikely a model built on the premise of flexibility can sustain a high level of quality.

SUMMARY COMMENTS

Requiring programs to adhere to all 12 critical elements maintains a commitment to quality while allowing flexibility in local service implementation. The specific elements outlined above were selected at the onset of the HFA initiative because they represented those indicators most frequently associated in the literature with positive participant outcomes. As HFA program sites mature and the knowledge base as to their effectiveness increases, revising some elements appears prudent. New thinking is particularly needed in the area of initial assessment, participant engagement and retention, service duration, service referrals, and advanced staff training. None of these changes suggest the current course of action was wrong or misguided. Rather, this process underscores the importance of programs and national initiatives remaining open to changes in light of emerging research and practice realities. Maintaining this commitment to flexibility is one aspect of HFA's evolution that will enhance its long-term viability and, ultimately, its success.

Achieving Universal Access

Beyond the issue of program structure, prevention advocates also must carefully consider how best to target their efforts to potential participants. Predicting future parenting behavior is a complex, and some would argue, impossible task (Starr, 1982). Despite such dire claims, numerous theoretical models exist which suggest that certain personal (Steele, 1987), familial (Straus & Kantor, 1987) and environmental factors (Garbarino, 1988) contribute to an elevated risk for maltreatment or, at a minimum, to poor parenting.

While such frameworks are useful in accurately predicting *groups* to be at an elevated risk for negative outcomes, misclassification of specific *individuals* is common (Browne, Davies, & Stratton, 1988). Risk assessment protocols and other screening devices used to determine access to child welfare services routinely identify individuals or families at risk who do not develop abusive or neglectful behaviors and fail to identify some individuals and families who later are involved in serious maltreatment (Cicchinelli, 1995; McDonald

& Marks, 1991; Murphy-Berman, 1994). In assessing the failure of these systems, many have argued that little empirical evidence exists which consistently ties any one variable or any combination of factors directly to poor parenting. Rather, it appears that any particular risk factor associated with negative outcomes for children is but one dimension of the total picture. Further, the evolving nature of human development and the changing demands of parenting as a child matures makes it highly unlikely that a single point risk assessment will be reliable over time. While the key to prediction may indeed be in understanding the interplay among individual skills, stressful events and social structure, determining a family's given status on these factors over time would require a level of personal surveillance intolerable in a free society.

As illustrated in Figure 3, the absence of perfect predictive capabilities is one of the most compelling reasons behind the expansion of universal, primary prevention. Since it is believed that most parents will fall victim to one or more risk factors over the course of their childrearing years, making educational and support services, including home visitation, available to all new parents has substantial theoretical appeal. This type of service delivery system also avoids the issue of stigmatization, a common criticism of secondary prevention. Though one might want to provide universal services, this strategy has its own set of limitations. While challenges to one's parenting abilities may indeed be universal, the level of risk and the need for service is not. All families may need some assistance, but some families most certainly need more intensive and long-standing support than others do. Any universal system, which provided the same, limited number of service contacts would not address the needs of multi-problem families. And universal services that provide intensive support to all families would represent an inefficient and overly costly intervention.

Since its inception, the HFA initiative has struggled over how best to structure services such that those families most in need of support have access to and enroll in prevention services. While most involved in HFA planning believe it is useful to include a comprehensive and consistent assessment of the challenges facing new parents as part of the model, there is no consensus as to how best to accomplish this task. This section of the paper reviews the procedures currently being used by the majority of HFA program sites to identify program participants, reports on recent research conducted by NCPCA to ex-

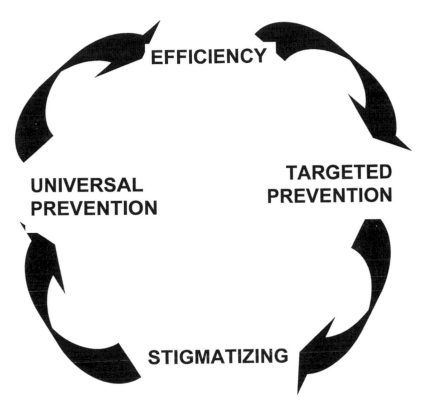

Figure 3. Prevention's circular debate

amine the validity of this approach, and outlines a possible alternative assessment strategy.

THE CURRENT ASSESSMENT APPROACH

HFA programs incorporate a two-part participant identification process pioneered by the Hawaii Healthy Start program (Breakey & Pratt, 1991; Mitchel-Bond & Cohn-Donnelly, 1993). The first stage involves a thorough review of the new mother's hospital records. This record screen consists of 15 items covering *demographic and socioeconomic factors* (e.g., marital status, educational level, employment status, income, stability of current living conditions, and access to a telephone); *current social contacts and emotional health* (e.g. extent of emergency contacts or family supports, late or limited prenatal care, an unsuccessful abortion attempt for present birth, attempts to place the child up for adoption, or marital or family problems); and *history of distress* (e.g., history of substance abuse, history of psychiatric care, history of abortions, history of depression). HFA assessment staff review hospital records for all new births to families residing in the program's catchment area on a regular basis, scoring each item as present, not present, or unable to assess due to missing or incomplete case records. A new mother is referred to the second stage of the assessment process if she is single; received late or no prenatal care; considered abortion for the present birth; or had a positive score on any 2 of the 15 items. If the case record is incomplete such that the majority of items cannot be assessed through the record screen, the mother also will be referred for an in-person interview. Approximately 60% of all new births are determined not to require additional services based upon this screening process.

The second risk assessment screen involves an in-person interview of the mother and partner, if possible, by HFA personnel. This interview, generally conducted in the hospital, is structured around the Family Stress Checklist (Murphy, Orkow, & Nicola, 1985). The checklist allows interviewers to summarize, in a standardized manner, each parent's response to ten risk factors: parental history of abuse as a child; parental history of criminal behavior, substance abuse or mental illness; prior parental contact with child protective services involving charges of child maltreatment; current low self-esteem, social isolation or depression; current multiple crises or stresses; violent outbursts between partners; rigid or unrealistic child expectations; belief in harsh punishment for a child; perception of the child as provocative or difficult; and parental ambivalence about the baby. Staff is trained to follow a structured interview format and clear guidelines are provided for scoring the respondent's statements. In each area, respondents are assigned a "0" if no risk is present, a "5" if a mild risk is present, and a "10" if a severe risk is present. If either the mother or her partner score over 20 on the FSC, the family is offered intensive home visitation services. About 50% of those families interviewed, or 20% of all births originally screened, are being offered HFA services around the country.

Evidence regarding the efficacy of this participant identification process included an early reliability study of the Family Stress Checklist (Murphy et al., 1985); a preliminary examination of the hospital screening tool's ability to identify families who would most likely be screened out after an in-person assessment (Stannard, 1988); and repeated comparisons of reported cases of maltreatment between those classified as high risk and those classified as low risk (Hawaii Department of Health, Maternal & Child Health Branch, 1992). In each case, the results supported the continued use of the existing system. Limitations in the design and scope of these prior studies, however, underscored the need for additional research. While these initial studies found the Healthy Start screening system a useful strategy for targeting services to a population facing initial challenges in providing for their children's well-being, it was unclear how well the system retained its validity over time. No systematic analysis had been done on how the level of risk for maltreatment varies as families faced new situations or challenges due to changes in the family structure or the child's developmental needs. Further, the only outcome measure assessed over time had been the rate at which the nonserved population was reported for maltreatment. This strategy is, at best, a crude indicator of success. The absence of a child abuse or neglect report cannot be equated with nonabusive or appropriate parenting (Olds, Henderson, Kitzman, & Cole, 1995). More specific observations of parent-child interactions and knowledge about both parents' skills and behaviors would be needed to determine if a nurturing relationship existed.

THE NCPCA RESEARCH

To address these and related questions, the federal National Center on Child Abuse and Neglect funded the NCPCA to conduct a randomized trial of Hawaii's Healthy Start program and evaluate the program's risk assessment system (Daro, McCurdy, & Harding, 1998). The risk assessment study sample involved a randomly selected group of 150 families, half of whom were screened out of service based upon the hospital check list (theoretically a "no risk" group) and half of whom were screened out of service based upon their score on the Family Stress Checklist (a theoretically "low risk" group). These families were interviewed and assessed using a variety of standardized measures when their infant turned both six months and one year of age. Measures included the Child Abuse Potential Inventory (Milner, 1987, 1989); the Michigan Screening Profile of

Parenting (Helfer, Hoffmeister & Schneider, 1978); Nursing Child Assessment Satellite Training (Barnard, 1978; Barnard, Hammond, Booth, Bee, Mitchell, & Spieker, 1989); the HOME Inventory (Caldwell & Bradley, 1984); and Maternal Social Support Index (Pascoe, Ialongo, Horn, Trinhart, & Perradatto,1998).

The study sought to address two specific aspects of the risk assessment problem—the ability of the program to accurately screen out families who are at limited risk, or at least, lower risk than the families whom they engage in services and the stability of a family's risk for maltreatment over time. Specifically, the study was designed to address the following hypotheses:

Families screened out of the program through the hospital record review process (theoretically, a "no risk" group) would have lower risk scores on standardized measures of child abuse potential than those families screened out on the basis of a personal interview (a "low risk" group).

Variation in risk levels as measured by scores on all measures would exist over time among families in both groups.

Families not offered home visitation will have more positive scores on standardized measures of child abuse potential and other indicators of family well being than families qualifying for Healthy Start services.

THE FINDINGS

Descriptive Characteristics A total of 96 women, or 49% of the original respondent pool, was interviewed at both 6 and 12 months post birth. There were no significant differences between these 96 participants and those that declined or were unavailable to be interviewed at both data points. Consequently, this sample is representative of the types of families generally excluded from Healthy Start services. Over two-thirds of the sample screened out of services were not on public assistance and most had annual household incomes of at least $25,000. Over 90% of those screened out of service had completed high school and over half attended college. The majority of those deemed ineligible for home visitation services were married (65%). Over half of the women not receiving services worked outside the home at the time they delivered their children. These women were, on average, 26.7 years of age and had, on average, 1.87 children. For those participants who were screened out of services based upon the Family Stress Checklist, no significant difference was found between the mother's total average score for those participating in the study and those who refused (t = -.98, p = .84, d.f. 100). Similarly, no significant difference between the two groups was found in the father's average score on this measure (t = 1.60, p = .11, d.f. 43).

Table 1 summarizes the descriptive characteristics for the present sample, dividing the group into those who were screened out of service based upon the hospital record screen (defined in this study as the "no risk" group) and those screened out of service based upon the Family Stress Checklist (defined in this study as the "low risk" group). As this table indicates, significant differences between these two groups existed on all but one (i.e., number of children) of the descriptive variables tested. Reflecting the structure of the hospital record screen, the "low risk" group included a significantly higher percentage of low-income families and public aid recipients. The women in the low risk group were more likely to be single (almost half had never been married), to have terminated their education at high school and to be unemployed. On average, the participants in the low risk group were almost six years younger than the no risk participants, although both groups had approximately the same average number of children (1.92 versus 1.82).

Variation in Personal Functioning Table 2 presents the 6 and 12 month average scores and range recorded on the study's standardized measures for each risk group. For purposes of comparison, this table also includes the comparable scores on these measures recorded by participants enrolled in the control group for the study's randomized trial. Following the logic of the assessment process, one would anticipate that the control group sample would perform more poorly on all of the study's standardized measures, reflecting their perceived higher risk for maltreatment. As this table illustrates, the hospital record screen appears to successful direct program resources to those families presently at relatively higher risk for maltreatment. Families screened out of service by the hospital record review process presented very few initial or subsequent difficulties in any of the domains tested. In addition, as a group, they appeared to have improved in most areas over the one-year observation period. Qualitative data reported elsewhere supports these patterns, particularly with respect

Table 1. *Study Participants: Descriptive Characteristics by Subgroup*

Variable	No Risk Sample[a]		Low Risk Sample[b]	
	%	n	%	n
Annual Household Income				
Under $15,000	2.4	1	17.9	7
$15,000–$24,999	14.3	6	17.9	7
$25,000 and over	76.2	32	38.5	15
Not Known	7.1	3	25.6	10
$X^2=14,00^{**}$ d.f. 4	100	42	100	39
Public Assistance				
Yes	14.0	7	47.8	22
No	82.0	41	50.0	23
Unknown	4.0	2	2.2	1
$X^2=13.01^{**}$ d.f. 3	100	50	100	46
Marital Status				
Married	96.0	48	30.4	14
Separated/Divorced	4.0	2	4.3	2
Cohabitating	-	-	17.4	8
Never Married	-	-	47.8	22
$X^2=48.56^{**}$ d.f. 4	100	50	100	46
Educational Level				
Less than High School	2.0	1	2.2	1
Some High School	2.0	1	10.9	5
High School Graduate	26.0	13	47.8	22
More than High School	70.0	35	39.1	18
$X^2=10.29^{**}$ d.f. 5	100	50	100	46
Employment Status				
Employed	68.0	34	39.1	18
Unemployed	32.0	16	60.9	28
Not Known	-	-	-	-
$X^2=8.04^{**}$ d.f. 2	100	50	100	46
Age				
Mean		29.5		23.8
(Standard Deviation)		(5.36)		(4.78)
n=		50		46
$t=5.50^{***}$ d.f. 94				
Number of Children				
Mean		1.92		1.82
(Standard Deviation)		(1.14)		(1.23)
n=		50		46
$t=.39$ d.f. 94				

[a]No risk includes those families screened out of services by the hospital checklist
[b]Low risk includes those families screened out of services by the Family Stress Checklist
Significance Levels: ***$p<.001$ **$p<.01$

to the types of discipline practices reported by these respondents. On balance, parents in this group were more likely than parents in the low risk sample to implement time out and other nonaggressive behavior modification strategies in managing their children's actions (Daro, McCurdy, & Harding, 1998).

In contrast, the targeting benefits of the Family Stress Checklist are less clear. While the FSC does appear to have concurrent validity (i.e., identifies a population at higher risk at the point of birth), our data suggest the predictive validity of the measure diminishes over time. As summarized in Table 2, the low risk group's mean scores moved closer over time to the control group's mean scores in virtually all areas tested. With the exception of the CAP, scores on all other measures parallel the control group's performance. Minimal differences existed between those screened into or out of the program based upon their FSC scores. This similarity in performance again was supported by the study's qualitative data. While notable percentages of participants in both risk categories reported a number of external stresses during the one year observation period, a higher proportion of participants in the low risk group reported legal difficulties, a decrease in their perceived and actual levels of social support, and a greater need to use physical discipline in modifying their child's behavior. Indeed, participants in the low risk group were three times more likely than parents in the no risk group to indicate that they had "slapped or hit" their one- year-old to control his or her behavior (Daro, McCurdy, & Harding, 1998).

Specificity (False Positives) Limited resources and the negative consequences of being labeled a potential child abuser suggests that caution is warranted in utilizing a risk assessment strategy which might inappropriately classify a sizable number of individuals at risk for maltreatment. In order to examine the extent to which the Healthy Start risk assessment system correctly identified specific individuals as being in need of service, we compared the specific scores individuals in the randomized trial's control group received on the study's various assessment measures to the average scores recorded for the "low risk" participants in the risk assessment study. We elected to focus on the average scores of the low risk group as the point of comparison because of the demographic similarities between this group and those in the randomized trial. This method allowed us

Table 2. *Mean Scores on Study Measures*

Variable	No Risk Sample[a]	Low Risk Sample[b]	Control Group[c]
Child Abuse Potential Inventory			
Mean 6 month (s.d.)	65.08 (61.53)	88.07 (66.11)	139.4 (85.1)
Range	2-278	5-255	15-290
n=	50	46	102
t=-1.76[d] d.f. 94			
Mean 12 month (s.d.)	66.40 (67.63)	82.67 (70.89)	129.3 (88.7)
Range	0-273	4-341	20-320
n=	50	46	102
t=-1.15[d] d.f. 94			
HOME Inventory			
Mean 6 month (s.d.)	36.49 (4.94)	35.17 (5.72)	30.5 (5.4)
Range	19-42	22-45	20-45
n=	35	41	126
t=1.06[d] d.f. 74			
Mean 12 month (s.d.)	39.41 (4.29)	35.03 (7.61)	34.2 (5.9)
Range	26-45	19-45	18-45
n=	37	36	101
t=3.04**[d] d.f. 71			
NCAST Feeding Scale			
Mean Parent—6 month (s.d.)	41.87 (4.63)	35.95 (7.27)	37.1 (6.6)
Range	32-50	21-48	20-51
n=	31	40	126
t=3.95***[d] d.f. 69			
Mean Parent—12 month (s.d.)	42.36 (5.30)	35.84 (7.86)	38.3 (8.5)
Range	29-50	18-49	15-50
n=	33	31	101
t=3.91***[d] d.f. 62			
Mean Child—6 month (s.d.)	21.16 (3.72)	18.97 (4.99)	19.4 (4.3)
Range	12-16	10-26	6-26
n=	31	40	126
t=2.04**[d] d.f. 69			
Mean Child—12 month (s.d.)	22.57 (2.88)	18.97 (5.28)	20.1 (3.7)
Range	14-26	4-25	8-25
n=	33	31	101
t=3.42***[d] d.f. 62			
Maternal Social Support Index			
Mean 6 month (s.d.)	26.72 (5.23)	24.90 (4.61)	22.8 (5.1)
Range	15-34	15-32	10-30
n=	36	42	126
t=1.63[d] d.f. 76			
Mean 12 month (s.d.)	27.41 (4.63)	25.11 (4.36)	22.8 (5.6)
Range	17-38	14-32	10-30
n=	37	37	104
t=2.20**[d] d.f. 72			

Continued

Table 2. *Mean Scores on Study Measures*

Variable	No Risk Sample[a]	Low Risk Sample[b]	Control Group[c]
Michigan Screening Profile of Parenting			
Expectations for Children			
Mean 6 month (s.d.)	5.10 (1.87)	5.12 (1.56)	4.5 (1.8)
Range	1-7	1-5	1-6
n=	41	46	126
t=.06[d] d.f. 85			
Mean 12 month (s.d.)	4.88 (1.89)	4.91 (1.85)	
Range	1-7	1-7	n.a.
n=	40	38	
t=.08[d] d.f. 76			
Relationship with Parents			
Mean 6 month (s.d.)	2.54 (1.83)	2.17 (1.65)	2.9 (1.9)
Range	1-7	1-7	(1-7)
n=	41	46	126
t=-1.02[d] d.f. 85			
Mean 12 month (s.d.)	2.38 (1.61)	2.21 (1.71)	
Range	1-7	1-7	n.a.
n=	40	38	
t=-.44[d] d.f. 76			
Coping Skills			
Mean 6 month (s.d.)	2.66 (1.84)	2.89 (1.82)	3.6 (1.9)
Range	1-7	1-7	(1-7)
n=	41	46	126
t=.62[d] d.f. 85			
Mean 12 month (s.d.)	2.13 (1.61)	2.55 (1.76)	
Range	1-7	1-7	n.a.
n=	39	38	
t=1.11[d] d.f. 76			
Emotional Needs Met			
Mean 6 month (s.d.)	1.95 (1.58)	1.90 (1.06)	2.5 (1.5)
Range	1-7	1-4	(1.6)
n=	34	39	126
t=-.18[d] d.f. 85			
Mean 12 month (s.d.)	1.46 (.84)	1.74 (1.06)	
Range	1-5	1-5	n.a.
n=	28	26	
t=1.08[d] d.f. 76			

[a]No risk includes those families screened out of service based upon the hospital checklist.
[b]Low risk includes those families screened out of service based upon the Family Stress checklist.
[c]Control—although qualifying for Healthy Start services at the time their babies were born, these families were randomly assigned to the randomized trial's control group and, therefore, did not receive the intervention.
[d]All t-tests results refer to the difference between the no risk and low risk sample scores.
Significance Levels: ***p<.001 **p<.01 p<.05

to control for any potential cultural and socio-economic biases that may be reflected in our pool of assessment instruments.

The percentage of randomized trial participants presenting risk profiles less serious than those enrolled in the risk assessment study was substantial. Depending upon the specific measure, one-quarter to two-thirds of the participants in the randomized trial's control group demonstrated *less risk* than the average parent screened out of service based upon the FSC at the time they gave birth. In the case of the HOME and CAP, the proportion of control group participants performing better than the average low risk participant increased over time. Looking across all of the measures, approximately one-quarter of the control group participants presented less relative risk on at least half of the scales utilized in this study at both the six and twelve month assessment points. Contrary to expectations, the FSC is not uniformly channeling services to those at greatest risk for poor parenting. Indeed, as many as one in four of families identified by their FSC score as "high risk" appear to fare better over time than the average family not offered the intervention based upon their relatively low FSC score.

Sensitivity (False Negatives) While issues of efficiency and individual liberties suggest concern with an assessment's specificity, child welfare concerns demand careful attention to an assessment's sensitivity, or its ability to correctly identify those parents who might abuse or neglect their child. The field is replete with examples of judgment errors that resulted in a child being retained in or returned to an abusive environment. For prevention efforts to have maximum impact, it is critical that they capture as large a percentage as possible of those parents facing various socio-economic or emotional challenges. Indeed, for many in the prevention field, providing services to those who may not need them is considered far less a concern than failing to provide early intervention services to a potentially abusive parent.

To explore the extent to which the Healthy Start risk assessment system missed families at risk, we examined how individuals in the no risk and low risk groups performed over time on the study's battery of assessment tools. Individuals were classified as being at risk for maltreatment if their score exceeded the accepted norm for the measure (e.g., above the 166 cut-off point for abuse on the CAP) or reflected a more negative score than had been true for the average participant in the randomized trial.

Approximately 10% of the risk assessment group recorded CAP scores above the 166 abuse cut-off score at both the 6 month and 12 month assessment points. Using the average score of the control group participants as the indicator of relative risk, the percentage of risk assessment participants presenting a more elevated level of distress was 16% at the 6 month assessment and 20% at the one year assessment. Of those scoring at the highest end of the CAP scale, half scored in excess of 214, an indication of very high risk for physical abuse, at both assessment points (Milner, 1986). Interestingly, these highest risk cases were not limited to participants in the low-risk study sample. While a greater proportion of the low-risk versus no-risk sample presented elevated CAP scores at the six-month period, these proportions were essentially equal at the one-year assessment. Further, those participants scoring above 214 on the CAP were equally divided between the two risk assessment samples, suggesting that the small percentage of parents at highest risk for physical abuse may be more equally distributed across the socio-economic spectrum than is often assumed (Drake & Zuravin, 1998). Focusing solely on those families with the most obvious demographic markers will inevitably lead to a system which may miss a small but very high risk population.

In contrast to the CAP findings, the proportion of study participants presenting higher levels of risk than the average participant in the control group across the other measures utilized in this study followed a more predictable and anticipated path. Overall, the percentage of risk assessment participants performing more poorly than the average control group member ranged from a low of 16% on the six month HOME to a high of 63% on the MSPP subscale relating to a parent's expectations for her child. In all but one case, a higher proportion of the low-risk sample presented elevated risk than did the no-risk group. The magnitude of these differences, however, varied greatly across the measures, with the greatest differences in the two groups being observed on the one-year NCAST, HOME and MSSI. These patterns underscore the findings discussed initially regarding the tendency of participants in the no risk group to improve over time while participants in the low risk group remained stable or declined.

On balance, these findings raise the spectra that a significant proportion of families screened out of service present, over time, as high or higher risk profile as the average family deemed eligible for Healthy Start services at the time they give birth. Indeed, looking across all of the measures utilized in this study, 46% of the full risk assessment sample scored more poorly than the average control participant on at least half of the assessment measures administered at 6 months. At 12 months, this percentage dropped to 28% primarily due to the fact that the MSPP, which had the highest percentage of risk assessment participants performing more poorly than the controls, was not administered at this assessment period. While there was no statistically significant difference in the proportion of those scoring poorly on multiple measures between the no and low risk groups at the six month assessment (X^2 = 2.43, p < .12, d.f. 2), this difference was significant at the one year assessment point (X^2 = 13.12, p < .00, d.f.2). Of the 21 study participants who presented elevated risk on at least half of the twelve month assessment measures, 17 (81%) were in the low risk sample.

AN ALTERNATIVE ASSESSMENT PROCESS

Appropriately targeting prevention services will require a more complex participant identification process than is currently offered through the HFA initiative. In conceptualizing this task, however, several aspects of the current system appear useful for both the program staff and the initiative's overall objectives. These features include:

a universal screening or review of all new parents;
a systematic assessment of how families are managing along a number of domains or constructs believed to be associated with poor parenting skills and/or negative outcomes for children;
a structured interview protocol which will assist staff in introducing difficult or sensitive issues to parents and allow for an accurate determination of needs; and
an empathic process of engaging families in the level and content of service most appropriate given their circumstances.

With these guidelines in mind, the HFA assessment process needs to be redesigned such that it more closely resembles an assessment *service* rather than a simple interview. Under this new design, efforts should be made to arrange for an in-home assessment visit for all new parents or, at a minimum, those identified by hospital personnel as facing unusual challenges due to such factors as young maternal age, low income, or limited social supports. This in-home assessment, described as a support and health service provided to women with newborns, would involve anywhere from a single visit to multiple visits over a two to three month period, depending upon the family's needs. The objective would be to provide the new mother with additional information and support and to conduct a comprehensive needs assessment.

During this series of home visits, the assessment worker would engage in a process involving observations, empathic listening, a focused assessment of the newborn, and completion of a standardized interview. The purpose of these visits would be to systematically review each respondent's strengths and challenges in a number of domains such as general parenting and child development knowledge, degree of formal and informal social supports, attitudes toward parenting, and personal well being. While some of these issues might be drawn from the existing FSC interview protocol, others might incorporate elements from various depression inventories, parent-child interaction observation scales and strength-based measures focusing on parenting attitudes and assumptions. During this assessment period, additional HFA staff or community service providers might be introduced to the families as a way of better integrating the assessment service into subsequent interventions.

The outcome of this assessment process would be a detailed profile of a family's needs rather than determining an absolute, numerical score. Depending upon a family's needs, they could be channeled to one of several options—intensive home visitation (e.g., the current HFA service model), group-based services, educational services, less intensive home-based support, etc. Outside of the HFA home visitation model, all other service options would be locally determined based upon available resources and participant characteristics. In all cases, this service component would be presented as a continuation of the assessment service not a new service or a service referral. At some sites (if not all), the worker who provided the assessment service might be one of the same workers providing the ongoing, intensive home visits.

This approach addresses many of the current system's shortcomings. First, it expands the assessment process to include multiple home visits. Such an approach creates a greater opportunity for a fuller, more accurate assessment of a family's needs than does a single interview session. Second, it explicitly assesses families on both strengths and weaknesses. This process is more reflective of the ecological theory of maltreatment developed Brofenbrenner (1979) and expanded upon by Cicchetti and Rizley (1981). Third, it provides a solid foundation for universal support for new parents, HFA's ultimate goal. Under this conceptualization, all new parents would receive some intervention, although for many this intervention would be minimal (e.g., a single home visit, a "welcome baby" packet, etc.). However, even a minimal level of support, if systematically delivered, would establish the normative standard of universal support. All parents, regardless of economic status or personal stability, would come to expect a systematic assessment of their parental capacity. Fourth, the assessment process gets out of the business of participant targeting. Respondents are no longer classified into either being eligible or not eligible for service based upon a single score. Rather the issue becomes using this assessment to determine the level or degree of future services. Fifth, creating an array of service options at the end of the assessment process allows HFA to explicitly encompass a broader array of services and existing support programs than is currently possible. Under this configuration, HFA is not simply a long-term, intensive home visitation *program* but rather an integrated family support *system*. Finally, the process may well facilitate the program's ability to successfully engage the most at-risk families into more intensive interventions. Families will no longer be asked to accept a new intervention based upon an identified set of limitations but rather to continue receiving parenting assistance on a more intensive basis. They will not be singled out for a specialized intervention; they will merely be given more of a universal, public good.

Realizing System Reform

Interest in early intervention and prevention programs is extraordinary at this time. A recent comprehensive review of state efforts conducted by NCPCA identified 37 separate major parent support initiatives operating in 25 states (Bryant, 1993). In addition to these publicly supported efforts, a number of carefully crafted family support programs, such as the Home Instruction Program for Preschool Youngsters (HIPPY), the Minnesota Early Learning and Development (MELD) program, and Parents As Teachers (PAT), among others, have been promulgated around the country (Dunst, 1995; Gomby, Carson, Lewit, & Behrman, 1993; Kagan et al., 1987; Weiss & Jacobs, 1988). Also, several major foundations, such as the Carnegie Corporation of New York and the Commonwealth Fund, have launched national initiatives to explicitly promote a more comprehensive and coordinated system of support for young children and their parents. Finally, federal legislation in the areas of child health, early education programs and child welfare services has opened new and substantial funding streams for early childhood and family support.

Ideally, all of these efforts would work together at the state level to produce the type of integrated system implied in the HFA vision. Unfortunately, system development is rarely that simple. Interventions are unlikely to group themselves in some logical sequence the way the human cells coordinate their efforts during fetal development. Such coordination, if it is to occur, will require explicit and continuous planning among all parties. "History clearly shows," writes Kagan, "that focusing on isolated inventions breed problems of scaling up which have rarely been successfully addressed. Normalization suggests an alternative strategy; it focuses on envisioning a wholly reconstituted system and suggests incremental strategies toward its accomplishment" (Kagan, 1996, p. 163).

While useful in achieving expanded resources for program participants, current HFA partnerships with public and private early childhood initiatives and support programs have not produced notable change in institutional practice or priorities. Using HFA as a catalyst for achieving this type of systemic change will require future partnerships to move beyond merely improving existing service delivery methods. They will need to create a shared vision, one that embraces HFA's theory of change. Specifically, those seeking an HFA affiliation will need to accept the concept of universal coverage for all new parents, agree to allow local responsibility and decision making within a program framework committed to quality, and refocus their operations to reflect participant, not provider, priorities.

Efforts to achieve this type of fundamental change face immense obstacles (Kagan, 1996; Schorr, 1997). Public provision of services is most commonly characterized by mandatory, not voluntary service provision in which the relationship between caregiver and recipient is perceived as paternalistic, not egalitarian. Whereas community based agencies seek to differentiate services based upon an individual's need and cultural standards, institutional care is best organized in pre-defined, uniform "packages" or options. And as noted in the current debate over welfare reform, public systems of care often foster continued dependency rather than offer a realistic path toward independence. Future HFA partnerships will need to challenge existing paradigms of service delivery and organizational structure if they are to move HFA toward its mission of system reform. Public entities will need to adopt new interpretations of standards and management, forestalling centralized control and adopting flexible, locally defined quality indicators. Private organizations and corporate entities will need to accept greater responsibility for supporting families within their sphere of influence. Public-private partnerships will be needed to forge strong, durable and universal support networks ultimately attractive to all new parents.

In much the same way the expansion of individual HFA sites built upon trends and programmatic reforms already underway in various states and local communities, achieving HFA's vision for system reform will need to build upon emerging policy trends within both the public and private sectors. Privatization of public services, managed care and its capitated funding strategies, and growing emphasis on personal responsibility and civic involvement are creating new flexibility in the way public dollars are allocated and public and private agencies interface (Berger & Neuhaus, 1996; Etzioni, 1993, 1996). Capitalizing on these changes to improve the relative position of preventive services and support for new parents is a major challenge for national as well as state HFA planners. Two areas—health care and child welfare services—are particularly important for realizing this type of system reform. The purpose of this section is to outline how these opportunities might be realized as well as to identify those issues impeding timely and steady progress.

IMPROVING HEALTH CARE ACCESS AND OUTCOMES

Beginning with adequate prenatal care during her mother's pregnancy and continuing through regular well-baby visits during her first few years of life, an infant's well being will be profoundly influenced by the availability of health care services. Considering this issue, the Carnegie Task Force on Meeting the Needs of Young Children recommended that any plan for national health care reform include specific strategies for improving access to family planning services, comprehensive prenatal care for expectant mothers, and universal primary and preventive care for young children. Key to ensuring expanded access is the need to establish a specific standard of health care coverage and services for all children (Carnegie, 1994).

The Survey of Parents with Young Children, conducted by the Commonwealth Fund in 1996, identified several pressures and concerns new parents face as they seek health information and medical guidance on how to best help their children grow and thrive. This telephone survey of 2,000 parents found that:

Most new mothers are discharged in one or two days and only 20% report receiving a follow-up nurse home visit.
Mothers are more likely to breast feed when encouraged to do so by a physician or nurse.
Only 30% of parents read or look at picture books with their children daily.
Parents want more information on how to help their child learn.
Parents who discuss with their physician how to help their child learn are more likely to read to their child.
Parents who receive special pediatric services such as a telephone information line are more likely to rate their doctor as excellent on quality of care.
Nearly half of children have parents who have received government assistance such as Medicaid or food stamps (Taaffe-Young, Davis, & Schoen, 1996).

Between 1960 and 1990, spending for health care grew at almost 6% per year (adjusted for inflation)—double the growth rate of the rest of the economy (Fuchs, 1997). Health expenditures in the U.S. are now approaching $1 trillion per year (or $4,000 for every person in the country) (Lee, Benjamin, & Weber, 1997). In part, the cost crisis is a consequence of medicine's success in preventing and treating acute disease, which has led to an extended life span and a growing population of elderly struggling with various chronic diseases. It also reflects the increasing availability of expensive drugs and medical technology in an environment in which economic incentives—such as fee-for-service and cost-based payment—actively encourage their use (Lasker, 1997). By the late 1970s, skyrocketing costs of Medicare, Medicaid and employer-sponsored health insurance, coupled with a troubled economy, forced government and business to confront the expenditure issue. Various strategies were implemented to reduce health cost inflation, including wage and price controls, prospective hospital payment, physician fee schedules, selective contracting and prepaid health plans (Bodenheimer & Grumback, 1995). When government-driven efforts at health reform failed in 1994, market forces took over the health care system, and a movement to reinvent government swept America (Gore, 1995; Osborne & Gaebler, 1992).

Given the historical ties between child abuse prevention and public health, HFA efforts have a unique opportunity and obligation to influence the direction of emerging health care reforms. As HFA moves into its next stage of development, capitalizing on current trends in Medicaid utilization patterns, public health service delivery systems, and health data management will be key to the initiative's success. First, as states move to managed care contracts and "medical home" initiatives to control costs in their Medicaid programs, many patients who previously received care through public hospitals and public health clinics are being shifted to "mainstream" medical settings (Robert Wood Johnson Foundation, 1996). Because these Medicaid populations are very different from the populations who have used managed care systems in the past, greater attention will be needed to bring these new recipients into the system. Effective care for many Medicaid recipients depends upon their ability to overcome physical, cultural and social barriers to care. Practitioners will increasingly need to get into the home environment and provide follow-up services and link patients with other relevant services and programs in the community. HFA's service delivery system is very well suited to accomplishing these objectives. Among the services frequently included in Medicaid packages are home visitation, transportation, translation, and childcare as well as referrals to existing public preventive and screening programs. Although home visitation has been a common feature of Medicaid practice for several years, it has generally been used on a limited basis to help high-risk parents cope with complex medical regimens or ensure compliance with health care plans. With the shift to managed care, many of these so-called "wraparound" public health and social services are now needed in mainstream medical settings. One immediate advocacy avenue for HFA state leaders is to work with Medicaid directors to ensure that these services are included in managed care contracts and that HFA sites or affiliates are funded to provide these services.

A second factor changing the mainstream health care system is tighter restrictions on where those insured by private carriers can go to receive service. Under the prior "unrestricted" plans, individuals could go to public health clinics or other venues to receive services they may not have wanted their private physician to know about, such as family planning, abortions, STD treatment, etc. Current managed care contracts offer recipients fewer options to "go out of the network" for their care (Lasker, 1997). Such a strategy has resulted in more traditional public health services being offered by a diversified pool of private providers. And although private providers and HMOs are required to document that immunizations are being given, the end result has not been full coverage (Bernier, 1994). To improve childhood immunization levels in today's environment, the medical sector's efforts need to be reinforced with strategies that can help clinicians identify and influence parents who are not seeking out indicated immunizations and account for children in their practices who are getting their immunizations elsewhere.

Because HFA programs work with the population in greatest need for immunizations (i.e., young children), this potential universal system of care can offer medicine valuable support in realizing this specific health outcome. Home visitors can provide education and outreach to new parents regarding the importance of immunizations as well as assist parents in securing recommended vaccinations for their children in a timely manner. Ongoing monitoring of HFA performance also will provide empirical data on the extent to which different incentives or strategies successfully overcome barriers to care such as a parent's misunderstanding of immunizations or difficulty in managing health care delivery systems. To augment efforts with individual families, HFA program managers can work with local public health officials to launch public education and media campaigns to help "funnel" patients in need of immunizations to their practitioners' offices; promote expanded wraparound services to address logistical barriers that some patients face in accessing care; and establish community-wide immunization registries. In addition, explicit links need to be made between HFA services and the reforms underway in the area of pediatric medicine (Zuckerman, Kaplan-Sanoff, Parker, & Taaffe-Young 1997).

Third, those engaged in health care delivery, like those engaged in child abuse prevention, are increasingly concerned with documenting changes in aggregate outcomes as well as proving the efficacy of their interventions. In order to successfully manage the financial risk inherent in managed care funding strategies, practitioners in both public health and general medicine need increased assurance that target populations are being effectively identified, offered appropriate service packages, successfully utilizing services and demonstrating the sought-after physical or mental health outcomes. Again, a universally delivered HFA system for new parents can help the two sectors better track the health outcomes of new borns over time. The HFA system offers public health a far more comprehensive tracking system on who engages in preventive services and the results of this engagement process. The data also will suggest communities and populations who will require more directed interventions either through the establishment of community-wide health promotion efforts or new engagement and retention strategies. As health care providers assume a greater percentage of the financial risk to deliver necessary services, they hopefully will become increasingly interested in promoting and utilizing effective prevention strategies.

Finally, HFA state leaders share an important advocacy mission with their colleagues in public health and medicine. Sustaining the safety net of public health services for those families who remain outside the private insurance and Medicaid systems is essential if all new parents and their infants are to have access to comprehensive and competent health care. As HFA plans for the future, it will be imperative that the national planning staff develop examples of how expanded services can be jointly developed between state health systems and HFA systems of support. Creating a well functioning, community-wide health care system is essential to ensuring that HFA program participants continue to receive the services they need after terminating their HFA involvement and that supportive services exist for families who do not effectively engage in HFA services. Advocacy efforts are needed to raise awareness that the well being of children is not merely a function of their parent's ability to care for them or the health care system to provide service. Rather, the solution lies in improving environmental quality and safety and to instilling in communities the value of rearing children in a supportive and nurturing context.

ACHIEVING MORE EFFECTIVE CHILD PROTECTION SYSTEMS

Child abuse prevention programs across the country are seeking stronger relationships with local child welfare agencies for a number of reasons. First, child welfare agencies are, by definition, society's designated caretakers for those children whose parents are unwilling or unable to ensure their safety. As such, this system serves as the primary intake source for children who are victims of or at risk for child abuse and neglect. Operating in most states since the mid 1960's, formal child abuse and neglect reporting and response systems provide the most widely recognized strategy for addressing maltreatment (Nelson 1984). Professionals and the general public are continuously encouraged to use this system as a means of securing assistance for families in need.

Indeed, the growing number of reports to local CPS agencies attest to public and professional familiarity with this system. In 1997, some three million children were reported to child protective service agencies for suspected maltreatment, a million of whom were confirmed victims (Wang & Daro, 1998). To a large extent, this overwhelming number of cases is the second reason child abuse prevention services are inclined to form formal service relationships with CPS agencies. The literature is replete with examples of CPS agencies failing to provide adequate protection for children referred to their care. Research has found that upwards of 50% of reports in some jurisdictions are not subjected to a formal, comprehensive investigation due to a lack of sufficient information or credible indication that a child is indeed at risk (Wells, Fluke, Downing, & Brown, 1989).

A recent analysis of reporting practices in California is illustrative of the issues facing child protective service workers nationwide. The research focused on reports made to Alameda County's Emergency Response Unit (ERU) from June 1, 1993 to May 31, 1994. During the study period, 17,566 official child abuse reports were recorded; 9,422 (54%) were closed after telephone intake and 8,133 (46%) were investigated by a ERU caseworker. Among these cases, 6,078 (75%) were closed after the caseworker's initial contact; the remaining 25%

received family services. In other words, only 12% of all reports filed during the study period received any formal services. Equally distressing was the degree of harm documented by the research team among a sample of children whose reports were not "substantiated." Researchers rated half of these cases as involving maltreatment and determined one-quarter of the children had suffered actual injury. Despite these injuries, these cases were "closed" because in the CPS worker's judgment there was a lack of evidence strong enough to justify court intervention; the actual injury was viewed as accidental (although the intent had clearly been abusive); no indication of immediate future danger existed; or the family presented various protective factors (e.g., the perpetrator was no longer in the home, the involvement of other service agencies, etc.) (Karski, Gilbert, & Frame, 1997). The inability of the child welfare system to provide assistance to all children who have experienced violence severe enough to generate a formal report underscores the need for reform and closer connection to voluntary service systems.

Finally, child abuse prevention services find partnerships with CPS agencies attractive because the relationship provides a ready-made participant population. To the extent some of the families reported to CPS have not yet abused or neglected their children, they are appropriate candidates for primary prevention efforts. In fact, many have argued that providing CPS agencies the option of referring these less severe cases to voluntary interventions offers an excellent strategy for achieving better coverage for all families and represent a more efficient use of resources (Farrow, 1997; Owen & Fercello, 1998).

It is difficult to deny the philosophical and pragmatic need for a strong relationship between public child welfare practice and community-based child abuse prevention programs; such a relationship, however, is not without its limitations, particularly in the case of HFA programs. At a minimum, an extensive partnership with CPS may freeze HFA programs at the level of secondary prevention and undermine the initiative's universal mission. Rather than casting a broad and inclusive net to identify families in need of support, this strategy limits HFA sites to working with families who have already exhibited behavior severe enough to warrant public intervention. It also potentially hinders programs from embracing the strength-based philosophy central to the delivery of effective family support services. For better or worse, child protective service interventions are viewed as mandated intrusion into the family, as the state intervenes to assume responsibilities birth parents are failing to adequately assume. In many communities, local CPS agencies and workers are not viewed as an effective source of support for parents. Rather, they are viewed as an agency that takes children from parents who, in the eyes of some community residents, are victims themselves of structural poverty and community violence. To the extent community residents have little faith in CPS agencies to accomplish their mission of child protection, an overt HFA-CPS partnership may result in residents extending this negative perception to prevention services.

Beyond this perception problem, strong, exclusive partnerships with CPS simply may not result in a strong support system for families, particularly those families facing the greatest challenges. At present, CPS practice is simply too fragmented and too overburdened to successfully engage in a partnership with a system as varied and dynamic as community-based family support. Further, the sheer number of reported cases not receiving any formal CPS intervention suggests that prevention program directors may soon find their services overwhelmed by the flood of families CPS will increasingly need to cast off to them. What often begins as having 10 to 20% of a program's caseload dedicated to CPS referrals can quickly become 70 to 80% as the need for CPS to place cases rapidly exceeds the capacity of prevention efforts to accept them. Without more careful attention to the full array of families in need of assistance and agencies needed to resolve the issue, any HFA-CPS partnership might easily result in two overburdened systems instead of one.

Indeed, despite the emphasis on family preservation embedded in the Public Law 96–272, the Adoption Assistance and Child Welfare Act of 1980, a recent analysis of child welfare caseload dynamics found a dramatic decrease in the number of children receiving child welfare services between 1977 and 1994. An estimated one million children were being served on March 1, 1994 compared to 1.8 million children on April 1, 1977. The major decrease was in children who received services while living at home. The number of children who received services at home declined from 1,244,400 in 1977 to 497,100 in 1994. And, despite the good intentions of reformers, this service system is increasingly relying upon foster care placement to protect children from harm. While 30% of the children served by the system in 1977 were placed in foster care, today that percentage has risen to 50% (USDHHS, 1997). The decline in in-home services and the increased proportion of children receiving foster care reflects a child welfare system that has evolved from a broad-based social service system into a system primarily serving abused and neglected children and their families.

In response to overburdening caseloads and increased dissatisfaction with public child welfare practice, advocates and public administrators have devoted significant resources to determining how best to recast child protection. The Executive Session on Child Protection, a think tank convened by the John F. Kennedy School of Government at Harvard University, in association with the Edna McConnell Clark and the Annie E. Casey Foundations is illustrative of the type of reform thinking common within the child welfare community (Farrow, 1997). This specific group met for three years in a series of intensive three-day meetings to share and examine new work in the field and the experiences of its members. The group concluded that rather than have child welfare the sole entity responsible for the safety of children, a "community partnership" was needed to provide a more rapid, intensive and effective response to the maltreatment dilemma. In crafting this "community partnership", the group advocates for a seven step process (Farrow, 1997).

Agreeing on the direction for change: CPS agency directors and state legislators need to recognize that a single, governmental agency cannot provide sufficient protections for all children.

Starting the partnership: Key partners cited by the group include parents, schools, substance abuse prevention and treatment providers, the police, domestic violence service providers and welfare service administrators.

Creating differential responses to the varied needs of families for child protection: This concept has been at the heart of child welfare reform for over two decades and reflects the perception that the diverse needs represented among child abuse reports require a diverse response system. At a minimum, advocates propose establishing two alternative responses: an "investigative track" for reports involving severe abuse or imminent harm and a "community service track" for cases involving potential maltreatment or less severe abuse. In the second option, emphasis would be placed on developing a comprehensive assessment of family strengths and needs rather than determining parental guilt.

Developing comprehensive neighborhood-based supports and services: This step involves reorganizing the delivery of public social and health services, expanding the network of available community-based options, and generating a greater array of informal supports (e.g., family, neighbors, friends, etc.).

Transforming public child protection services: This step calls for CPS to change their internal policies and practices while playing a leadership role in creating and sustaining the community partnerships. Mainstays of this change identified by the Executive Session include more comprehensive assessments, engaging families and natural networks of support, understanding the dynamics of substance abuse, domestic violence and other risks to children, and teaming with colleagues in other systems and the community.

Shifting intake and follow-up services for low risk cases to a community-based system: If this can be achieved, and many believe it is possible, a sizable number of families could be diverted off existing CPS caseloads and on to the caseloads of various community-based service programs.

Instituting community governance and accountability for protecting children: While a variety of agencies and systems will assume responsibility for delivering services, communities will need to establish a system to ensure overall accountability, general system effectiveness, and data collection and management. The Executive Session proposed that in this final developmental stage local systems may elect to form formal boards that assume responsibility for keeping children safe.

Under this new conceptualization, the child protective service agency of the future will retain a central role in creating the partnerships and managing the outcomes. "They will now act as the catalysts, organizers, and leaders in the development of community partnerships. Moreover, they will directly oversee the initial response to maltreatment reports (even though they may not provide that response itself); they will provide protective supervision for highest-risk cases; and they will supervise foster care and adoption services for families for whom voluntary services are not sufficient and for whom the oversight and/or custody of the CPS agency is required" (Farrow, 1997, p. 43).

Rather than simply reflect a theoretical model of what "might be," the steps outlined above are based on the actual experiences in many states and local communities around the country. Indeed, the concept of shared responsibility and calls for "community systems of care" have been common place for at least a decade (Daro, 1988; Kamerman & Kahn, 1990; USDHHS, 1990, 1991). Two things, however, make the current reform particularly promising for prevention advocates in general and for HFA efforts in particular.

First, new funding structures at the federal level create explicit incentives for child welfare administrators to embrace a more comprehensive approach to service delivery. Passage of the federal Family Support and Preservation Act offered a unique opportunity for child welfare administrators to refocus their efforts in terms of a broader target population. Included as part of the Omnibus Budget Reconciliation Bill of 1993 (OBRA), the bill authorizes child welfare administrators to begin spending money on prevention services rather than merely focusing resources on families who have already demonstrated abusive or neglectful patterns of behavior. Through Fiscal Year 1997, Congress appropriated $623 million for grants to states to conduct planning activities and fund family preservation and support services for the first time. An additional $52 million was set aside for court enhancement studies, grants to Indian tribes and federal evaluation, research and training activities. The Fiscal Year 1998 appropriation level, the final year of the current legislation, was set at $255 million. Recent reauthorization of the legislation continues the program through Fiscal Year 2002. The legislation's planning component as well as its infusion of new monies offer child welfare administrators an excellent opportunity to create a more useful system and to build stronger collaborative service networks in partnership with local, community-based family support efforts.

The Government Accounting Office (GAO) conducted a review of spending patterns under this legislation in late 1996. This review found that all states had established a specific action plan and that most were using these revenues to partially support services to new populations, specifically those families at risk who had not yet abused or neglected their children. In the last two years, states budgeted 56% of their service dollars to family support and 44% to family preservation. GAO analysts concluded that the somewhat greater emphasis on family support services reflects priorities established through state and community planning efforts (GAO, 1997). Equally plausible, however, is the growing frustration many in state government have felt with the limited utility of family preservation services and their exclusive focus on those families who are on the verge of losing their children to the foster care system (Mac Donald, 1994; Notkin, 1994; Pelton, 1997; Rossi, 1991). The family support concept of engaging families prior to the onset of maltreatment strikes many in the child welfare system as a more productive point of intervention.

Second, HFA and its broad scale, national implementation offers child welfare administrators a consistent and comparable service partner. Rather than interfacing with a large number of small, community-based agencies with diverse mission statements and participant populations, child welfare agencies now have the option of establishing a collaborative relationship with a sizable and focused prevention effort. Indeed, HFA's potential for universal assessment and diversified service options for all new parents might well offer child welfare the alternative response system suggested by reform advocates. Despite the good intentions of such study groups, and a body of evidence that suggest such reorganization is indeed doable and once done, successful, the model outlined by the Executive Session may not represent significant change. In essence, the model continues the current "hands off" policy for social interventions into the parenting process. Reporting a family for failure or potential failure continues to be required before a family can access help. If the reform effort, however, was integrated into a comprehensive, universal system of support for all new parents, the concept becomes quite powerful. The assessment of parental capacity becomes normalized as the community seeks to provide support to all new parents, with the specific level of support and degree of social intervention determined by community standards of care.

This approach, while promising, faces formidable obstacles. Unanswered questions exist regarding ultimate responsibility and authority. If the new system is instituted, how will sensitive issues such as participant confidentiality and family privacy be addressed? Will data regarding parental functioning be shared openly among participating agencies? How will information be fed back into the system such that needed policy or practice reform can be readily identified? How will decisions be made regarding which families are offered more coercive interventions and which families are offered community-based options? To what degree will participants be given authority to determine which services they will utilize and which they will not? And, until prevention capacity is sufficient to meet the demands of all families, how will service resources be allocated?

Answers to these and similar questions are far from self-evident. However, the potential of identifying a new gatekeeper for child protection, one that does not carry the historical baggage of current child protective services holds great promise. In addressing these questions, state and local communities will be able to approach the task with freer thinking and a new normative framework, one which seeks protection and support for children rather than the determination of parental guilt and punishment.

Conclusions

No system of universal support for new parents, regardless of scope or quality, will solve the plethora of social ills. Despite the best efforts of prevention advocates, some number of children will experience injury or limited social and cognitive development because their parents are unable or unwilling to care for them. In a sense, the more we learn about planning and implementing prevention services the more we realize how little we know about the appropriate scope for these efforts and their ultimate impacts. In this sea of uncertainty, however, the HFA experience has identified several concepts worth incorporating into any large-scale prevention initiative.

First, the new imagery, one that casts prevention services in a vertical rather than horizontal framework, is the correct imagery for future planning. When a social dilemma is multifaceted and rooted in a diverse array of personal, familial and societal causes, prevention advocates will be wise to begin with a strong foundation which offers a certain degree of universal assessment. Once the specific degree of need is established for each individual or family, more specialized or intensive services can be built upon this essential foundation.

Second, although quality issues are paramount, prevention efforts need to remain flexible both in establishing new innovations as well as in replicating the most promising of our approaches. No single program or delivery system will be correct for all participants or all communities. Those interested in preventing child abuse and supporting new parents need to draw from the empirical findings and clinical experiences generated by thoughtful program evaluators and practitioners and use this knowledge to craft workable programs for their community and target population. This type of careful and rational planning is necessary if prevention efforts are to be responsive to the uniqueness of a given community and to generate the type of ownership and investment necessary to sustain efforts over the long term.

Finally, prevention advocates need to force themselves to think at a systems level, to understand that it is as critical to build relationships among providers in a given community as it is to build relationships between individual parents and their children. Such integration efforts need to engage a variety of disciplines, professionals and the public at large. Unless such an effort is undertaken, HFA and other large-scale prevention efforts will fail to create the familial and societal conditions necessary for the consistent and positive nurturing of all children.

References

Anderson, P., & Fenichel, E. (1989). *Serving culturally diverse families of infants and toddlers with disabilities.* Washington DC: National Center for Clinical Infant Programs.

Azar, S. (1988). Methodological considerations in treatment outcome research in child maltreatment. In G. Hotaling, D. Finkelhor, J. Kirkpatrick, & M. Straus (Eds.), *Coping with family violence: research and policy perspectives* (pp. 288–289). Beverly Hills: Sage.

Barnard, K. (1978). *Nursing child assessment satellite training learning resource manual.* Seattle WA: University of Washington.

Barnard, K., Hammond, M., Booth, C., Bee, H., Mitchell, S., & Spieker, S. (1989). Measurement and meaning of parent-child interaction. In F. Morrison, C. Lord, & D. Keating (Eds.), *Applied developmental psychology* (Vol. III, pp. 40–81). San Diego CA: Academic Press.

Belsky, J. & Vondra, J. (1990). Lessons for child abuse: The determinants of parenting. In D. Cicchetti, & V. Carlson (Eds.), *Child maltreatment: Theory and research on the causes and consequences of child abuse and neglect* (pp. 153–202). Cambridge: Cambridge University Press.

Berger, P. & Neuhaus, R. (1996). *To empower people: From state to civil society.* Washington DC: American Enterprise Institute.

Berlin, L., O'Neal, C., & Brooks-Gunn, J. (1998). What makes early intervention programs work? The program, its participants and their interaction. *Zero to Three, 18(4)* (February/March), 4–15.

Bernier, R. H. (1994). Toward a more population-based approach to immunization: Fostering private-and public-sector collaboration. *American Journal of Public Health, 84,* 1567–1568.

Besharov, D. (1986). Unfounded allegations: A new child abuse problem. *The Public Interest, 83,* 18–33.

Besharov, D. (1990). *Combating child abuse.* Washington DC: AEI Press.

Bodenheimer, T. S. & Grumbach, K. (1995). *Understanding health policy: A clinical approach.* Norwalk CT: Appleton & Lange.

Bowlby, J. (1969). *Attachment.* New York: Basic Books.

Bowlby, J. (1973). *Attachment and loss: Volume 2 separation.* New York: Basic Books.

Bowlby, J. (1980). *Loss.* New York: Basic Books.

Brazelton, T. B. (1992). *Touchpoints: Your child's emotional and behavioral development.* Hawaii: Addison-Wesley.

Breakey,G., & Pratt, B. (1991). Healthy growth for Hawaii's Healthy Start: Toward a systematic statewide approach to the prevention of child abuse and neglect. *Zero to Three, 11:4* (April), 16–22.

Bronfenbrenner, U. (1979). *The ecology of human development: experiments by nature and design* Cambridge MA: Harvard University Press.

Brookings Institute. (1998). *Learning what works: Evaluating complex social interventions. Report on the symposium held October 22, 1997.* Prepared by the Brookings Institute and Harvard University, Project on effective interventions. Washington DC: The Brookings Institute.

Browne, K., Davis, C., & Stratton, P. (1988). *Early prediction and prevention of child abuse.* New York: Wiley and Sons.

Bryant, P. (1993). *Availability of existing statewide parent education and support programs and the need for these programs nationwide.* Chicago: National Committee to Prevent Child Abuse.

Caldwell, B. & Bradley, R. (1984). *Home observation for measurement of the environment* (Rev. ed.). Little Rock: University of Arkansas.

Carnegie Task Force on Meeting the Needs of Young Children (1994). *Starting points: Meeting the needs of our youngest children.* New York: Carnegie Corporation of New York.

Chalk, R. & King, P. (Eds). (1998). *Violence in families: Assessing prevention and treatment programs.* Washington DC: National Academy Press.

Cicchetti, D. & Rizley, R. (1981). Developmental perspectives on the etiology, intergenerational transmission, and sequelae of child maltreatment. *New Directions for Child Development, 11,* 31–55.

Cicchinelli, L. (1995). Risk assessment: Expectations and realities. *The APSAC Advisor, 8*(4), 3–8.

Cohn, A. (1986). *An approach to preventing child abuse.* Chicago: National Committee to Prevent Child Abuse.

Cowan, W. M. (1979). The development of the brain. *Scientific American, 241*(3), 113–133.

Cross, T. Bazron, B., Dennis, K., & Isaacs, M. (1989). *Toward a culturally competent system of care.* Washington DC: Child and Adolescent Service

System Program Technical Assistance Center, Georgetown University Child Development Center.

Daro, D. (1988). *Confronting child abuse.* New York: Free Press.

Daro, D. (1991). *The child abuse prevention movement: Aggregate gains and shortcomings.* Chicago: National Committee to Prevent Child Abuse.

Daro, D. (1993). Child maltreatment research: Implications for program design. In D. Cicchetti & S. Toth (Eds.), *Child abuse, child development, and social policy* (pp. 331–367). Norwood NJ: Ablex.

Daro, D. (1996). Preventing child abuse. In J. Briere, L. Berliner, J. Bulkley, C. Jenny, & T. Reid (Eds.), *The APSAC handbook on child maltreatment* (pp. 343–358). Thousand Oaks CA: Sage.

Daro, D. & Cohn, A. (1988). Child maltreatment evaluation efforts? What have we learned? In G. Hotaling, D. Finkelhor, J. Kirkpatrick, & M. Straus (Eds.), *Coping with family violence: Research and policy perspectives* (pp. 275–287). Newbury Park CA: Sage.

Daro, D. & Harding, K. (1999). Healthy Families America: Using research in going to scale. *The Future of Children, 9*(1), 152–176.

Daro, D., Jones, E., & McCurdy, K. (1993). *Preventing child abuse: An evaluation of services to high-risk families.* Philadelphia: William Penn Foundation.

Daro, D., McCurdy, K., & Harding, K. (1998). *The role of home visiting in prevention child abuse: An Evaluation of Healthy Start.* Chicago: National Committee to Prevent Child Abuse.

Daro, D. & Wang, C. (1998). *Current trends in child abuse reporting and fatalities: The results of the 1997 annual fifty state survey.* Chicago: National Committee to Prevent Child Abuse

Daro, D. & Winje, C. (1998). *Healthy Families America: Profile of program sites.* Chicago: National Committee to Prevent Child Abuse.

de Mause, L. (1974). The evolution of childhood. *Historical Childhood Quarterly, 1,* 503–75.

Drake, B. & Zuravin, S. (1998). Bias in child maltreatment reporting: Revisiting the myth of classlessness. *American Journal of Orthopsychiatry, 68,* 295–304.

Dunst, C. (1995). *Key characteristics and features of community-based family support program.* Chicago: The Family Resource Coalition.

Edelwich, J. & Brodsky, A. (1980). *Burnout.* New York: Human Sciences Press.

Ellwood, A. (1988). Prove to me that MELD makes a difference. In H. Weiss & F. Jacobs (Eds.), *Evaluating family programs* (pp. 303–314). New York: Aldine.

Epstein, H. (1979). Correlated brain and intelligence development in humans. In M. Hahn, C. Jensen, & B. Dudek (Eds.), *Development and evolution of brain size.* New York NY: Academic Press.

Etzioni, A. (1993). *Spirit of community: Rights, responsibilities and the communitarian agenda.* New York NY: Crown.

Etzioni, A. (1996). *The new golden rule: Community and morality in a democratic society.* New York NY: Basic Books.

214

MOTIVATION AND CHILD MALTREATMENT

Farrow, F. (1997). *Child protection: Building community partnerships . . . Getting from here to there.* Cambridge MA: John F. Kennedy School of Government, Harvard University.

Forum on Child and Family Statistics (1997). *America's children: Key national indicators of well-being.* Washington DC: Federal Interagency Forum on Child and Family Statistics.

Frankel, H. (1988). Family-centered, home-based services in child protection: A review of the research. *Social Service Review, 62*(1), 137–157.

Fuchs, V. R. (1997). Managed care and merger mania. *Journal of the American Medical Association, 277,* 920–921.

Garbarino, J. (1988). *The future as if it really mattered.* Longmount CO: Book-makers Guild.

Garbarino, J., Cohn, A., & Ebota, A. (1982). *The significance of cultural and ethnic factors in preventing child abuse: An exploration of research findings.* Chicago: National Committee for Prevention of Child Abuse.

Gomby, D., Larson, C., Lewit, E., & Behrman, R. (1993). Home visiting: Analysis and recommendations. *The Future of Children, 3*(3) (winter), 6–22.

Gore, A. (1995). *Reinventing government: National performance review.* Washington DC: Office of the Vice President of the United States.

Government Accounting Office (GAO). (1997). *Child welfare: States' progress in implementing family preservation and support services.* (GAO/HEHS-97-34)(February) Washington DC: U.S. Government Printing Office.

Gueron, J. M., & Pauly, E. (1991). *From welfare to work.* New York NY: Russell Sage Foundation.

Gutterman, N. (1997). Early prevention of physical abuse and neglect: Existing evidence and future directions. *Child Maltreatment, 2*(1), 12–34.

Halpern, R. (1984). Lack of effects for home-based early intervention? *Some possible explanations. American Journal of Orthopsychiatry, 54*(1), 33–42.

Halpern, R. & Larner, M. (1987). Lay family support during pregnancy and infancy: the Child Survival/Fair Start Initiative. *Infant Mental Health Journal,8*(2), 130–143.

Hawaii Department of Health, Maternal and Child Health Branch. (1992). *Healthy start.* Honolulu HI: Department of Health, Maternal and Child Health Branch.

Helfer, R. (1982). A review of the literature on the prevention of child abuse and neglect. *Child Abuse and Neglect, 6,* 251–261.

Helfer, R., Hoffmeister, J., & Schneider, C. (1978). *MSPP manual (Michigan Screening Profile of Parenting).* Boulder CO: Test Analysis and Development Corporation.

Howing, P., Wodarski, J., Kurtz, P., & Gaudin, J. (1989). Methodological issues in child maltreatment research. *Social Work Research and Abstracts, 25*(3), 3–7.

Johnson, D. L. & Walker, T. (1991). A follow-up evaluation of the Houston Parent-Child Development Center: School performance. *Journal of Early Intervention 15*(3), 226–236.

Kagan, S. L. (1996). America's family support movement: A moment of change. In E. Zigler, S. Kagan, & N. Hall (Eds.), *Children, families & government: Preparing for twenty-first century* (pp. 156–170). Cambridge: Cambridge University Press.

Kagan, S., Powell, D., Weissbourd, B., & Zigler, E. (Eds.). (1987). *America's family support programs.* New Haven CT: Yale University Press.

Karoly, L. A., Greenwood, P. W., Everingham, S. S., Hoube, J., Kilburn, M. R., Rydell, C. P., Sanders, M., & Cheisa, J., (1998), *Investing in our children: What we know and don't know about the costs and benefits of early childhood interventions.* Santa Monica CA: Rand.

Kahn, Robert. (1993). *An experiment in scientific organization: The MacArthur Foundation program in mental health and human development.* Chicago: The MacArthur Foundation.

Kamerman, S. & Kahn, A. (1990). Social services for children, youth and families in the United States. *Children and Youth Services Review, 12*(1/2).

Karski, R., Gilbert, N., & Frame, L. (1997). Evaluating the emergency response system's screening, assessment and referral of child abuse reports. *CPS Brief,9*(5), 1–11.

Larner, M. (1992). Realistic expectations: Review of evaluation findings. In M. Larner, R. Halpern, & O. Harkavy (Eds.), *Fair start for children: Lessons learned from seven demonstration projects* (pp. 218–245). New Haven CT: Yale University Press.

Lasker, R. (1997). *Medicine and public health: The power of collaboration.* New York: The New York Academy of Medicine, Committee on Medicine and Public Health.

Lee, P., Benjamin, A., & Weber, M. (1997). Policies and strategies for health in the United States. In R. Detels, W. Holland, J. McEwevy, & G. Omenn (Eds.), *Oxford textbook of public health.* New York: Oxford University Press.

Leeds, S. J. (1984). *Evaluation of Nebraska's intensive services project: Lincoln and McCook, Nebraska, March 1983-February 1984.* Iowa City IA: National Resource Center on Family Based Services.

Lutzker, J. & Rice, J. (1984). Project 12-ways: Measuring outcome of a large in-home service for treatment and prevention of child abuse and neglect. *Child Abuse and Neglect, 18*, 519–524.

Lutzker, J. & Rice, J. (1987). Using recidivism data to evaluate Project 12-ways: An ecobehavioral approach to the treatment and prevention of child abuse and neglect. *Journal of Family Violence, 2*(4), 283–290.

Mac Donald, H. (1994). The ideology of family preservation. *The Public Interest, 115* (spring), 45–60.

Mann, J. (1990). Drawing on cultural strengths to empower families. *Protecting Children, 7*(3), 3–5.

McCurdy, K. (1996). *Home visiting.* Washington DC: U.S. Department of Health and Human Services, National Center on Child Abuse and Neglect.

McDonald, T. & Marks, J. (1991). A review of risk factors in child protective services. *Social Service Review, 65*(1), 112–132.

Milner, J. S. (1986). *The Child Abuse Potential Inventory: Manual.* Webster NC: Psytech.

216

MOTIVATION AND CHILD MALTREATMENT

Milner, J. S. (1987). *Additional cross-validation of the Child Abuse Potential Inventory.* Paper presented at the meeting of the National Family Violence Research Conference, Durham NH.

Milner, J. S. (1989). Additional cross-validation of the Child Abuse Potential Inventory. *Journal of Consulting And Clinical Psychology, 1*, 219–223.

Mitchel-Bond, L. & Cohn-Donnelly, A. (1993). Healthy Families America: Building a national system. *The APSAC Advisor, 6*(4), 9–10, 27.

Murphy, S., Orkow, B., & Nicola, R. (1985). Prenatal prediction of child abuse and neglect: A prospective study. *Child Abuse and Neglect, 9*, 225–235.

Murphy-Berman, V. (1994). A conceptual framework for thinking about risk assessment and case management in child protective services. *Child Abuse and Neglect, 18*, 193–201.

Musiak, J., Bernstein, B., Percansky, C., & Stott, F. (1987). A chain of enablement: Using community-based programs to strengthen relationships between teen parents and their infants. *Zero to Three, 8*(2) (December), 1–6.

National Association of Pubic Child Welfare Administrators (NAPCWA). (1988). *Guidelines for a model system of child protective services.* Washington DC: American Public Welfare Association.

National Commission to Prevent Infant Mortality. (1989). *Home visiting: Opening doors for America's pregnant women and children.* Washington DC: National Commission to Prevent Infant Mortality.

National Vaccine Advisory Committee. (1991). The measles epidemic: The problems, barriers, and recommendations. *The Journal of the American Medical Association, 266*, 1547–1552.

Nelson, B. (1984). *Making an issue of child abuse: Political agenda setting for social problems.* Chicago: University of Chicago Press.

Notkin, S. (1994). *The Edna McConnell Clark Foundation program for children strategy statement.* Background paper prepared for the Edna McConnell Clark Foundation.

Olds, D., Eckenrode, J., Henderson, C. R. Jr., Kitzman, H., Powers, J., Cole, R., Sidora, K., Morris, P., Pettitt, L., & Luckey, D. (1997). Long-term effects of home visitation on maternal life course, child abuse and neglect and children's arrests: Fifteen-year follow-up of a randomized trial. *Journal of the American Medical Association, 278*, 637–643.

Olds, D., Henderson, C., Chamberlin, R., & Tatelbaum, R. (1986). Preventing child abuse and neglect: A randomized trial of nurse home visitation. *Pediatrics, 78*, 65–78.

Olds, D., Henderson, C., Kitzman, H., & Cole, R. (1995). Effects of prenatal and infancy nurse home visitation on surveillance of child maltreatment. *Pediatrics, 95*, 365–372.

Olds, D. & Kitzman, H. (1993). Review of research on home visiting for pregnant women and parents of young children. *The Future of Children, 3*, 53–92.

Osborne, D. E. & Gaebler, T. (1992). *Reinventing government: How the en-*

trepreneurial spirit is transforming the public sector. Reading MA: Addison-Wesley.

Owen, G. & Fercello, C. (1998). *Reducing child maltreatment among high-risk families: The results of a three year field experiment to assess the impact of the family option program.* St. Paul MN: Wilder Research Center.

Pascoe, J., Ialongo, N., Horn, W., Trinhart, M., & Perrradatto, D. (1998). The reliability and validity of the Maternal Social Support Index. *Family Medicine, 20*(4), 271–276.

Pelton, L. (1997). Child welfare policy and practice: The myth of family preservation. *American Journal of Orthopsychiatry, 67*(4) (October), 545–553.

Purves, D. (1994). *Neural activity and the growth of the brain (Lezioni Lincee).* New York: Cambridge University Press.

Quint, J. C., Polit, D. F., Bos, H., & Cave, G. (1994). *New chance: Interim findings on a comprehensive program for disadvantaged young mothers and their children.* New York: Manpower Demonstration Research Corporation.

Ramey, C. & Ramey, S. (1998). Early intervention and early experience. *American Psychologist, 53*(2), 109–120.

Robert Wood Johnson Foundation. (1996). *Annual report.* Princeton NJ: The Robert Wood Johnson Foundation.

Rossi, P. (1991). *Evaluating family preservation programs—A report to the Edna McConnell Clark Foundation.*

St. Pierre, R. G., Layzer, J. I., Goodson, B. D., & Bernstein, L. S. (1997). *National impact evaluation of the Comprehensive Child Development Program: Final report.* Cambridge MA: Abt Associates.

St. Pierre, R. G., Swartz, J., Gamse, B., Murray, S., Deck, D., & Nickel, P. (1995). *National evaluation of the Comprehensive Child Development Program: Interim report.* Cambridge MA: Abt Associates.

Sandler, J. (1979). *Effects of adolescent pregnancy on mother-infant relations: A transactional model.* Report to the Center for Population Research. Bethesda MD: National Institutes of Health.

Sameroff, A. & Chandler, M. (1975). Reproductive risk and the continuum of caretaking casualty. In F. Horowitz, M. Hetherington, S. Scarr-Salapatek & G. Siegal (Eds.), *Review of Child Development Research.* (Vol. 4, pp. 187–244). Chicago: University of Chicago Press.

Schore, A. N. (1994). *Affect regulation and the origin of the self: The neurobiology of emotional development.* Hillsdale NJ: Erlbaum.

Schorr, L. (1997). *Common purpose: Strengthening families and neighborhoods to rebuild America.* New York: Doubleday Books.

Schorr, L. & Schorr, D. (1985). *Within our reach.* New York: Anchor Press/Doubleday.

Sedlek, A. & Broadhurst, D. (1996). *Third national incidence study of child abuse and neglect (NIS-3): Executive summary.* Washington DC: U.S. Department of Health and Human Services, ACYF, NCCAN.

Seitz, V., Rosenbaum, L. K., Apfel, N. H. (1985). Effects of family support intervention: A ten-year follow-up. *Child Development, 56,* 376–391.

Slaughter-DeFoe, D. (1993). Home visiting with families in poverty: Introducing the concept of culture. *The Future of Children, 3*, 172–183.

Specht, H. & Courtney, M. (1994). *Unfaithful angels: New social work has abandoned its mission*. New York: Free Press.

Stannard, M. (1988). *A Study of the Healthy Start project assessment process conducted at the Kap'iolani Women's and Children's Medical Center*. Prepared for Maternal and Child Health Branch, Family Health Services Division, Department of Health for the Sixteenth Legislature State of Hawaii.

Starr, R. (1982). *Child abuse prediction: Policy implications*. Cambridge MA: Ballinger.

Steele, B. (1987). Psychodynamic factors in child abuse. In R. Helfer & R. Kempe (Eds.), *The battered child* (4th ed., pp. 81–114). Chicago: University of Chicago Press.

Straus, M. & Kantor, G. (1987). Stress and child abuse. In R. Helfer & R. Kempe (Eds), *The battered child*. (4th ed., pp. 42–59). Chicago: University of Chicago Press.

Taaffe-Young, K., Davis, K., & Schoen, C. (1996). *The Commonwealth Fund survey of parents with young children*. New York: The Commonwealth Fund.

TenBensel, R., Rheinberger, M., & Radbill, S. (1997). Children in a world of violence: The roots of child maltreatment. In M. E. Helfer, R. Kempe, & D. Krugman (Eds.), *The battered child*. (5th ed., pp. 3–28). Chicago: University of Chicago Press.

Thompson, R. (1995). *Preventing child maltreatment through social support: A critical analysis*. Thousand Oaks CA: Sage.

U.S. Department of Health and Human Services (USDHHS), Children's Bureau. (1997). *National study of protective, preventive and reunification services delivered to children and their families*. Washington DC: U.S. Government Printing Office.

U.S. Department of Health and Human Services (USDHHS), U.S. Advisory Board on Child Abuse and Neglect. (1990). *Child abuse and neglect: Critical first steps in response to a national emergency*. Washington DC: U.S. Government Printing Office.

U.S. Department of Health and Human Services (USDHHS), U.S. Advisory Board on Child Abuse and Neglect. (1991). *Creating caring communities: Blueprint for an effective federal policy for child abuse and neglect*. Washington DC: U.S. Government Printing Office.

U.S. Department of Health and Human Services (USDHHS), U.S. Advisory Board on Child Abuse and Neglect. (1995). *The continuing child protection emergency: A challenge to the nation*. Washington DC: U.S. Government Printing Office.

Wasik, B. H. (1993). Staffing issues for home visiting programs. *The Future of Children, 3*, 140–157.

Wasik, B. H., Bryant, D. M., & Lyons, C. M. (1990). *Home visiting: Procedures for helping families*. Newbury Park CA: Sage.

Wang, C. T. & Daro, D. (1998). *Current trends in child abuse reporting and fatalities: The results of the 1997 annual 50 state survey.* Chicago: National Committee to Prevent Child Abuse.

Weiss, H. (1993). Home visits: Necessary but not sufficient. *The Future of Children, 3,* 113–128.

Weiss, H. & Jacobs, F. (Eds.). (1988). *Evaluating family programs.* New York: Aldine.

Wells, S., Fluke, J., Downing, J., & Brown, C. H. (1989). *Final report screening in child protective services.* Washington DC: The American Bar Association.

Wieder, S., Poisson, S., Lourie, R., & Greenspan, S. (1988). Enduring gains: A five-year follow-up report on the Clinical Infant Development Program. *Zero to Three, 8*(4), 6–11.

Willis, D., Holden, E. W., & Rosenberg, M.. (Eds.). (1992).*Prevention of child maltreatment: Developmental and ecological perspectives.* New York: Wiley.

Zuckerman, B., Kaplan-Sanoff, M., Parker, S., & Taaffe Young, K. (1997). The Healthy steps for young children program. *Zero to Three, 17*(6) (June/July), 20–25.

Balancing Research and Treatment in Child Maltreatment: The Quest for Good Data and Practical Service

John R. Lutzker

University of Judaism

Many scientific disciplines have been around for centuries. Psychology is now well over 100-years-old. Social work has become an established field. Yet, the field of child abuse and neglect was only formally professionally recognized in the 1960s (Kempe, Silverman, Steele, Droegemueller, & Silver, 1962). Further, dealing with this serious societal problem requires the combined efforts of law enforcement, the legal system, social work, psychology and other mental health disciplines, medicine, rehabilitation, public welfare agencies, schools, the media, and religious organizations.

Thus, the multidisciplinary nature of research and treatment in child maltreatment, while necessary and useful on one hand, may on the other hand, mitigate against the formation of streamlined theory, research, and treatment. That said, given the comparatively short history of efforts to understand and treat child maltreatment, good models exist from which to move forward, although combining research and treatment in this area represents a true challenge. Sometimes research and treatment actually seem to have competing agendas. For example, even the collection of pretreatment or baseline data can sometimes be problematic. Agencies may have such pressing needs for service for a given family or group of families that the collection of pretreatment or baseline data may be precluded so that the family or families are able to receive immediate treatment services.

Agencies or individual families may resist the collection of certain intake/demographic data and information. They may resist or refuse to allow the implementation of certain standardized assessment techniques. For example, Kapitanoff, Lutzker, and Bigelow (2000) have suggested that cultural/ethnic issues and variables may make the administration of various assessment techniques difficult or impossible. Many such tools are invasive and can run against the grain of establishing rapport with a family.

Presented here will be a review of the features of good applied research, programs that have combined good research and treatment in child maltreatment, factors that work against combining research and treatment in child maltreatment, and suggestions for overcoming some of these obstacles.

What Is Good Applied Research?

Good applied research should have several features. What makes for *applied* research is that it has social relevance (Baer, Wolf, & Risley, 1968). Surely, the area of child maltreatment fulfills this criterion. The maltreatment of children is an extraordinary problem of social significance. Interventions should be conducted and reported in such a way that they have specific behavioral definitions and can be replicated. Unfortunately, many treatment programs, and some research programs in child maltreatment have not reported clear, replicable procedures.

It is better yet if the treatment has expert content validation. For example, in examining parent-child relationships, experts on children and experts on parent training should be formally queried through questionnaires as to the relevance of both measurement tools and treatment strategies. This kind of validation is frequently overlooked in much applied research.

An example of content validation was described by Lutzker, Megson, Webb, and Dachman (1985) who were interested in teaching affective adult-child interaction skills to staff who worked with families reported for child maltreatment. To determine which skills to teach the staff, these researchers examined the early childhood literature to find interactions that had been suggested by experts. Then, they developed a list of these skills and formally surveyed early childhood experts, child behavior therapists, and preschool teachers as to which skills to incorporate into the staff training protocols. Further, they then videotaped teachers interacting with children in a childcare center. The teacher-child interactions were scored against the content validated skills that had been recommended by the experts. The teachers' rates of the use of these skills were then used as the criterion measures against which to compare the staff who received training. This research was replicated with many more child maltreatment staff (McGimsey, Lutzker, & Greene, 1994).

An underutilized area of research methodology is single-case research design, especially in child maltreatment (Lutzker, Wesch, & Rice, 1984). I have long argued that good applied research should have five components: clinical, case studies, single-case experiments, research with multiple families addressing many research questions, and program evaluation (Lutzker, et al., 1984; Lutzker, 1992). By clinical, I mean that if we collect data on families involved in child maltreatment, the data should always and primarily be from direct observations that are reliable and valid. That is, even though we may not be able to use the data for research, the collection of data should be as rigorous as possible so that the data can be trusted to represent real change. Thus, to be valid, we must rely on accurate operational definitions which, when possible, as indicted above, should be content validated by experts. Further, data should be reliable. Thus, observers should be trained to performance criteria on their ability to accurately record the behaviors that are directly observed, live or by video tape. The observers' data should be reliable to a minimum 80% criterion. That is, two independent observers' data should agree at least 80% of the time. Reliability observations should be made on at least 25% of all sessions.

Indirect measures such as ratings, self-report inventories, surveys, and personality scores should always be secondary measures in the assessment of families involved in child maltreatment. Thus, from these direct observational data, much information is gleaned from the family.

Although much data can be generated from families, the difficulties faced by the applied researcher in working with these families often causes much of the data to be insufficient for publication. These "first level" data are the data to which I refer as "clinical" and they are not without value. Clinical data can be used for several good purposes. First, they can be used to demonstrate the parents' or family's progress (or the lack thereof) in the intervention program. Second, they can have a positive reactive effect. For example, we once worked with a mother who was very critical of her son. We defined "critical" and asked her to keep baseline data on the frequency she was critical of her child. We did this, of course, with the intent of developing a treatment program aimed at reducing the criticisms. In this case, however, the mere collection of the baseline data made the mother aware of how critical she was and her criticisms dropped to nearly zero with no other treatment. This is a positive reactive effect.

Of further use, clinical data are important for supervision. As they are useful for showing the family directly how they are progressing through treatment, these same data are quite helpful for staff to show supervisors progress or lack thereof in cases and can be used to problem-solve.

The next level of single-case methodology is the case study. A case study is a thorough detailed description of a novel technique applied to a person or family. It is one step more sophisticated than "clinical" data. Kazdin (1982) eloquently described the value and requirements of case studies in the published literature. In fact, most of applied psychology and behavioral psychology began with the publication of case studies.

In order to have value to the consumer of professional literature, a case study needs to be described in sufficient detail as to be replicable. Further, a case study should describe new treatment of a previously intractable problem and that new treatment should produce dramatic outcome.

An illustrative case study from Project SafeCare is the case of Julie, a 33-year-old Caucasian female referred for physically abusing her 4-year-old son. Project SafeCare (Lutzker, Bigelow, Doctor, Gershater, & Greene, 1998) was a four-year grant-funded research and service project that provided and examined training in bonding, home safety, and child health care skills to young parents who were either reported for child maltreatment or were referred for being at risk for child maltreatment.

When counselors assessed Julie at her home they found her profoundly deficient in parenting skills, child health care skills, and her home was filled with hazards accessible to her son. Further, administration of the Beck Depression Inventory (BDI; Beck & Steer, 1993) showed Julie to be in the severely depressed range. The Parenting

Stress Index (PSI; Abidin, 1990) showed parenting stress above the clinical cut-off score, and the Child Abuse Potential Inventory (CAPI; Milner, 1986) showed high risk.

The first service offered to Julie was the home safety program. This was because of fear that the many hazards accessible to her son could cause him imminent injury. Thus, Julie was provided with safety latches and a five-part video series on how to make her home safer. This service also included some counselor reminders such as saying to the parent, "Please remember what the video said about latches." By the end of the home safety program hazards had been reduced by over 95%.

Planned Activities Training (PAT) (Lutzker, Huynen, & Bigelow, 1998) was the next intervention. In five sessions, a counselor taught Julie how to plan activities, use incidental teaching, establish and state rules, review performance, and apply consequences. There were dramatic increases in this mother's performance of these skills and the frequency in which she engaged her child. There was a profound increase in the child's instruction-following after the mother's experience with PAT. This is a frequent generalized outcome of PAT (Bigelow & Lutzker, 1998).

Finally, a five-part child health care training program was implemented. This involved, through role-playing, teaching Julie how to identify, treat, or report to medical personnel, her child's illnesses. After the 15-week research/service program that Project SafeCare provided to Julie the scores on the BDI decreased from severe to mild, the PSI scores fell below the clinical level, and the CAPI scores showed significantly less risk. This case study reflects the use of clinical data and demonstrates a dramatic change in a serious problem of child maltreatment.

Single-case experiments are the next level of evaluation using single-case designs. Single-case experiments are conducted with one individual or one family. Despite this, these designs are robust, showing excellent internal validity (Kazdin, 1982). They differ from case studies in that they do meet scientific criteria. Through the single-case research design that may be utilized a functional relationship is shown between the treatment and the outcome. Also, these designs require reliability observations demonstrating a high percentage agreement between independent observers. These criteria are often lacking in case studies.

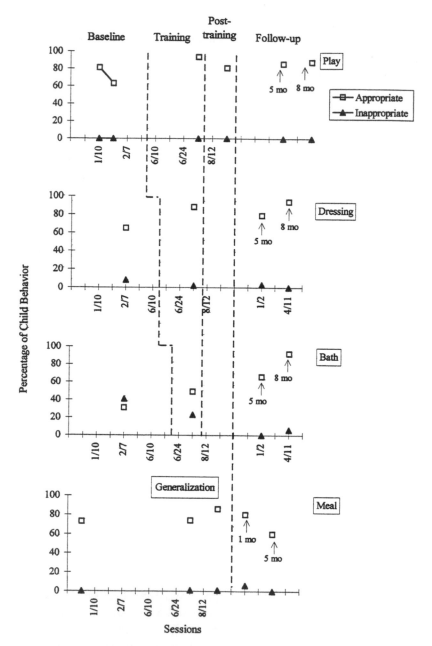

Figure 1. Planned activities/parent-child interactions training child behavior. From Cordon, Lutzker, Bigelow, & Doctor (1998). Evaluating Spanish protocols for teaching bonding, home safety, and health care to a mother reported for child abuse, *Journal of Behavior Therapy & Experimental Psychiatry*, 29, 41–45.

With single-case experiments, the data are gathered from reliable direct observations. That is, a second observer at least 25% of baseline and treatment observation sessions collects reliability data. The usual minimally acceptable interobserver agreement is 80%. The experimental designs can be from the following: ABAB (withdrawal) design, multiple baseline design across behaviors, settings, or individuals, changing criterion design, or alternating treatments design. An ABAB design is used when there is no ethical concern that the temporary withdrawal of treatment will cause any lasting damage. Thus, in this design the "A" condition is baseline and the "B" condition is treatment. When the second A and B conditions are implemented in this design, two elements of the reason that makes these designs robust are fulfilled. The first is that we have validated a prediction, that being that if it were not for treatment, baseline would have continued at the same level without improvement. The second "A" condition, that is the withdrawal of treatment, substantiates the prediction if the performance thus returns to near the baseline level. The second aspect of this design that has been achieved is replication. The second AB results demonstrate that the treatment was once again effective. Replication is very important in establishing internal and external validity.

Kazdin (1982) and Hersen and Barlow (1976) are excellent guides for the conducting and understanding single-case research designs. The primary limitation of a single-case experiment is a lack of external validity. Obviously, little can be said about generality from one subject or family. Nonetheless, single-case experiments are valuable contributions to the applied literature because they provide empirically validated internally valid data on treatment strategies that can then be replicated to help establish their generality.

An example of a single-case experiment was provided by Cordon, Lutzker, Bigelow, and Doctor (1998) who described the evaluation of Spanish protocols for teaching bonding, home safety, and health care skills to a mother reported for the physical abuse of her six-year-old son. The effects of Planned Activities Training (PAT) and home safety training were evaluated by using multiple baseline designs (see Figures 1 & 2). PAT was sequentially introduced across the following training settings: play, dressing, and bath. Meal time observations allowed for measures of generalization. As can be seen in Figure 1, appropriate child behavior improved, including in the generalization setting (meals), whenever the mother received PAT in each new setting.

Figure 2 shows the mother's PAT skills across settings and generalization to the meal setting in which she did not receive any training. She also demonstrated considerable improvement each time training was introduced. She began generalizing her skills in the meal setting after she had received training in the other three settings. Her skills were maintained at five-month follow-up. Hazards accessible to the child were reduced dramatically and demonstrated through a multiple baseline design across rooms. Health care skills also improved dramatically after training, and these data were presented in a case study format (i.e., positive treatment effects demonstrated after baseline).

Research with more than one person or family represents the next level of evaluation in child maltreatment. Over the years, through our ecobehavioral model we have described a number of examples of the use of single-case research designs with multiple families to demonstrate the efficacy of a treatment protocol. On Project SafeCare we demonstrated the effects of video parent training across families (Bigelow & Lutzker, in press). Multiple baseline designs were used to show the internal validity a video training program has on improving parenting skills.

These designs have been used within the ecobehavioral model to teach nutritious meal-planning and shopping skills to an illiterate mother who was referred because of child neglect due to her previous inability to plan and shop for nutritious meals (Sarber, Halasz, Messmer, Bickett, & Lutzker, 1983). The designs were also used to show the effects of parent training with a mother referred for neglect (Dachman, Halasz, Bickett, & Lutzker, 1984), to demonstrate the efficacy of a training program aimed at teaching young parents to recognize and treat their infants' illnesses (Delgado & Lutzker, 1988), to teach staff and parents affective adult-child interaction skills (Lutzker, Megson, Webb, & Dachman, 1985; McGimsey, Lutzker, & Greene, 1994), and to teach young mothers how to provide infant stimulation (Lutzker, Lutzker, Braunling-McMorrow, & Eddleman, 1987). By "ecobehavioral" it is meant that services are delivered insitu, assessment and treatment are multifaceted, treatment involves the direct teaching of skills rather than a focus on counseling, and

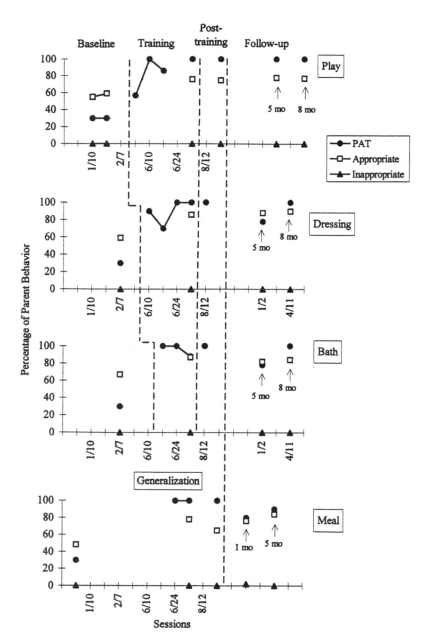

Figure 2. Planned activities/parent-child interactions training parent behavior. From Cordon, Lutzker, Bigelow, & Doctor (1998). Evaluating Spanish protocols for teaching bonding, home safety, and health care to a mother reported for child abuse, *Journal of Behavior Therapy & Experimental Psychiatry*, 29, 41–45.

generalization of skills is actively programmed. Humanistic counseling skills are used by counselors to be able to relate to consumers
(participants); however, direct observation of behavior (performance)
and the teaching of specific skills represent the primary strategies of
the ecobehavioral model (Lutzker, 1984).

Application of the ecobehavioral model to child maltreatment
began with the creation of Project 12-Ways in 1979. The undergirding
philosophy of this model applied to child maltreatment is that problems as complex and multifaceted as child maltreatment are in need of
multifaceted assessment and treatment. The ecobehavioral model approaches assessment and treatment in-situ. That is, both assessment
and treatment are conducted in natural settings, not offices. There are
two important reasons for this in child maltreatment. Foremost is that
the likelihood of the new skills taught to parents and children generalizing across behavior, time, and settings, is enhanced by providing
the training in the natural setting. The second reason is that families
reported for maltreatment are not prone to want to attend sessions
in offices and may often have transportation difficulties and other
obstacles that make it difficult for them to attend clinic sessions. This
has especially been the case in rural settings. The ecobehavioral model
(Lutzker, 1984) also relies on direct observation of behaviors as the
primary assessment tool. It utilizes the single-case research designs
described here in order to examine functional relationships between
treatment variables and outcome in each family. Treatment strategies
are skill-based and taught directly. There is little reliance in more
traditional counseling techniques other than to establish rapport and
in utilizing problem-solving strategies.

Recently, in our replication of Project 12-Ways, Project SafeCare,
we have used single-case research designs to demonstrate parent
training of a mother referred for neglect (Lutzker, Bigelow, Doctor,
Gershater et al., 1998), the use of video to reduce home safety hazards
(Mandel, Bigelow, & Lutzker, 1998), the use of video to teach Planned
Activities Training to families reported for child abuse (Bigelow &
Lutzker, 1998), and the evaluation of Spanish protocols for teaching
bonding, home safety, and health care skills to a mother reported for
child abuse (Cordon et al., 1998).

To some degree, clinical data, and to a much larger degree case
studies, single-case experiments, and research with multiple fami-

lies provides documentation that particular procedures can be effective to change behaviors of families involved in child maltreatment. The behaviors targeted for change presumably are relevant factors that contribute to child maltreatment; thus, for example, teaching a mother at risk for neglect skills such as Planned Activities Training and child health care would seem to be logical strategies aimed at preventing neglect. Nonetheless, if the proof is in the pudding, then program evaluation is needed in all programs addressing larger questions such as incidence and recidivistic incidence of child maltreatment during and after treatment. The National Research Council (1993) has suggested that these kinds of data are all too frequently absent from programs. Program evaluation is still all too rare in child maltreatment literature. Very few program descriptions include such evaluation tools as recidivism rates of the described project examined against a comparison or control group.

Project 12-Ways underwent three program evaluations. The first evaluation (Lutzker & Rice, 1984) examined recidivism by 50 families served by Project 12-Ways who were then compared to 45 matched comparison families. The recidivism rate of the Project 12-Ways families was 10% after services had been terminated, while the rate was 21% for the comparison families. These rates were significantly different at the $p < .05$ level.

Lutzker, Wesch, and Rice (1984) examined a number of demographic variables from Project 12-Ways over a four-year period. Among the data examined, they noted that the modal type of referral was for prevention, followed by abuse, and then neglect. The modal type of service provided was parent-child training, followed by basic skills training for the children and health maintenance and nutrition training for the parents. Three years of recidivism data showed lower rates for families served by Project 12-Ways than comparison families.

Wesch and Lutzker (1991) examined a number of variables on 232 families served by Project 12-Ways and created a matched comparison group of equal numbers. The primary conclusion of this evaluation was that families served by Project 12-Ways may have been more "problematic" than the comparison families based on three variables: the frequency of pretreatment contacts with the child protective service as measured by abuse or neglect reports and foster placements or adoptions.

In addition to recidivism, placement can be used as a measure of program evaluation (Lutzker & Campbell, 1994). That is, whether a child or children remain in the home or placed in foster homes. Others have suggested that cost analyses should also be examined in any large-scale programs. The actual costs of a given project should be calculated. These costs can be compared, for example, to similar services offered by community mental health centers or other programs.

Finally, social validation represents another component of program evaluation. This takes the form of asking the consumers of the research and services their opinions of the goals, processes, and outcomes of the services which they received. Data are collected on these dimensions using Likert-type scales. In addition to asking consumers these questions, O'Brien, Lutzker, and Campbell (1993) also asked agency personnel who interacted with a large ecobehavioral project serving families who had children with developmental disabilities about the goals, processes, and outcomes related to the families served. They also asked about the professionalism of the staff.

Asking about the professionalism of the staff allowed the researchers to determine if the staff were conducting themselves in a manner deemed professional by the agency personnel. Thus, even though a staff member might have good clinical skills, if professional skills are lacking, the services could be hampered or even terminated. It is therefore important to address such questions as whether the staff dress properly, are timely in attending meetings and returning phone calls, are accurate in their written reports, and so on. If these areas are lacking, corrective feedback can be used to improve these skills.

Social validation can have several purposes. It can confirm empirical outcome data. That is, although data from services may show clear behavior change in families, to have families rate outcome as favorable provides a validation of the data collected by others. If the consumers' outcome ratings are lower than those achieved through direct observation data, the validity of the data collection methods my be questioned.

If the outcome is favorable, but the consumers are unsatisfied with the process, this may indicate a problem with the predicted durability of treatment effects. That is, if the consumer does not like the treatment, even though outcome might initially look favorable, it is unlikely that the consumer will continue to carry out the treatment program when the researchers/service providers withdraw (Lundquist & Hansen, 1998).

The service provider can adjust the quality of services when data from social validation are consistently below set criteria (standards). Thus, for example, if the direct service providers (staff) were routinely scored by families as lacking empathy, more training in the use of empathic counseling techniques would be in order.

Program evaluation should be considered ethically essential in any broad-scale project aimed at addressing child maltreatment. To fail to do so may cause a lack of consumer confidence, a lack of funder confidence, and should cause researchers and service providers a similar lack of confidence.

Successful Programs

Fantuzzo, Weiss, and Coolahan (1998) have described a community-based, partnership-directed, applied research project aimed at improving prosocial skills of child victims of abuse. First, and of considerable importance in conducting applied research, these researchers formed linkages with community-based agencies. Next, they created a multisystems level intervention strategy. Additionally, Fantuzzo et al. collaborated with their community partners to implement the treatment program which involved using resilient skilled peers whom they called "play buddies" to help teach social skills to peers who were victims of child abuse and who lacked adaptive social behavior compared to other children their age. The community partners were the parents who participated in the local Head Start Program. Parent training was also provided to these children's parents by other community parents who participated in the creation of the program. This research provides an outstanding example of producing favorable outcome by incorporating community partners in designing assessment and treatment strategies.

Feldman (1998) has conducted considerable applied research with a challenging population, parents with intellectual deficits. These parents represent one of the highest risk situations for child maltreatment. Using direct observation methodology and single-case and group research designs, Feldman has shown that several crucial parenting skills can be taught to these parents by using pictorial cues in the instructional strategies. Skills that have been taught include

234
MOTIVATION AND CHILD MALTREATMENT

feeding, hair washing, sleep safety, bottle cleaning, nutrition, crib safety, diapering, bathing, and treating diaper rash. After training, the parents with intellectual deficits demonstrated skills equal to parents without intellectual deficits.

Violence prevention has been the goal of applied research conducted by Pittman, Wolfe, and Wekerle (1998). Using cognitive-behavioral treatment strategies, these researchers have taught a number of relationship and problem-solving skills to Canadian adolescents in their Youth Relationships Project. Direct observation and criterion performance is combined with a series of validated assessment scales to evaluate outcome. Among the variables that have been examined and successfully improved are the youths' coercion behaviors, emotional abusive behaviors, and positive communication.

Wrap-around (multifaceted) services for rural Utah families have been provided and evaluated by Striefel, Robinson, and Truhn (1998). The core services that have been provided to families reported for or at-risk for child maltreatment, have been: early childhood education and development services; early intervention for children at risk for developmental delays; nutritional services for children and their families; child care; child health services; prenatal care; mental health services; substance abuse education; parent education in child development, health, nutrition, and parent training; and vocational training.

The Family Interaction Skills Project (FISP) utilized multiple services, assessments, and outcome measures (Hansen, Warner-Rogers & Hecht, 1998) in rural West Virginia. Families were assessed for histories and risk of child maltreatment, parental psychopathology and substance abuse, knowledge and expectations about child development and behavior, child management skills, stress and anger control deficits, problem-solving and coping skills, social contacts and support, and adult relationships. As with other good applied research, direct and indirect measures were used to assess these many family characteristics.

Direct skill training in such areas as parenting and problem-solving skills was used. Families showed gains in behaviors measured directly and were evaluated using single-case research designs. Further, program evaluation data documented the broader success of the program across families.

The projects described here provide models of applied research in that they document behavior change in individual families, they evaluate program outcome, they prevent child maltreatment, and they use direct behavioral strategies to teach skills. Another component of these projects is that participants must demonstrate criterion performance of the trained skills.

Professional Challenges in Child Maltreatment

The nature of the population in child maltreatment provides challenges to conducting meaningful research and providing effective treatment. We know that families reported for child maltreatment have a low probability of treatment adherence. We know that they are prone to move (re-locate) much more frequently than other families. We know that they are prone to problems of substance abuse, unemployment, and were often victims themselves of family violence. Some findings suggest that being mandated for treatment increases the probability of favorable treatment outcome. There are no data to suggest that admitting or not to abuse may be related to outcome or adherence. It is clear, however, that adherence is more likely to occur in families reported for abuse than neglect. This is probably so because whether or not the family admits to abuse, they are aware of the scrutiny of the agency and the public about this form of maltreatment and are most often aware that they are in danger of having a child or their children removed from their home. This is not as apparent for families reported for neglect. Often the neglect is long-standing and often intergenerational. The family may view their lifestyle as something that should not come under the purview of an agency or social service. Thus, they may be frequently puzzled as to why they should adhere to a treatment program.

Many factors contribute to problems of treatment adherence in families involved in child maltreatment. Lundquist and Hansen (1998) have suggested a number of strategies for improving treatment adherence. One potential barrier to adherence that needs to be considered is the assessment process. For example, Fantuzzo et al. (1998) have suggested that many assessments are outright insulting to families, focusing on deficits rather than strengths. They have urged researchers to revise assessments with input from community members such as parents, and local HeadStart professionals and aids.

Lundquist and Hansen (1998) have also suggested antecedent

and consequent strategies for improving treatment adherence such as written homework assignments, directly asking families about adherence, ensuring that counselors show appropriate empathy, feedback, shaping procedures, and positive reinforcement. Incentives have been offered but often seem impractical.

Kapitanoff et al. (2000) have noted that cultural differences can affect adherence in child maltreatment families. Cultural factors may also cause difficulties in the definition of child maltreatment and differing opinions as to the role of agencies or government in families' lives. For example, rather severe corporal punishment is considered acceptable in many cultures. When members of these cultures immigrate to the United States or Canada they bring these values with them; yet, these values can be in conflict with North American definitions of child maltreatment. Treatment recommendations such as frequent verbal praise may run counter to some cultural beliefs against such reinforcement for positive behavior. Finally, gender roles and expectations, which differ widely across cultural groups, may also be influential.

Korbin (1991) suggested several factors that should be considered in examining child abuse from a multicultural perspective. These factors are also important in examining issues of adherence and include the cultural value of the child, the culture's beliefs about disabilities, beliefs about developmental patterns, and child-rearing styles.

In our own work in urban Los Angeles (Lutzker, Bigelow, Doctor, & Kessler, 1998) we have found that there are cultural nuances that, when known, and attempted by the service provider, can help insure assessment or treatment adherence. The service provider or researcher must view problems of adherence with perspective.

For example, we have learned that it is not prudent to have a male staff member provide services alone to a Latina or Middle-Eastern mother. We have learned that organizational styles of Middle-Eastern families are very different from those of the U.S. and that it is helpful to have staff from a Middle-Eastern background when possible to serve those families. Although these families are not comfortable having male counselors alone in the homes with the mothers, they seem to appreciate when there is a male supervisor available. This has to do with authority issues.

Finally, male children seem to have more freedom than female children in these households. The service provider or researcher must view problems of adherence with a cultural perspective.

Despite the serious nature of the problem of child maltreatment and the possible argument that perpetration causes a family to have everyday rights or freedoms diminished, it must be noted that investigation, assessment, and treatment services represent major invasions into the private lives of families. When we seek help from professionals such as the dentist, a physician, an attorney, or a mental health provider, we tend to be discriminating consumers, at least after we have sampled the professional's services. That is, if we become uncomfortable with the services or are not pleased with the outcome, we are prone to terminate our relationship with that professional and seek help from another provider. This option is frequently not available to the family referred for child maltreatment. They have been mandated to accept the service or have at minimum been told that their failure to be involved puts them at risk of more serious agency scrutiny, even so far as have the child or children removed from the home.

Thus, there are multiple factors that make it difficult to conduct research and treatment with families involved in child maltreatment. Nonetheless, ethical and cultural issues must be taken into account in our research and treatment efforts.

Striking the Balance

In this discussion and in the literature, it has been suggested that research and treatment in child abuse and neglect has been less than "hard-nosed." Recommended here has been a series of evaluations ranging from case studies to sophisticated program evaluation. Also, recommended here are multiple forms of assessment such as interview, standardized measures, and direct observation. All of these strategies have been used, but each poses practical roadblocks to service and research. The problems all researchers and service providers face in the field of child maltreatment, especially adherence problems, may in part be a function of our attempts at tight science and sophisticated assessment within an environment that is not conducive for such efforts.

How do we successfully provide service and use adequate research strategies while effecting behavior change and increasing adherence And, along with these issues, how do we remain culturally responsive? This is no easy challenge. We may simply have to "ease" some of our research and assessment strategies. We may need to more routinely accept available comparison groups instead of randomly selected control groups. We *should* rely more on single-case research designs with multiple replications.

Services must be well received by the consumers of them. We need to use consumers more frequently in the design of our assessments and treatments. It may be fruitful to train previous consumers (i.e., graduates of our treatment programs) to become future teachers/trainers (i.e., service providers).

In order to provide effective treatment and thus be able to conduct better research, more subjects need to complete our service projects and programs. That is, we need to lower attrition rates. Thus, the issues of cultural sensitivity and responsiveness, along with these issues of the design of assessment, treatment, and research strategies, become paramount. We *can* strike a balance between research and treatment but new flexibility is needed.

Future Efforts

At the risk of cliché, prevention certainly seems to be the first line of defense against child maltreatment. Thus, it is imperative to ask the questions, "what efforts can lead to effective prevention programs?" The literature is relatively encouraging as to the effects of wrap-around, large-scale, and ecobehavioral prevention services for families (Wasik, 1998). Wasik has suggested that early intervention programs must be evaluated. She points to the clear evidence that poverty is predictive of several poor developmental outcomes such as lower school performance, poor language skills, grade retention, and school drop-outs. On the other hand, children who participate in child-focused prevention programs show increases in IQ scores by the end of such programs.

Wurtele (1998) has suggested implementation of a human development curriculum stretching perhaps from preschool into college. Children and older students in such a curriculum could be taught nonaggressive problem-solving strategies appropriate to their developmental level. For example, teaching of these strategies could occur on the playground for young children. For adolescents, learning to deal with relationships would be useful in such a curriculum (Pittman et al., 1998). These programs, as many authors have suggested, should be skill-based and empirically validated. The work of Fantuzzo and his colleagues (1998) also suggests that utilizing peers as therapeutic agents might be an additional bonus to such programs. There is increasing evidence that cognitive-behavioral strategies are effective in skill building in the prevention of interpersonal violence. These strategies could be incorporated into a curriculum.

The media represents an area of concern for efforts to prevent child maltreatment. Garbarino (1995) has expressed concern that we have become inured to violence in the media, that we are so sensitized to it that we do not recognize the degree to which our own standards have dropped. Evidence over the past 30 years from developmental, social, and behavioral research has suggested that children imitate violent depictions from film/video and that children already prone to aggressive behavior are probably adversely affected by violent modeling (Josephson, 1987). Thus, given the escalation of violence in the media, in both movies and television (including news, and especially local news), those of us conducting research and providing services in child maltreatment should be especially concerned.

What to do about the escalating violence in media is another issue that may affect family violence and child maltreatment. Attempts such as rating systems have been made; however, there are arguments that ratings may actually exacerbate the problem, making accessible "PG" and "R" rated films more appealing and alluring to children. One possible means of "treating" the violence problem in the media without tampering with or tempering the First Amendment would be for parents and professionals to organize boycotts of sponsors and producers of violent programming.

Summary

Child maltreatment is a relatively new field. It is also an interdisciplinary field. Thus, the field's youth and its interdisciplinary nature have caused it to lack the focus of more established human service fields. Nonetheless, theory is emerging (Lutzker, 1998), and research, assessment, and treatment services are improving. Lutzker has suggested that the field has lacked an empirical base, but there are a

240

MOTIVATION AND CHILD MALTREATMENT

number of researchers and service providers who have offered an empirical perspective.

Applied research must have clear social significance. This is readily apparent in the child maltreatment field. Behaviors under study should be clearly and operationally defined. Portwood, Reppucci, and Mitchell (1998) have suggested that the legal arena also lacks some of the empiricism that could advance the field. That is, definitions of child maltreatment and standards of optimal parenting are sorely needed. This notwithstanding, there has been some improvement in providing empirically derived, content validated assessments and treatment protocols in the field of child maltreatment.

Although there has been considerable growth in the amount of research, two areas still seem lacking. One is the use of single-case research design (Kazdin, 1982) in which much is learned about the individual family. The other is program evaluation. More research needs to include measures such as recidivism and to make use of treatment and comparison groups.

Families involved in child maltreatment present special challenges to researchers and service providers. They often are not willing participants and thus they present challenges in conducting research and treatment adherence. A number of strategies to improve adherence are available and should be considered when conducting research and treatment in child maltreatment. Cultural sensitivity (or better said, "responsiveness") and the proper training of staff in cultural sensitivity ("responsiveness") should be at the forefront of research and treatment programs.

Child maltreatment is a field in which the media and the public may play more of a role than in other fields. The dilemma is that incidence of abuse continues to rise and treatment funding has diminished. This would seem to all the more suggest that prevention efforts should be strengthened.

Several empirical and successful programs in treatment and prevention are available. The field needs to be more aware of and attend to issues such as understanding prophylactic practices of families in abject circumstances who are not involved in child maltreatment. There are concerns as to the role that the media plays in family violence.

If the American and Canadian economies continue to flourish one would expect that increased funds should be available to prevent and treat child maltreatment. As Wurtele (1998) has suggested, advancing a human development curriculum, perhaps from preschool into college, that includes much skill training to prevent interpersonal and family violence may be the best route to take. Having the funding to do so would be the first place to start.

References

Abidin, R. R. (1990). *Parenting Stress Index* (2nd ed.). Charlottesville VA: Pediatric Psychology Press.

Baer, D. M., Wolf, M. M., & Risley, T. R. (1968). Some current dimensions of applied behavior analysis. *Journal of Applied Behavior Analysis, 1,* 91–98.

Beck, A. T., & Steer, R. A. (1993). *Beck Depression Inventory: Manual.* San Antonio TX: Psychological Corporation.

Bigelow, K. M., & Lutzker, J. R. (1998). Using video to teach planned activities to parents reported for child abuse. *Child & Family Behavior Therapy, 20,* 1–14.

Cordon, I. M, Lutzker, J. R., Bigelow, K. M., & Doctor, R. M. (1998). Evaluating Spanish protocols for teaching bonding, home safety, and health care skills. *Journal of Behavior Therapy and Experimental Psychiatry, 29,* 41–54.

Dachman, R. S., Halasz, M. M., Bickett, A. D. & Lutzker, J. R.(1984). A home-based ecobehavioral parent-training and generalization package with a neglectful mother. *Education and Treatment of Children 7,* 183–202.

Delgado, L. E. & Lutzker, J. R. (1988). Training young parents to identify and report their children's illnesses. *Journal of Applied Behavior Analysis, 21,* 311–319.

Fantuzzo, J., Weiss, A., & Coolahan, K. C. (1998). Community-based partnership-directed research: Actualizing community strengths to treat child victims of physical abuse and neglect. In J. R. Lutzker (Ed.), *Handbook of child abuse research and treatment* (pp. 213–237). New York: Plenum Press.

Feldman, M. (1998). Parents with intellectual disabilities: Implications and interventions. In J. R. Lutzker (Ed.), *Handbook of child abuse research and treatment* (pp. 401–420). New York: Plenum Press.

Hansen, D. J., Warner-Rogers, J. E., & Hecht, D. B. (1998). Implementing and evaluating an individualized behavioral intervention program for maltreating families: Clinical and research issues. In J. R. Lutzker (Ed.), *Handbook of child abuse research and treatment* (pp. 133–158). New York: Plenum Press.

Hersen, M., & Barlow, D. H. (1976). *Single case experimental designs.* New York: Pergamon Press.

Garbarino, J. (1995). *Raising children in a socially toxic environment.* San Francisco: Jossey-Bass.

Josephson, W. L. (1987). Television violence and children's aggression: Testing the priming, social script, and disinhibition predictions. *Journal of Personality and Social Psychology, 53,* 882–890.

Kapitanoff, S., Lutzker, J. R., & Bigelow, K. M. (2000). Cross cultural issues in disabilities and child abuse. *Aggression and Violent Behavior, 5,* 227–2AA.

Kazdin, A. E. (1982). *Single-case research designs: Methods for clinical and applied settings.* New York: Oxford University Press.

Kempe, C. H., Silverman, F. N., Steele, B. Droegemueller, W., & Silver, H. R., (1962). The battered child syndrome. *Journal of the American Medical Association, 181,* 17–24.

Korbin, J. (1991). Cross-cultural perspectives and research directions for the 21st century. *Child Abuse and Neglect, 15,* 67–77.

Lundquist, L. M., & Hansen, D. J. (1998). Enhancing treatment adherence, social validity, and generalization of parent training interventions with physically abusive and neglectful families. In J. R. Lutzker (Ed.), *Handbook of child abuse research and treatment* (pp. 449–471). New York: Plenum Press.

Lutzker, J. R. (1984). Project 12-Ways: Treating child abuse and neglect from an ecobehavioral perspective. In R. F. Dangel & R. A. Polster (Eds.), *Parent training: Foundations of research and practice* (pp. 260–291). New York: Guilford Press.

Lutzker, J. R. (1992). Developmental disabilities and child abuse and neglect: The ecological imperative. *Behaviour Change, 9,* 149–156.

Lutzker, J. R. (1998). Child abuse and neglect: Weaving theory, research and treatment in the twenty-first century. In J. R. Lutzker (Ed.), *Handbook of child abuse research and treatment* (pp. 563–570). New York: Plenum Press.

Lutzker, J. R., Bigelow, K. M., Doctor, R. M., Gershater, R. M., & Greene, B. F. (1998). An ecobehavioral model for the prevention and treatment of child abuse and neglect: History and applications. In J. R. Lutzker (Ed.), *Handbook of child abuse research and treatment* (pp. 239–266). New York: Plenum Press.

Lutzker, J. R., Bigelow, K. M., Doctor, R. M. & Kessler, M. (1998). Safety, healthcare, and bonding within an ecobehavioral approach to treating and preventing child abuse and neglect. *Journal of Family Violence, 13,* 163–185.

Lutzker, J. R., & Campbell, R. V. (1994). *Ecobehavioral family interventions in developmental disabilities.* Pacific Grove CA: Brooks/Cole.

Lutzker, J. R., Huynen, K. B., & Bigelow, K. M. (1998). Parent training. In V. B. van Hasselt & M. Hersen (Eds.), *Handbook of psychological protocols for children and adolescents* (pp. 467–500). Mahwah NJ: Erlbaum.

Lutzker, S. Z., Lutzker, J. R., Braunling-McMorrow, D., & Eddleman, J. (1987). Prompting to increase mother-baby stimulation with single mothers. *Journal of Child and Adolescent Psychotherapy, 4,* 3–12.

Lutzker, J. R., Megson, D. A., Webb, M. E., & Dachman, R. S. (1985). Validating and training adult-child interaction skills to professionals and to parents indicated for child abuse and neglect. *Journal of Child and Adolescent Psychotherapy, 2,* 91–104.

Lutzker, J. R., & Rice, J. M. (1984). Project 12-Ways: Measuring outcome of a large-scale in-home service for the treatment and prevention of child abuse and neglect. *Child Abuse and Neglect: The International Journal, 8,* 519–524.

Lutzker, J. R., Wesch, D., & Rice, J. M. (1984). A review of Project 12-Ways: An ecobehavioral approach to the treatment and prevention of child abuse and neglect. *Advances in Behaviour Research and Therapy, 6,* 63–73.

Mandel, U., Bigelow, K. M., & Lutzker, J. R. (1998). Using video to reduce home safety hazards with parents reported for child abuse or neglect. *Journal of Family Violence, 13,* 147–162.

McGimsey, J. F., Lutzker, J. R., & Greene, B. F. (1994). Validating and teaching affective adult-child interaction skills. *Behavior Modification, 18,* 209–224.

Milner, J. S. (1986). *The Child Abuse Potential Inventory: Manual* (2nd ed.). Webster NC: Psytec.

National Research Council (1993). *Understanding child abuse and neglect.* Washington DC: National Academy Press.

O'Brien, M. P., Lutzker, J. R. & Campbell, R. V. (1993). Consumer evaluation of an ecobehavioral program for families with children with developmental disabilities. *Journal of Mental Health Administration, 20,* 278–284.

Pittman, A. L., Wolfe, D. A., & Wekerle, C. (1998). Prevention during adolescence: The Youth Relationships Project. In J. R. Lutzker (Ed.), *Handbook of child abuse research and treatment* (pp. 341–356). New York: Plenum Press.

Portwood, S. G., Reppucci, N. D., & Mitchell, M. S. (1998). Balancing rights and responsibilities: Legal perspectives on child maltreatment. In J. R. Lutzker (Ed.), *Handbook of child abuse research and treatment* (pp. 31–52). New York: Plenum Press.

Sarber, R. E., Halasz, M. M., Messmer, M. C., Bickett, A. D., & Lutzker, J. R. (1983). Teaching menu planning and grocery shopping skills to a mentally retarded mother. *Mental Retardation, 21,* 101–106.

Striefel, S., Robinson, M. A., & Truhn, P. (1998) Dealing with child abuse and neglect within a comprehensive family-support program. In J. R. Lutzker (Ed.), *Handbook of child abuse research and treatment* (pp. 267–289). New York: Plenum Press.

Wasik, B. H. (1998). Implications for child abuse and neglect interventions from early educational interventions. In J. R. Lutzker (Ed.), *Handbook of child abuse research and treatment* (pp. 519–541). New York: Plenum Press.

Wesch, D. & Lutzker, J. R. (1991). A comprehensive evaluation of Project 12-Ways: An ecobehavioral program for treating and preventing child abuse and neglect. *Journal of Family Violence, 6,* 17–35.

Wurtele, S. K. (1998). School-based child sexual abuse prevention programs: Questions, answers, and more questions. In J. R. Lutzker (Ed.), *Handbook of child abuse research and treatment* (pp. 501–516). New York: Plenum Press.

Understanding the Dynamics of Child Maltreatment: Child Harm, Family Healing, and Public Policy (Discussant's Commentary)

Ross A. Thompson
University of Nebraska

For almost a half-century, the Nebraska Symposium on Motivation has profiled many of the evolving themes and issues at the heart of psychology. It has also documented, less directly, changes in society. When the symposium was inaugurated in 1951, child maltreatment was a sad reality of life for many children, but it was not a topic of considerable professional attention. With the identification of the "battered child syndrome" (Kempe, Silverman, Steele, Droegemueller, & Silver, 1962) in the early 1960s, however, professional concern with the plight of abused and neglected children quickly grew. National attention to child maltreatment also increased as public concern about family poverty escalated in the late 1960s, the incidence of reported sexual abuse grew in the late 1970s and early 1980s, and anguish over drug-exposed babies and the effects of homelessness on children emerged during the past decade. During the same period, media reports of abuse-related fatalities in families who were well-known to social service personnel and of children who became "lost" in the foster care system focused critical scrutiny on the inadequacies of the child protection system. These reports also revealed how the growing national problem of child maltreatment had become linked to other social ills, such as urban and rural poverty, the drug culture, neighborhood dysfunction, and the changing patterns of family life and child care (Thompson & Wyatt, 1999). A symposium devoted to child maltreatment would have been almost unimaginable when the symposium began in 1951, but the chapters of this 46th Annual Nebraska Symposium on Motivation reveal how much we have learned about this extraordinarily complex and challenging problem of human motivation.

As psychologists have studied child maltreatment, three questions have been at the heart of their inquiry. First, *what are the effects of abuse or neglect on its child victims?* Psychological research has revealed that the sequelae of maltreatment extend significantly beyond bruises and broken bones to include damaged self-esteem, distrust in close relationships, conduct problems, and other harms. Often the psychological effects of maltreatment are the most significant sequelae, but understanding why abuse leaves enduring scars for some children but has transient consequences for others is a significant research challenge. Second, *how can families be healed?* Psychological research has highlighted the multifaceted contributors to family risk for child maltreatment, such as adult psychopathology, the child-related belief systems of parents, economic stress, family disorganization, domestic violence, and deteriorating neighborhoods. These and other etiological considerations are profound, and their diversity and complexity make it uncertain how often—and how—abusive families can be psychologically reconstituted to become healthy environments of child nurturance. Third, *how can public policy reduce child maltreatment?* Psychological research has shown that abuse and neglect occurs within family, neighborhood, community, and broader social ecologies that must each be included in intervention, but how to accomplish this with limited public resources remains a formidable challenge. This is especially so if the goal is not merely to intervene to stop abuse that has occurred, but to prevent child maltreatment in families at risk.

These three questions—concerning child harm, family healing, and public policy—underlie contemporary research in child maltreatment. Although each question contributes crucially to our understanding, researchers have not always studied these questions in complementary ways. The breadth of definitions of child maltreatment varies significantly, for instance, depending on whether the focus is on child victimization, family healing, or public policies (English, 1998; Thompson & Jacobs, 1991). Likewise, the essential elements of effective intervention are conceptualized very differently depending on whether the primary concern is remediating the effects of abuse on children, reconstituting the family, reducing abuse re- cidivism, or addressing complex public priorities concerning family welfare (Thompson & Flood, in press). This can make the study of child maltreatment resemble the proverbial blind men inspecting the elephant, with each characterizing the beast differently depending on his special perspective.

The contributors to this symposium volume provide compelling, state-of-the-art perspectives on these central questions of child harm, family healing, and public policy. In so doing, each contributor also frames the questions that define an agenda for future research on these issues. Although each has a unique perspective to child mal- treatment, none of these experts is blind to the additional, sometimes alternative perspectives that are essential to a more complete un- derstanding of this social problem. Each is also thoughtful about the difficulties in studying, as well as treating and preventing, this complex social phenomenon. As a result, this collection of papers highlights some of the ways that the study of child maltreatment can be more thoughtfully conceptualized, and better integrated, than has been true in the past. The goal of this short commentary is to show how this is true by discussing some of the more important themes emerging from this symposium volume.

Child Harm: The Consequences of Child Maltreatment

How are children affected by abuse or neglect? The answer to this question is neither obvious nor simple. As the contributors to this volume explain, the consequences of maltreatment are complex and contingent. Consequences are complex because they can affect the full range of developmental competencies that are rapidly emerging in childhood and adolescence: not just physical trauma but psycholog- ical and relational sequelae are apparent in child victims. Moreover, children and youth are especially susceptible to the detriments of abuse and neglect because the rapid pace of their growth means that developing physical and psychological capacities are vulnerable to insult, detriments are likely to cumulate rapidly as the child matures, and coping capacities as well as resiliency are limited. This makes an understanding of the complex consequences of child maltreatment important to treatment and prevention, and also to our understanding of the processes of development itself.

Consequences are contingent because they are not apparent in all children who are victimized by abuse or neglect, and while some sequelae are enduring, others are more transient. The effects of child maltreatment are often complexly tied to other risk factors in the child's home and neighborhood. This means that rather than assuming that maltreatment has comprehensively devastating effects on a child's psychological functioning, individual patterns of vulnerability and compensation are the rule. As Widom (this volume) notes, abuse or neglect meaningfully heightens a child's psychosocial risk, but does not make dysfunction inevitable.

The contributors to this volume explain why this is so. Children vary significantly in the kind of maltreatment they experience, as well as the frequency, intensity, and chronicity of their victimization. Widom and Cicchetti and Toth (this volume) each describe research findings indicating that these variations in the kind and severity of maltreatment contribute to meaningfully different outcomes for children, despite the comorbidity of different forms of child victimization. Furthermore, Milner's chapter (this volume) surveys research studies indicating that parent belief systems differ significantly for adults who are physically abusive or neglectful, contributing further insight to the associations between type of maltreatment and child outcomes. The term "maltreated children" thus describes a heterogeneous population of children whose victimization varies significantly in its effects on the child, in the parental and family processes associated with harm, and quite likely also in the child's own self-regard and personal construction of the experiences contributing to victimization.

Each of the contributors to this symposium reminds us also that child maltreatment occurs in a complex social ecology that begins with but extends beyond the family system. This is relevant to prevention (as Daro notes in this volume) and treatment (Lutzker's ecobehavioral model) as well as to understanding the consequences of maltreatment. As Lutzker (this volume) notes, for example, the social ecologies in which children and families live include social networks, school-based associations, religious institutions, work (or lack of work), and other ecologies. Children who are abused or neglected are thus affected also by homes that may be colored by domestic violence, economic stress, substance abuse, single parenting, welfare reliance, and other ills that contribute their own risks to healthy psychosocial growth. Children may also live in neighborhoods that are impoverished, dangerous, unstable, or which otherwise undermine healthy intellectual or socioemotional growth. As Widom notes—and as she and Cicchetti and Toth thoughtfully describe in their research—the risk to children from maltreatment interacts with other risk factors in the child's environment. This means that many of the sequelae of child abuse or neglect are also outcomes of the cumulation of other risk factors in the child's life experience. Indeed, for children at heightened psychosocial risk, Widom's "saturation model" suggests that experiences of maltreatment may not in themselves significantly heighten risk much further than what the child already experiences (Widom, Ireland, & Glynn, 1995). What we often regard as the consequences of maltreatment may be created instead by the broader family conditions associated with abuse.

A thoughtful and sensitive understanding of the life experience of victimized children requires consideration not only of risk factors, but also of buffers or protections. The social ecologies of some children, even in conditions of risk, offer them access to a supportive adult outside the family (such as a grandparent, teacher, counselor, or the parent of a friend) who can provide assistance in coping with victimization (Thompson, 1995). As Cicchetti and Toth show from their research, sometimes the resources of resiliency come from within the child, such as the positive self-esteem and ego-resiliency that some maltreated children in their sample maintained despite their victimization. Knowledge of the psychosocial protections that exist along with risk factors is important not only because it contributes to a more accurate assessment of the quality of a child's life experience, but also because it provides a foundation for therapeutic or preventive interventions. Indeed, many of the strategies outlined by Daro and Lutzker to reduce child maltreatment consist of strengthening the psychosocial buffers in the child's life or in the family ecology.

Contributing further complexity to predicting the effects of child maltreatment are the dynamics of individual development and of family life. The effects of abuse or neglect emerge over time and appear in a developmentally changing individual. This can account for the well-known "sleeper effects" by which certain sequelae are not immediately apparent, but gradually emerge over time as new developmental challenges are encountered and as the child's capacities to master those new challenges are undermined by earlier victimization. The changes, challenges, and opportunities of psychosocial growth can also account for the amelioration of immediate harms over time as well, and patterns of developmental adaptation can be seen in the findings presented by Widom and by Cicchetti and Toth. Just as children develop, families also change over time. Some family changes can increase risk for child maltreatment, and others may reduce it. To Daro, understanding changing family risk status over time is crucial to providing appropriate preventive interventions; to Cicchetti and Toth, it is necessary for maintaining appropriate comparison between maltreated and nonmaltreated groups. In each case, changing family risk over time reflects the family dynamics that also color a child's life experience related to maltreatment.

These considerations related to the hetereogeneity of child maltreatment, the multifaceted risk factors in the lives of victimized children, consideration of protective factors, and the dynamics of individual development and family life have important methodological implications that are also elucidated by the contributors to this symposium. They suggest, for example, that the sequelae of child maltreatment should be better distinguished from those of correlated risk factors in research on child victimization (see also Emery & Laumann-Billings, 1998). Because maltreated children are likely to come from families and neighborhoods in which they are prone to many psychosocial risks, distinguishing the harms they experience that arise uniquely from abuse or neglect is a formidable research challenge. Another challenge is to develop better empirical and theoretical models to characterize processes of psychosocial adaptation and resiliency that maltreated children experience. To the extent that theoretical expectations provide a prism through which researchers interpret their findings, general expectations of psychosocial dysfunction arising from maltreatment may cause researchers to miss important evidence for constructive coping and psychosocial adaptation when it appears. Yet if abuse or neglect do not inevitably foreshadow psychological decline, and if individual patterns of vulnerability and compensation are instead the rule, then greater attention to processes of psychosocial coping as well as harm may be appropriate.

These and other considerations suggest that more complex research strategies are needed in the study of child maltreatment, as Lutzker argues insightfully in his description of clinical research methods. This is a difficult task in the limited current funding environment for research on abuse and neglect (Thompson & Wilcox, 1995). Yet in contrast to the "hourglass methodology" that has often characterized research into child maltreatment—in which a variety of antecedent risk factors are predictively associated with child maltreatment and in which maltreatment is used as a single predictor of a host of sequelae—more incisive (and expensive) research designs are required to ask more insightful questions concerning distinctive risk factors, patterns of compensation and adaptation, and the dynamics of individual development and family life. Fortunately, the contributors to this symposium provide useful models of how to do so. Widom's large-sample, prospective longitudinal cohorts design, incorporating a matched control group, exemplifies the kind of research strategy necessary to distinguish the sequelae of child maltreatment from those of other risk factors in children's lives. Her research design also enables careful assessment of alternative theoretical portrayals of the unfolding of risk over the course of individual lives. Cicchetti and Toth's prospective longitudinal research design incorporates ecological and developmental systems views to sensitively document the unfolding of the psychosocial consequences of maltreatment as children mature. Each study offers lessons to current researchers (and research funders) about the scale of the research effort required to address the most important questions concerning child victimization.

Not just more sophisticated research methodologies but more sophisticated theoretical schemas may also be needed in future studies of the consequences of maltreatment for children. Concepts from the interdisciplinary study of developmental psychopathology may be especially useful because scientists in this field must address the complexities of psychosocial risk and psychological dysfunction in a thoroughly developmental framework (Cicchetti & Cohen, 1995; Cicchetti & Rogosch, 1997; Sroufe & Rutter, 1984). Several principles that have emerged from the field of developmental psychopathology may be especially relevant to research on the effects of child maltreatment. First, the principle of *equifinality* emphasizes that there are multiple pathways leading to the development of childhood disorders. As earlier noted, in studies of the sequelae of maltreatment, it is important to remember that the outcomes observed in child victims are likely to have complex and multifaceted origins in which abuse or neglect is often one of many factors shaping adjustment. Second, the principle of *multifinality* underscores that any risk factor can lead to diverse outcomes depending on other influences on the child. In this regard, as the studies described in this volume illustrate, child maltreatment is linked to diverse psychological outcomes that can be maladaptive (e.g., increased aggression, anxiety, depression, conduct problems) but some may be psychologically adaptive in the circumstances in which children live. The consequences of maltreatment may be best understood in the context of other influences on the child.

Third, developmental psychopathologists caution against searching for single, direct causes of pathology and emphasize that "the action is in the interaction" over time among multiple internal and external influences on development. The interactive, compounding impact of psychosocial risks is likely to be greater than the additive effects of each risk factor taken alone. Risks must be viewed in the context of protections and of sources of adaptation and compensation. In research on the consequences of child maltreatment, it is likewise valuable to remember that child victimization—itself a heterogeneous phenomenon—is likely to interact in complex ways with other psychosocial influences from within the child (e.g., developing self-concept, ego resiliency) and in the child's social ecology (e.g., social support, disadvantaged minority status).

Keeping these principles in mind will help researchers view child maltreatment within the context of the multiple psychosocial influences that shape individual patterns of adjustment for victimized children and to devise research strategies incorporating these considerations. Keeping these principles in mind will also help researchers distinguish marker variables that are associated with child maltreatment from causal influences that are etiologically relevant, as Joel Milner (using a memorable illustration of the association between the earlobe crease and heart attack risk) reminded the symposium audience during his presentation.

Finally, developmental psychopathologists emphasize that children at risk should be regarded as developing persons, who face the same psychological changes, challenges, and opportunities in their growth as do children in more typical conditions. As illustrated especially in the work of Cicchetti and Toth and of Widom, a comprehensively developmental orientation to the study of child maltreatment is essential to a sensitive portrayal of its consequences.

Family Healing: Changing Representations and Relationships

Another principle of developmental psychopathology is that individuals help to construct their own developmental pathways. They do so primarily through the representations that guide their self-awareness, relationships with others, interpretations of events, and perceptions of the broader world. In recent years, new insight into the sequelae of child maltreatment has been achieved as researchers have borrowed concepts from attachment theory, social information processing theory, and other formulations to consider the nature of the "internal working models" that are created from early experiences of abusive or neglectful care. Widom's inquiry into the "cycle of violence" inaugurated by child maltreatment draws substantially on these cognitively-based formulations, as does Cicchetti and Toth's examination of the developmental outcomes of maltreated children. Their findings, and those of others (e.g., Dodge, Bates, & Pettit, 1990), suggest that some of the most important sequelae of abuse and neglect may be in children's representations of self, relationships, and the family that derive from their victimization.

Representations are important to understanding not only the experience of victimized children, but of the parents who abuse them. Milner's provocative chapter provides a theoretical expansion of the social information processing model that has been heuristically powerful in understanding the core deficits of troubled, abuse-prone parents. This model also has implications for effective intervention. Milner's discussion emphasizes the quasi-sequential steps of social information-processing that contribute to child abuse, beginning with biased perceptions of child behavior, leading to abuse-prone interpretations and evaluations of the meaning and significance of the child's acts, followed by inadequate information integration and response selection, and concluding with poor response implementation and monitoring processes. Milner's discussion highlights also the diversity of the parental belief systems that must be considered in understanding the adult representations that contribute to maltreatment. As he thoughtfully indicates, parents have core beliefs related

254

MOTIVATION AND CHILD MALTREATMENT

to the nature of children, the motives underlying their behavior, children's responsibility for misbehavior, and expectations for age-appropriate conduct. Parents also have core beliefs concerning their role as parents, their attitudes toward behavior control, and views about the nature of the parent-child relationship. Perhaps most importantly, parents have representations of themselves in the world that contribute to the threat-oriented schemas, low perceptions of self-efficacy, external locus of control, and diminished self-esteem that also contribute to risk for maltreatment. Many of the most important self-referent beliefs prognostic of abuse may be unarticulated, unrecognized, perhaps even unconscious, influences on parental behavior.

Research on the representations underlying abusive parenting is consistent with vigorous study of the representational facets of typical parenting in developmental psychology. Just as child maltreatment researchers are beginning to incorporate an understanding of parental representations into their studies of the personality, ecological, and other factors influencing maladaptive parenting, developmental psychologists are following the same path in their understanding of normative parent-child relationships. They are discovering the importance, for example, of the multiple (and sometimes conflicting) goals, expectations, and relational schemas—for both parent and offspring—that underlie the success of discipline encounters (Dunn, Brown, & Maguire, 1995; Grusec & Goodnow, 1994; Grusec & Kuczynski, 1997; Kochanska & Thompson, 1997; Parke & Buriel, 1998). Developmental researchers are investigating the content and origins of the parent belief systems that function consciously (and often unconsciously) as implicit frameworks of assumptive understanding guiding parental actions (Goodnow & Collins, 1990; Harkness & Super, 1996; Sigel, McGillicuddy-DeLisi, & Goodnow, 1992; Smetana, 1994). Recent investigators are also exploring the differences between automatic and controlled cognitive processes governing parental actions, inquiring (as does Milner) into how interventions to strengthen competent parenting can alter schemas enlisted automatically and improve the quality of controlled cognitions during encounters with offspring (Bugental & Goodnow, 1998). Those seeking to understand the parental representations that contribute to abusive behavior would be wise to explore these developmental literatures because of the conceptual tools they offer to elucidating the belief systems of abuse-prone adults, and also because of their implications for family healing.

These representations have diverse origins in a parent's personality and life history, cultural and subcultural ethnotheories of development, current experience with children, and the marital and family ecology—although these origins are not well-understood (Holden, 1995; Okagaki & Divecha, 1993; Smetana, 1994). They also originate, as attachment theorists remind us, in the parent's prior experience of close relationships (Crittenden, 1993, 1996). In this view, a child's early attachment to parents helps to shape emergent representations of what other people are like, what relationships are like, and how one participates in relationships, and these representations contribute to trust or distrust in intimacy. These early experiences also shape broader representations of self that contribute to a sense of security or uncertainty in relating to partners. These representations of self, other people, and relationships constitute the "internal working models" arising from early attachments that are, to some extent, continuously modified and updated as new relationships are formed with other caregivers, and later with close friends, romantic and marital partners (Thompson, 1998). Adults thus experience parenting as another close relationship—albeit a relationship of unique qualities—to which these long-developing representations are applied. As Milner describes in his research review, adults who experience diminished self-efficacy and loss of self-esteem as parents, who are insensitive to and unempathic with children's emotional cues, who perceive their offspring negatively and expect children to betray them with disobedience, and who relate negatively to their children may be reflecting a relational history that has become internalized in biased interpretations of offspring behavior, inappropriate behavioral strategies, and negative self-regard.

Family healing thus may begin with an understanding of the representations underlying parental behavior, and the relationships (both past and current) that contribute to those representations. It is not surprising to find that this conclusion has implications for treating troubled families and for preventing child maltreatment from occurring. Many of the treatment programs described in Lutzker's chapter, including the author's own Project 12-Ways and Project Safe-Care based on his ecobehavioral model of family services, emphasize strengthening family relationships and the relational representations they reinforce through strategies that include personal counseling, developing supportive relationships with community parents, improving interpersonal problem-solving strategies, and social skills development. The child abuse prevention efforts described by Daro also reveal the importance of relationships when young families are offered a sensitive, compassionate home visitor who is concerned about the parent's and child's well-being as well as providing access to needed services. Furthermore, the Healthy Families America initiative that she describes emphasizes strengthening the formal and informal social supports that typically characterize well-functioning families—in extended family networks, workplace settings, and the neighborhood and community—but are often absent or dysfunctional for families at risk of child maltreatment (Thompson, 1995). Taken together, in the context of the approaches outlined by Milner that directly address the social information-processing deficits of abuse-prone adults, there may be considerable value in considering treatment and prevention strategies that provide adults with supportive relationships that inspire trust and provide care. In a sense, such "rehabilitative attachments" in the adult years may contribute also to reworking the "internal working models" that have developed from past relationships, and contribute to more healthy representations related to parenting. In the words of campaign sloganeering, one might conceive of the origins of child victimization and of the bases of family healing as "it's the relationships, stupid."

Public Policy: A New Approach to Prevention

Treatment heals the wounds caused by prior victimization on a family-by-family basis. But a public problem like child maltreatment deserves a public response, hopefully one that addresses the social ills that lead to abuse and neglect. Unfortunately, Daro's compendium of the problems in local and national child protection efforts is consistent with those of other critics of the system (e.g., National Commission on Children, 1991; Pelton , 1992, 1997; Select Committee on Children, Youth, and Families, 1987; U.S. Advisory Board on Child Abuse and Neglect, 1990, 1991). Local CPS workers are not perceived by families as helpful or accessible sources of assistance because they also have the power to remove children from their homes and thus are regarded as having dual, mutually inconsistent, responsibilities.

The typical practices of CPS agencies are unduly inflexible, personnel too overburdened, and relevant services needlessly categorized and fractionated to provide effective assistance to troubled families. Child protection agencies devote considerable time and effort to investigating reports of suspected abuse, with few resources remaining to meaningfully aid families so identified. When interventions are provided, they are rarely integrated into the natural fabrics of family life and social networks to provide a structure for enduring support for healthy family functioning after time-limited interventions have ended. Moreover, the interventions that are provided to troubled families are often ineffective and, when children are concerned, may actually be harmful (such as many foster care placements). Most strikingly, children rarely receive the treatment they need for coping with the consequences of their victimization.

Perhaps the most central and significant limitation of CPS agencies is their mandate to intervene only after a report of suspected child maltreatment, leaving other troubled families unaided until they reach the point that a child is victimized. Although there are many programs that can provide assistance to families (e.g., WIC, Title XX assistance), none are oriented toward the unique problems of abuse-prone families and the stresses that lead to child victimization. Child protection agencies, by contrast, are specialized to work with such families but do so only after a child has been harmed, rarely preventively. It is reasonable to ask whether a society has made a serious commitment to reducing child maltreatment when families are helped only after, not before, their troubles have reached the threshold of child harm.

These considerations make it easy to concur with Daro's contention that prevention is the crucial effort to combating child maltreatment. But prior prevention efforts have yielded mixed and inconsistent results, whether their success is defined in terms of reducing the incidence of child maltreatment, improving family functioning, or strengthening child development. What is new and significant about the proposals Daro discusses is the focus on prevention efforts that are *universally available* to families, offered within a *flexible framework* that can be tailored to the specific needs of family members, oriented toward embedding families within a *network of supports* that can continue to foster healthy family functioning after intervention has ended, and with the eventual goal of *systemic reform* of health and social services to better serve family members. These ambitious goals are not just theoretical proposals: the Healthy Families America initiative that Daro describes has already succeeded in implementing many of these goals in the provision of preventive services to families throughout the country.

The Healthy Families America initiative is part of a national shift of perspective concerning the most effective strategies for reducing child maltreatment. As reflected also in the report of the Executive Session on Child Protection profiled in Daro's chapter, as well as reports of the U.S. Advisory Board on Child Abuse and Neglect (1990, 1991, 1993a, 1993b) and other agencies (e.g., the National Commission on Children, 1991; the National Research Council, 1993), thoughtful students of the child protection system are urging a redirection of focus from short-term interventions to strengthen the parenting skills of abusive adults to a broader focus on neighborhood-based supports and services that can strengthen healthy family functioning. Moreover, this new shift of perspective includes greater concern with the experience of children in troubled families, and attention to their developmental needs through direct services and by improving the capacities of parents to provide appropriately for them. The central focus of this shift in national perspective is on enabling troubled families to receive assistance before their problems have reached a crisis.

This new national perspective to child maltreatment is reflected in the Healthy Families America initiative, and in other approaches also. One of these is the proposal of the U.S. Advisory Board on Child Abuse and Neglect (1990, 1991, 1993a, 1993b) that a comprehensive national abuse prevention strategy should be neighborhood-based and child-centered. The view that child protection should be "neighborhood-based" means that effective abuse prevention efforts should be decentralized and local in their orientation, and should strengthen and rely on the informal support systems that typically characterize healthy neighborhoods and well-functioning families (Melton & Thompson, in press). National and local child protection efforts should seek to support community-based initiatives that strengthen the capacities of neighbors to help each other through the advice, material assistance, referrals, and other supportive aids that family members naturally offer other families within caring communities. The "neighbor helping neighbor" goal is complemented by the view that child protection should also be "child-centered," which means that it includes a focus on the needs of children (Thompson & Flood, in press). This includes individualized treatment and other services for children who are victimized by abuse, but it also includes community-based initiatives that improve the support that all children receive from neighbors, school personnel, community programs, and other agencies and individuals who are regularly involved in their lives.

Another way of conceiving this new national perspective to child maltreatment is that it is oriented toward "preventive family preservation". By strengthening community networks of support that can provide enduring assistance to troubled families, and offering services that can be flexibly tailored to the needs of individual family members, the overarching goal is to enable families to function better before they ever come to the attention of child protection agencies. Such an approach to prevention is far more broadly-based than the targeted services conventionally offered to identified families, but given the enormous expense of the current child protection system it is also likely to be more cost-effective. Healthy Families America is thus a contributor to the new landscape of child protection efforts that seek to help families before a child has been harmed.

Conclusion

The contributors to the 46th Annual Nebraska Symposium on Motivation offer insightful perspectives on the dynamics of child maltreatment and, in doing so, address broader questions concerning human motivation. In elucidating the complex and contingent sequelae of maltreatment, their discussions of child harm highlight the complex interaction of risk factors and the interplay of risks and protections in the life experience of victimized children. In considering the importance of the representations and relationships that contribute to abusive parenting, their discussions of family healing underscore the importance of the internal, relational dynamics of troubled parent-child interaction. In presenting new perspectives to child protection, their discussions of preventive strategies emphasize how troubled families are embedded in neighborhoods and communities that can either support healthy family functioning or undermine it. Consistent with the field of human motivation more generally, these chapters are

260

MOTIVATION AND CHILD MALTREATMENT

a reminder of how challengingly complex, but crucially important, is our understanding of these forces in the lives of children, their families, and the communities in which they live.

References

Bugental, D. B., & Goodnow, J. J. (1998). Socialization processes. In W. Damon (Ed.), *Handbook of child psychology* (5th ed., Vol. 3). *Social, emotional, and personality development* (N. Eisenberg, Vol. Ed.) (pp. 389–462). New York: Wiley.

Cicchetti, D., & Cohen, D. J. (1995). Perspectives on developmental psychopathology. In D. Cicchetti & D. J. Cohen (Eds.), *Developmental psychopathology: Vol. 1. Theory and methods* (pp. 3–20). New York: Wiley.

Cicchetti, D., & Rogosch, F. A. (1997). Equifinality and multifinality in developmental psychopathology. *Development and Psychopathology, 8,* 597–600.

Cicchetti, D., & Toth, S. L. (this volume). Developmental processes in maltreated children. In D. J. Hansen (Ed.), *Motivation and child maltreatment. Nebraska Symposium on Motivation, Vol. 46. Motivation and Child Maltreatment.* Lincoln: University of Nebraska Press.

Crittenden, P. M. (1993). An information-processing perspective on the behavior of neglectful parents. *Criminal Justice and Behavior, 20,* 27–48.

Crittenden, P. M. (1996). Research on maltreating families: Implications for intervention. In J. Briere, L. Berliner, J. A. Bulkey, C. Jenny, & T. Reid (Eds.), *The APSAC handbook on child maltreatment* (pp. 158–174). Thousand Oaks CA: Sage.

Daro, D. (this volume). Child abuse prevention: New directions and challenges. In D. J. Hansen (Ed.), *Motivation and child maltreatment. Nebraska Symposium on Motivation, Vol. 46. Motivation and Child Maltreatment.* Lincoln: University of Nebraska Press.

Dodge, K. A., Bates, J. E., & Pettit, G. S. (1990). Mechanisms in the cycle of violence. *Science, 250,* 1678–1683.

Dunn, J., Brown, J. R., & Maguire, M. (1995). The development of children's moral sensibility: Individual differences and emotion understanding. *Developmental Psychology, 31,* 649–659.

English, D. J. (1998). The extent and consequences of child maltreatment. *The Future of Children, 8,* 39–53.

Emery, R. E., & Laumann-Billings, L. (1998). An overview of the nature, causes, and consequences of abusive family relationships: Toward differentiating maltreatment and violence. *American Psychologist, 53,* 121–135.

Goodnow, J. J., & Collins, W. A. (1990). *Development according to parents.* Hillsdale NJ: Erlbaum.

Grusec, J. E., & Goodnow, J. J. (1994). The impact of parental discipline methods on the child's internalization of values: A reconceptualization of current points of view. *Developmental Psychology, 30,* 4–19.

Grusec, J. E., & Kuczynski, L. (Eds.) (1997). *Parenting and children's internalization of values: A handbook of contemporary theory.* New York: Wiley.

Harkness, S., & Super, C. M. (Eds.) (1996). *Parents' cultural belief systems: Their origins, expressions, and consequences.* New York: Guilford.

Holden, G. W. (1995). Parental attitudes toward childrearing. In M. H. Bornstein (Ed.), *Handbook of parenting. Vol. 3. Status and social conditions of parenting.* Hillsdale NJ: Erlbaum.

Kempe, C. H., Silverman, F., Steele, B., Droegemueller, W., & Silver, H. (1962). The battered child syndrome. *Journal of the American Medical Association, 181,* 17–24.

Kochanska, G., & Thompson, R. A. (1997). The emergence and development of conscience in toddlerhood and early childhood. In J. E. Grusec & L. Kuczynski (Eds.), *Parenting and children's internalization of values* (pp. 53–77). New York: Wiley.

Lutzker, J. R. (this volume). Balancing research and treatment in child maltreatment: The quest for good data and practical service. In D. J. Hansen (Ed.), *Motivation and child maltreatment. Nebraska Symposium on Motivation, Vol. 46. Motivation and Child Maltreatment.* Lincoln: University of Nebraska Press.

Melton, G. B., & Thompson, R. A. (in press). The conceptual foundation: Why child protection should be neighborhood-based and child-centered. In G. B. Melton, R. A. Thompson, & M. A. Small (Eds.), *Toward a child-centered, neighborhood-based child protection system.* Westport CT: Praeger.

Milner, J. S. (this volume). Social information processing and child physical abuse: Theory and research. In D. J. Hansen (Ed.), *Motivation and child maltreatment. Nebraska Symposium on Motivation, Vol. 46. Motivation and Child Maltreatment.* Lincoln: University of Nebraska Press.

National Commission on Children (1991). *Beyond rhetoric: A new American agenda for children and families.* Washington DC: U.S. Government Printing Office.

National Research Council, Panel on Research on Child Abuse and Neglect (1993). *Understanding child abuse and neglect.* Washington DC: National Academy Press.

Okagaki, L., & Divecha, D. J. (1993). Development of parental beliefs. In T. Luster & L. Okagaki (Eds.), *Parenting: An ecological perspective* (pp. 35–67). Hillsdale NJ: Erlbaum.

Parke, R. D., & Buriel, R. (1998). Socialization in the family: Ethnic and ecological perspectives. In W. Damon (Ed.), *Handbook of child psychology* (5th ed., Vol. 3). *Social, emotional, and personality development* (N. Eisenberg, Vol. Ed.) (pp. 463–552). New York: Wiley.

Pelton, L. H. (1992). A functional approach to reorganizing family and child welfare interventions. *Children and Youth Services Review, 14,* 289–303.

Pelton, L. H. (1997). Child welfare policy and practice: The myth of family preservation. *American Journal of Orthopsychiatry, 67,* 545–553.

Select Committee on Children, Youth, and Families (1987). *Abused children in America: Victims of official neglect.* Washington DC: U.S. Government Printing Office.

Sigel, I. E., McGillicuddy-DeLisi, A. V., & Goodnow, J. J. (Eds.) (1992). *Parent belief systems* (2nd ed.). Hillsdale NJ: Erlbaum.

Smetana. J. G. (Ed.) (1994). *Beliefs about parenting: Origins and developmental implications.* (New Directions for Child Development Series #66; W. Damon, General Editor). San Francisco: Jossey-Bass.

Sroufe, L. A., & Rutter, M. (1984). The domain of developmental psychopathology. *Child Development, 55,* 17–29.

Thompson, R. A. (1995). *Preventing child maltreatment through social support: A critical analysis.* Thousand Oaks CA: Sage.

Thompson, R. A. (1998). Early sociopersonality development. In W. Damon (Ed.), *Handbook of child psychology* (5th ed., Vol. 3). *Social, emotional, and personality development* (N. Eisenberg, Vol. Ed.) (pp. 25–104). New York: Wiley.

Thompson, R. A. & Flood, M. F. (in press). Toward a child-oriented child protection system. In G. B. Melton, R. A. Thompson, & M. A. Small (Eds.), *Toward a child-centered, neighborhood-based child protection system.* Westport CT: Praeger.

Thompson, R. A., & Jacobs, J. E. (1991). Defining psychological maltreatment: Research and policy perspectives. *Development and Psychopathology, 3,* 93–102.

Thompson, R. A., & Wilcox, B. L. (1995). Child maltreatment research: Federal support and policy issues. *American Psychologist, 50,* 789–793.

Thompson, R. A., & Wyatt, J. M. (1999). Current research on child maltreatment: Implications for educators. *Educational Psychology Review, 11,* 173–201.

U. S. Advisory Board on Child Abuse and Neglect (1990). *Child abuse and neglect: Critical first steps to a national emergency.* Washington DC: U.S. Government Printing Office.

U. S. Advisory Board on Child Abuse and Neglect (1991). *Creating caring communities: Blueprint for an effective federal policy on child abuse and neglect.* Washington DC: U.S. Government Printing Office.

U. S. Advisory Board on Child Abuse and Neglect (1993a). *The continuing child protection emergency: A challenge to the nation.* Washington DC: U.S. Government Printing Office.

U. S. Advisory Board on Child Abuse and Neglect (1993b). *Neighbors helping neighbors: A new national strategy for the protection of children.* Washington DC: U.S. Government Printing Office.

Widom, C. S. (this volume). Motivation and mechanisms in the "cycle of violence." In D. J. Hansen (Ed.), *Motivation and child maltreatment. Nebraska Symposium on Motivation, Vol. 46. Motivation and Child Maltreatment.* Lincoln: University of Nebraska Press.

Widom, C. S., Ireland, T., & Glynn, P. J. (1995). Alcohol abuse in abused and neglected children followed-up: Are they at increased risk? *Journal of Studies on Alcohol, 56,* 207–217.

Subject Index

childhood victimization/violence
and race or ethnicity findings
by, 11–13, 12*t*
childhood victimization/vio-
lence/gender findings by, 9–11,
10*t*
conclusions of, 29–32
criminal behavior findings by, 8–
9
empirical findings by, 6–15
follow-up interviews by, 4–6
on importance of neglect, 15–17
risk of arrest finding by, 7–8*t*
sample identification/tracing of
criminal histories, 3–4
violence begets violence findings
by, 13–15, 14*t*

Department of Social Services
(DSS), 7, 91
deprived relatedness, 113
desensitization, 18–20
developmental outcomes
caregivers as contributors to,
108–122
emotion processes as contributors
to, 122–131
exosystem level influences on
maltreatment and, 96–100
human development curriculum
to aid in, 238–239
interventions at exosystem level,
140–141
interventions at individual level,
142–144
interventions at microsystem
level, 141–142
maltreatment and resilience, 132–
140
maltreatment experiences and
ontogenic, 103–107
microsystem level influences on
maltreatment and, 100–103
developmental pathway construction, 253
DIS-III-R, 4

discipline
choice of, 68–69
conflicting goals/expectations of,
254
corporal punishment beliefs and,
53
disengaged relatedness, 113

ecobehavioral model, 228, 230
ecological-transactional model
on caregivers as development
contributors, 108–122
on child maltreatment, 91–96
on developmental outcome, 96–
103
on emotion processes and development, 122–131
implications for developmental
interventions of, 140–144
on ontogenic development, 103–
107
on resilience functioning, 132–
140, 145
Edna McConnell Clark Foundation,
206
Emergency Response Unit (ERU)
[Alameda County, California],
203–204
emotion processes
importance of attention to, 130–
131
maltreated children and development of, 122–131
Emotional Quality, 112, 113
empathy
development of, 25
relevant to effective parenting,
56–57
equifinality principle, 251–252
ethnic differences. *See* race/eth-
nicity differences
event related potentials (ERPs),
105–106, 107
Executive Session on Child Protection, 206, 258
external stimulation needs, 19

Author Index